BRITAIN'S MILITARY AIRFIELDS 1939~45

BRITAIN'S MILITARY AIRFIELDS
1939~45

David J. Smith

Patrick Stephens Limited

First published in 1989

British Library Cataloguing in Publication Data

Smith, David J. (David John), *1943-*
  Britain's military airfields.
  1. Great Britain. Air bases, 1912-1945
  I. Title
  358.4'17'0941

  ISBN 1-85260-038-1

All plans are based on official publications.

Front endpaper *Snetterton Heath, Norfolk, almost completed. A Class A airfield which was destined to become an 8th Air Force Fortress base* (IWM CH15427).

Rear endpaper *A Fortress of the 305th Bomb Group on final approach to Chelveston, Northants, in the spring of 1944* (IWM CH13007).

Patrick Stephens Limited is part of the Thorsons Publishing Group, Wellingborough, Northamptonshire, NN8 2RQ, England

Printed and bound in Great Britain by Butler & Tanner Ltd, Frome and London

Typeset by MJL Limited, Hitchin, Hertfordshire

10 9 8 7 6 5 4 3 2 1

Contents

Author's introduction and acknowledgements

I have set out within the following pages to describe the development of military airfields in Britain from the days before the First World War to 1945 when their numbers reached an all-time high. The book is intended to complement PSL's *Action Stations* series with which it is assumed that the reader is familiar. Strategic requirements, site selection, planning and construction are discussed, as is the sorry tale of the paved runway debate. Royal Naval Air Stations and flying boat bases are not neglected, neither are the little known Satellite Landing Grounds used for aircraft storage, the Advanced Landing Grounds in south-east England, and supporting functions such as bombing and firing ranges and shadow factories. Detailed notes will be found on how to research airfield histories and investigate the sites themselves and, for the first time, there is a comprehensive list of airfield memorials. The standard airfield building types are all described, as are the various lighting, navigation and Flying Control aids provided.

Abandoned airfields dot the landscape from one end of Britain to the other, an eyesore to some but a piece of our heritage to others. Few people live more than 10 miles away from at least one of them and there is an increasing awareness of their historical importance, fuelled by the PSL *Action Stations* series and a number of privately-published individual histories. It is unfortunate, however, that this enlightenment does not always extend to landowners, as too many airfield buildings are still being demolished without regard for their historical significance. At the time of writing there are very few aeronautical structures which have achieved listed status and those of Second World War vintage have yet to aspire to any official protection.

Although many airfields were built to a similar pattern, each has its own special character. Some are virtually obliterated, others intact but derelict. Richard Hough in his book *One Boy's War* describes his impressions of them in their heyday:

'I know of nothing more distinctive and memorable than a wartime airfield. To the outside world they may have all looked the same. To anyone who was going to live there for a while — and maybe die there — each stamped its nature indelibly on your mind. Most had an ominous demeanour, especially those like Watton with great dark camouflaged hangars with their zigzag roofs and steel girder extensions like gibbets at each corner to accommodate the giant sliding doors when they were opened. By the very nature of their function, and unlike Army barracks, airfields were stark and open to the sky. There were few tall trees near them, and from a distance the first thing you usually saw was the water tower, then the crouching hangars, the grey concrete control tower, then the living quarters and scattered Nissen huts, and last of all the olive drab aircraft themselves, widely dispersed about the perimeter in their bays. It was the absence of bright colour as much as the destructive function of wartime airfields that contributed to their ominous character.'

1942 was the peak year for the largest construction programme in our history and one which resulted in Britain being referred to as 'a vast aircraft carrier anchored off the northwest coast of Europe'. An American pilot put it in a more homely fashion in 1944 when he claimed that England's airfields were 'thicker than fleas on a dog's back'. Ignoring the slur on American dogs, this was hardly an exaggeration! It is easy to become bogged down in pure statistics about wartime airfield building, but some of the more enlightening figures are as follows.

The Air Ministry's Directorate General of Works spent £600 million in the five years of war. The total area of concrete laid in runways, perimeter tracks and dispersal points was approximately 160 million square yards and Sir Archibald Sinclair, Secretary of State for Air, compared this with a 9,000 mile long 30 ft wide highway stretching from London to Peking. In addition, 30 million tons of hardcore and 18 million cu ft of wood were used and 336,000 miles of electricity cables were laid. In 1945 some 360,000 acres of land were occupied by airfields in Britain.

A book of this nature inevitably owes a large debt to friends and correspondents. I should like to thank Alan W. Hall, Editor of *Aviation News* magazine, for permitting me to adapt and expand some of the material about airfields which I have written for him over the past decade. I am also grateful to the Airfield Research Group and many of its members for help with photographs and information, in particular Aldon P. Ferguson, Guy Jefferson, Fred Cubberley, Ken West, Paul Francis and Julian C. Temple. Thanks are due to Ernie Cromie, Tony Hooper, Brian Martin, Dave Welch and the Pembrokeshire Aviation Group, all of whom helped in various ways, including the supply of present-day aerial photographs. Mick Burrow kindly liaised with Len Lovell at the FAA Museum at Yeovilton and located a number of interesting photographs. Other rare material came from Roy Bonser, Dr Atholl Duncan, Peter H.T. Green and Zdenek Hurt, all of whom dug deep into their photo collections to illustrate various points in my manuscript. Ron Blake in his capacity as Senior Lecturer in Town and Country Planning at Trent Polytechnic, Nottingham, tends to see airfields in a different light from the average enthusiast and thus provided me with many useful and refreshing pointers. My main source material came from the Public Record Office but the official Royal Air Force history *Works*, published in 1956, also proved very useful. Finally, thanks to my publishers, Patrick Stephens Limited, for all their help and support.

David J. Smith
Bebington

Abbreviations

ACG   Airfield Construction Group
ACS   Airfield Construction Squadron
ADGB   Air Defence of Great Britain
AGS   Air Gunners School
ALG   Advanced Landing Ground
AM   Air Ministry
AMWD   Air Ministry Works Directorate
AOC   Air Officer Commanding
AOP   Air Observation Post
APC   Armament Practice Camp
ASU   Aircraft Storage Unit
ATA   Air Transport Auxiliary
BG   Bombardment Group
CCRC   Combat Crew Replacement Centre
CFS   Central Flying School
D/R   Dead Reckoning
DZ   Drop Zone
EAB   Engineer Aviation Battalion
ECFS   Empire Central Flying School
EFTS   Elementary Flying Training School
ELG   Emergency Landing Ground
FAA   Fleet Air Arm
FG   Fighter Group
FTC   Flying Training Command
FTG   Fighter Training Group
FTS   Flying Training School
GS   Gliding School
GTS   Glider Training School
HCU   Heavy Conversion Unit
HF   High Frequency
IWM   Imperial War Museum
MoD   Minstry of Defence
MoS   Ministry of Supply

MoW   Ministry of Works
MU   Maintenance Unit
ORB   Operations Record Book
OTU   Operational Training Unit
PAFU   (Pilot) Advanced Flying Unit
PBS   Prefabricated Bitumenized Surfacing
PoW   Prisoner of War
PR   Photographic Reconnaissance
PRG   Photo-Recce Group
PRO   Public Record Office
PSP   Pierced Steel Planking
PTS   Parachute Training School
RAE   Royal Aircraft Establishment
RAAF   Royal Australian Air Force
RCAF   Royal Canadian Air Force
RLG   Relief Landing Ground
RNAS   Royal Naval Air Station
SFTS   Service Flying Training School
SLG   Satellite Landing Ground
SMT   Square Mesh Track
TAF   Tactical Air Force
TBR   Torpedo-Bomber-Reconnaissance
TCG   Troup Carrier Group
TRE   Telecommunications Research
          Establishment
USAF   United States Air Force
USAAF   United States Army Air Force
VHB   Very Heavy Bomber
VHF   Very High Frequency
VR   Volunteer Reserve
WO   War Office
W/T   Wireless Telegraphy

Chapter 1

Airfield development 1912-39

The first military airfield in Britain was established at Larkhill on Salisbury Plain in 1911 on a site which was already in use by civilian aviators. Today the spot is marked by a small concrete plinth and brass plaque. On the outbreak of the First World War there were only seven service aerodromes: Eastchurch, Farnborough, Gosport, Larkhill, Montrose, Netheravon and Upavon. In those days any flat, reasonably dry piece of land was considered sufficient for landing and taking off. Whether as a legacy of the Army's preoccupation with horses or by coincidence, racecourses were often chosen as likely aerodromes. As early as 1912 it was suggested that a national network of military airfields should be sited next to Roman roads so that they could be recognized easily from the air. No specific action was taken but Stamford, later to be renamed Wittering, and Waddington were two of those which fulfilled this requirement.

The word aerodrome, incidentally, was derived from Greek words meaning 'aerial racecourse'. The Americans corrupted it sometimes to airdrome, but it was their term air-

Stonehenge, a training aerodrome opened in 1917 (Via Dr A.A. Duncan).

Spad S.7 B6796 and DH 5 A9355 with an Avro 504J in the background. The location is uncertain but typical of the basic aerodromes of the era (Via Dr A.A. Duncan).

field which eventually came into universal use. The original word is not extinct, however. British Air Traffic Controllers' Licences still include an 'Aerodrome Control Rating'.

By 1917 a total of 73 aerodromes were available in Britain, most of them temporary in nature as is shown by Sir Arthur Harris's reminiscence of an incident in his early career.

> 'I was sent to start Sutton's Farm air station as a night-flying anti-Zeppelin station. I landed there and the aerodrome consisted of a large field full of sheep, an infuriated farmer and a still more infuriated dog. So when we'd cleared off the sheep and I'd appeased the farmer and been billeted on him, I formed a Flight there.'

This was the site, developed and renamed Hornchurch, which was to see so much action during the Battle of Britain.

Sites were often discovered in a haphazard fashion. For example, long before 1914 Major Atcherley, father of the brothers who were to play such a prominent part in the history of the RAF, force-landed a hot air balloon in Shropshire. He reported to the War Office that the point where he came down would make a good aerodrome. However, it was not until 1916 that they acted upon his advice, Tern Hill being the result. In 1917 Sholto Douglas, a young pilot later to become Marshal of the Royal Air Force, was given the task of selecting eight sites in Ireland on which training schools could be set up. The specification was simple; grass fields which would give runs of 500 to 600 yd in any direction. He set off in

the summer of 1917 and picked such locations as Collinstown (today's Dublin Airport), Baldonnel and Aldergrove, which is now Belfast Airport.

Certain First World War aerodromes in Britain were referred to as Flight Stations, others as Landing Grounds, Class 1, 2 or 3. Flight Stations were aerodromes at which a Flight of aeroplanes were deployed by a Home Defence Squadron. The three classes of landing ground were peculiar also to Home Defence and were graded according to the quality of their aerial approaches. Class 1 signified that they were unrestricted from any direction, Class 2 meant subject to hazards (usually trees and buildings) from one direction, while Class 3s were obstructed on more than one side. They were further sub-divided into Day and Night Landing Grounds and changes of their status both in class and facilities were quite frequent during their operational life.

At the end of the First World War there were, according to one source, 301 aerodromes or landing grounds in existence in Britain, some 256 being relinquished during 1919 and 1920. Most of those where accommodation was confined to canvas hangars, huts and tents soon disappeared from the landscape as they returned to agriculture. The nucleus retained by the greatly depleted RAF obviously tended to be the ones at which permanent hangars and domestic accommodation had been built. By 1924 there were only 27 service and 17 civil aerodromes in the whole of Great Britain, each covering an average area of 200 acres.

A rare survivor from 1914-18, the armoury at Leighterton, a training station in Gloucestershire.

Early in the 'thirties, the Air Ministry Works Directorate was formed with responsibility for planning and organizing the construction of new airfields and the maintenance of existing ones. In 1935, the first year of expansion, the total expenditure on Works Services was just under £5 million out of an overall RAF budget of £27.5 million. The peak was to be reached in 1942 when £145 million was spent on works. The organization was divided into geographical areas covering the whole of Great Britain and Northern Ireland, there being 20 by the middle of the war.

Practically all the existing airfields were products of the Great War and their surfaces had received little or no maintenance since the date of construction. Most of the fighter stations were sited around London — Biggin Hill, Kenley, North Weald and Northolt all being built on wet clay. As aircraft landing speeds became higher, accidents directly attributable to rough surfaces became such a problem that the RAF brought pressure to bear to have them improved, but there was no effective long-term planning, the work being done piecemeal over a number of years. The barracks, hangars and landing ground at Biggin, for example, were rebuilt in 1931/32, the same being performed at Kenley during the next two years.

The final phase of the RAF's inter-war evolution is known as The Expansion, brought about by Hitler's seizure of power in January 1933, the withdrawal of Nazi Germany from the League of Nations in October and the consequent collapse of the International Peace Conference at Geneva. The emergent *Luftwaffe*, secretly training under the guise of glid-ing clubs and airline flying, caused great concern in Britain and in November 1933 a committee was set up 'to examine the worst deficiencies in national and imperial defence'. Early in 1934 it reported two salient conclusions, namely that (a) Nazi Germany was now the 'ultimate potential enemy' and (b) London would not be the only target in a future war. From that point on, RAF strategy shifted to a mixed doctrine of defence and offence and found expression in the 'Re-Orientation Scheme' devised in July 1934 by Air Chief Marshal Sir Robert Brooke-Popham, Commander-in-Chief of Air Defence of Great Britain.

The ensuing Expansion was executed through a succession of 13 alphabetically-coded schemes, five of which ('A', 'C', 'F', 'L' and 'M') were ratified in Parliament, although none was fully implemented because of the rapidly changing political climate. Of those to bear fruit, Scheme 'A' was most notable for extending fighter cover northwards to the Tees so that England's main industrial areas could be properly defended from air attack across the North Sea. Scheme 'C', approved in March 1935, placed renewed emphasis on deterrence and envisaged 1,500 first-line aircraft distributed largely among 70 bomber and 35 fighter squadrons. Priority here was given to a strike force capable of reaching Berlin in a straight line, which meant developing bomber aerodromes north of the Wash. This was the context in which Lincolnshire and Yorkshire first emerged as 'bomber country'.

Scheme 'F', approved in February 1936, foresaw an expanded Home Defence force of

Bristol Scout 'C' 3051 with a General Service hangar of the mid-war period (Via Dr A.A. Duncan).

1,736 aircraft in 124 combat squadrons, still with an approximate 2:1 ratio of bombers to fighters but with a rising component of coastal reconnaissance.

Under the scheme, Air Defence of Great Britain (ADGB) was scrapped in July 1936 and replaced by four Commands — Fighter, Bomber, Coastal and Training. After two years of indecision, the next major revision was ratified in March 1938, in which Scheme 'L', as it was known, was devised in response to Germany's annexation of Austria and provided for 2373 first-line aircraft in 152 squadrons. Although the overall balance was still in favour of bombers, priority was now given to building up fighter strength and to this end all Auxiliary Squadrons were transferred from Bomber to Fighter Commands pending appropriate re-equipment. A substantial increase in training schools was also sanctioned.

To meet the airfield requirements of RAF Expansion, the Air Ministry Aerodromes Board was formed within Air Ministry Works Directorate (AMWD) on 26 May 1934 with two retired officers, AVM C.A.H. Longcroft, CB, DSO, AFC and AC the Hon J.D.Boyle, CBE, DSO at its head. Longcroft had been with No 1 Squadron in 1912 and had made some of the Royal Flying Corps's longest cross-country flights at that time. One of them was a non-stop trip from Montrose in Scotland to Farnborough.

The Board worked closely with the Air Ministry Lands Branch whose officers performed the complicated legal and administrative tasks relating to the acquisition of the necessary land. Prior to the Second World War, the Air Ministry had to rely on the archaic and cumbersome procedures of the Defence Act of 1842 for the compulsory purchase of land. Fortunately, the Defence Regulations made under the Emergency Powers (Defence) Act, 1939, permitted the taking of immediate possession of land and buildings when approved by a competent authority, a process commonly called requisitioning.

The Aerodromes Board was instructed to look for sites at least three miles apart but, with commendable foresight, it tried to work to five miles. Likely sites were pinpointed by the simple method of studying the 1 in Ordnance Survey map and marking off the possible flat areas which were free from obstructions within a circle of approximately 1,100 yd. In general, areas below 50 ft above mean sea level were avoided owing to the risk of flooding and over 600 ft because of low cloud base. The selected areas were then visited and walked field by field, the maximum space for landing being plotted. If available, the local geological map was studied to ascertain the soil structure. No consideration was given to paved runways at that time so well-drained land was essential.

From the beginning of 1935 to the outbreak of war, approximately 100 new service air-

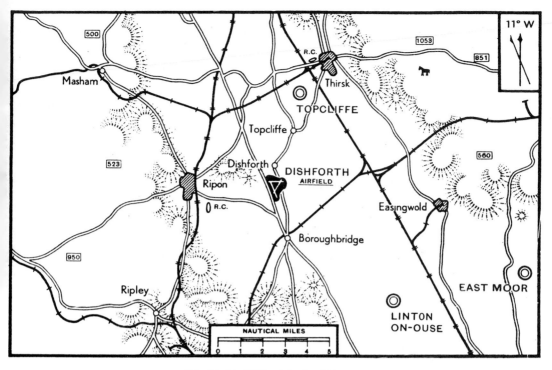

ALL HEIGHTS IN FEET ABOVE MEAN SEA LEVEL

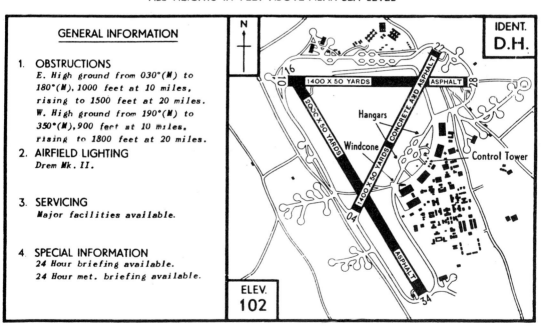

GENERAL INFORMATION

1. **OBSTRUCTIONS**
   *E. High ground from 030°(M) to
   180°(M), 1000 feet at 10 miles,
   rising to 1500 feet at 20 miles.
   W. High ground from 190°(M) to
   350°(M), 900 feet at 10 miles,
   rising to 1800 feet at 20 miles.*

2. **AIRFIELD LIGHTING**
   Drem Mk. II.

3. **SERVICING**
   Major facilities available.

4. **SPECIAL INFORMATION**
   *24 Hour briefing available.
   24 Hour met. briefing available.*

IDENT.
D.H.

ELEV.
102

*Expansion station to which runways and dispersals were added during wartime: Dishforth,
Yorks.*

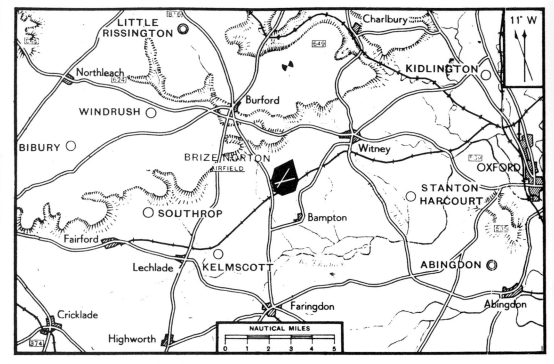

ALL HEIGHTS IN FEET ABOVE MEAN SEA LEVEL

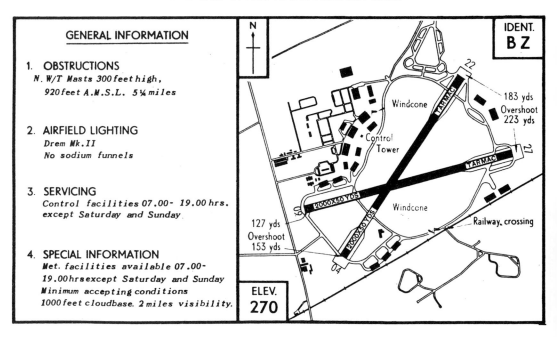

Expansion station to which runways and dispersals were added during wartime: Brize Norton, Oxfordshire.

fields were established, including many whose names were destined to become famous. They followed a roughly similar circular pattern with a grass landing ground to a standard diameter of 1,100 yd. Although the best shape was accepted to be a rectangle or square which gave full length runs from every direction, even if a portion of the edge was blocked by buildings or other obstructions, the 1,100 yd diameter was dictated by the need for the so-called 'bombing circle'. This provided a safe practice bombing area on the station itself, thus avoiding the necessity of acquiring other land for the purpose.

The siting of the airfield buildings dictated the alignment of the obstruction-free 'flight-ways', rather than the other way round in the case of the later runway airfields. However, by 1938 the likely provision of the Lorenz blind approach system within the RAF necessitated the laying down of definite flying lanes for every airfield. Although it was not intended that these planned flightways should constitute confined landing areas on grass airfields, they inevitably concentrated operations on certain strips of turf with attendant wear, and gave more than a hint of the need for paved runways. When these were built at some future date, they tended to follow the existing flightways which were not always consistent with prevailing wind directions. The result was a number of airfields with main runways almost permanently out of wind. The worst was probably Turnhouse, now Edinburgh Airport, which had to build an entirely new runway in the 1970s.

The number of stations required for the first years of Expansion was relatively small, which allowed prime sites from an engineering point of view to be selected. Only when a site was essential in a particular location for strategic reasons were less than ideal conditions accepted. As the RAF increased in size, so did the degree of compromise in the acceptance of new locations which were of minimal standard.

Aerodrome drainage was somewhat different from other forms of land drainage in one respect, namely that it was vital that any water that fell on to the surface was removed from it or through it to natural or artificial drainage as soon as possible. There was much experimentation into the evaporation and absorption of water by special grasses, the Chester seed firm of James Hunter Ltd being well to the fore with their much-vaunted *Hunterized* surface. The head of the company, Claude Hunter, was himself a pilot and graduated from supplying the seed to the laying of whole aerodromes. It was said that he made Fairey's Great West Aerodrome so perfect that he had

to go back and 'roughen' the south-west corner so that the Fairey Company could bump aircraft wheels on it hard enough to test the undercarriages!

Other agricultural processes were aimed at improving soil conditions and turf-growing, and involved mechanical methods such as sub-soiling (consolidating the soil immediately beneath the turf), as well as with the importation of suitable soils and materials like sand, ballast and clays, together with chemical processes using lime, fertilizer and manure. The rudimentary but effective criterion for an acceptable surface was that a light car could be driven over the aerodrome at 20 mph without undue discomfort to the occupants. This test still applies today, although the speed has been increased by the Civil Aviation Authority to 30 mph! Claude Hunter, perfectionist as always, had worked to 50 mph! The Air Ministry's bearing capacity test consisted of slowly running a loaded 3 ton lorry over the ground.

The effect of a roughly circular plan meant that the hangars were laid out in a curve following the boundary. Unfortunately, the siting of hangars and other buildings to reduce their obstruction to flying was sometimes adversely affected by civilian regulations such as the Ribbon Development Act. In many instances the latter meant building further out into the flying area or further along the aerodrome boundary than would otherwise have been necessary.

Such was the prevailing mood of pacifism in the 1930s that the urgently-needed new airfields had to meet the stringent requirements of both the Royal Fine Arts Commission and the Society for the Preservation of Rural England. There was no attempt at dispersal of accommodation, the technical buildings being located immediately to the rear of the hangars. The airmen's quarters were normally grouped around an open area behind the technical buildings, with officers' and sergeants' messes provided as separate groups, somewhat more isolated but still in close proximity to both the technical and airmen's buildings. In the case of training stations, instructional buildings were located so as to be equally convenient to the technical and domestic sites.

The first of the Expansion stations, begun in 1935, were Marham, Feltwell, Stradishall, Cranfield, Harwell, Tern Hill, Waddington, Church Fenton, Manby, Thorney Island and Odiham. Some existing stations, namely Catterick, Cranwell, Halton, Hornchurch, Leuchars, North Weald, Sealand, Tangmere, Turnhouse, Upper Heyford and Wittering, were modernized to bring them into line with current standards and to provide for increased

Halfpenny Green, originally known as Bobbington, a training station of pre-war design before dispersal became the keynote (DoE).

establishments. In 1936 new permanent stations were started at Debden, Dishforth, Driffield, Finningley, Hemswell, Hullavington, Leconfield, Scampton, Shawbury, Upwood and Wyton. The same year, the planning and construction of Aircraft Storage Units was begun. To economize on construction, most of them were co-located with other units on the same airfield so that HQ and other buildings could be shared.

New armament training camps and observer schools did not conform to the elaborate standards of the main Expansion stations, being of hutted construction. Among them were Penrhos, West Freugh, Evanton, Acklington and Jurby. They did, however, require technical and instructional buildings of special design. Other hutted stations for Auxiliary Air Force squadrons were started at Detling, Doncaster and Dyce and accommodation was provided for Volunteer Reserve training centres at Shoreham and Stapleford Tawney, amongst others. Lyneham, now the RAF's main transport base, was to have had permanent build-

ings but these were substituted by hutted accommodation.

Further hutting was erected at a number of municipal airports for VR training and at the new Flying Training School at Kinloss some of the buildings were permanent, others being wooden huts. An ASU was subsequently added at this Scottish airfield, along with a similar unit at nearby Lossiemouth, where it was planned that temporary accommodation would eventually be replaced by brick buildings. To facilitate this the huts were laid out in a similar fashion to a permanent station. If such an improvement was not envisaged, the same balanced layout was followed but the spacing of the buildings was substantially reduced. Good examples of this concentration were Bobbington and Cranage, although only the hut floors can be seen today.

The last permanent stations to be constructed before the war were Binbrook, Bramcote, Middle Wallop, Newton, Topcliffe, Leeming, North Luffenham, Swinderby, Syerston, Waterbeach, Oakington, Middleton St

George, Coningsby, Swanton Morley, West Malling and Ouston. At the same time, new ASUs were begun at Dumfries, Hawarden, Lichfield and Limavady. Limavady, however, was never completed as such and was transferred to Coastal Command's control.

The opening of hostilities presented the RAF with a large number of requisitioned civil aerodromes, most of which had been established during the previous decade. Some owed their origin to the urging of the Air Ministry in October 1928 for all towns with more than 20,000 inhabitants to build an airport, although few councils followed the advice. The early 1930s, however, saw a rise in air-mindedness and many local authorities hastily established municipal airports. Some of the sites were hardly suitable but prestige was at stake.

Sir Alan Cobham had done more than anyone to bring aviation to the masses and in the summer of 1929 he and Lady Cobham made a 10,000 mile air tour in search of suitable sites for municipal airports. Every town from Inverness to Penzance was visited and whenever possible its mayor was persuaded to take a flight. By the end of that year only eight municipal airports were in existence; at Blackpool, Manchester, Nottingham, Hull, Stoke, Carlisle, Bristol and Plymouth. Privately-owned airports totalled seven; Heston, Hanworth, Woodley. Maylands, Hesketh Park, Haldon and Shoreham. There were proposals for 42 more and most of them were eventually completed. A few of the towns and cities which failed to develop an airport later regretted their decision. One of the largest, Sheffield, is still talking about building one today. Llanfair-p-g, the Welsh village with the longest name, planned an aerodrome and caused *Flight* magazine to comment: 'The difficulty is can a landing field be found big enough for blazoning the name on the ground as is now the custom at all the big aerodromes?'

A few of the well-known airports were privately-owned. They included Heston, Gatwick and de Havilland's Stag Lane. Heston rivalled Croydon, having a concrete hangar, radio equipment and advanced lighting, while as early as 1928 Stag Lane was claiming to be the busiest aerodrome in the world. An average of 1,000 landings were recorded on a

Chipping Warden, Northants, seen in 1987. Built in 1940, it had temporary technical buildings in a similar layout to that of the Expansion Period but with dispersed living sites (Tony Hooper).

Middle Wallop, Hants, one of the last of the Expansion stations and not completed until after the war began (Roy Bonser Collection).

typical fine summer's day by the London Aero Club and private owners. It was not destined to survive for long, however, de Havilland selling the site for building in the early 1930s and moving to Hatfield.

In September 1939, virtually all the municipal airports were requisitioned for military use but few were suitable for modern high performance aircraft, being generally too small and/or dangerously close to built-up areas. Those with adjacent shadow factories - Elmdon, Speke and Yeadon for example - soon acquired runways, but the majority were relegated to elementary flying training, repair work and other mundane but essential activities.

There was a further class of civil aerodrome to be considered - the AA Landing Ground. In 1932 the Automobile Association extended its terms of reference to cater for the private flyer as well as the motorist. In October of that year the *AA Register of Aircraft Landing Grounds* was first published detailing temporary sites, some of which were disused World War aerodromes, mainly located in areas where permanent aerodromes had not yet been established. Often to be found near country hotels, their use was arranged by the AA with landowners and farmers who agreed to keep them clear of livestock. Petrol was supplied from a local garage with an AA patrolman acting as liaison, and all sites were guaranteed tested by an aircraft.

The *Register* was amended regularly, some landing grounds often being withdrawn from use or relocated to allow for crop rotation. When the war began, the AA handed over all their information to the Air Ministry, but though the sites were inspected few were found suitable for development into military airfields. However, it is evident that the surveyors often found better stretches of land in the immediate vicinity. RAF Finmere, for example, was built about half a mile from the landing ground at Tingewick, and Wallingford was close to RAF Benson.

AA sites which *were* developed to varying degrees included Leeming, Newmarket, Clifden Hampden in Oxfordshire which became RNAS Culham, Bury St Edmunds (Westley), Ronaldsway in the Isle of Man and Christchurch in Hampshire. Today's St Mawgan owes its origins to the AA Landing Ground known as Newquay which later became RAF Trebelzue. This site in turn was swallowed by the entirely new airfield built in 1942. The unwanted AA sites were obstructed in the summer of 1940 as all the locations would have been known to German intelligence.

On 3 September 1939 the number of RAF airfields in the UK was 116, almost twice that five years earlier and about four times that in 1925, the nadir of its fortunes. Many of the new permanent stations would endure to the present day, their hangars housing a Tornado as readily as a Heyford, Whitley or Lancaster.

Chapter 2

Paved runways, taxi-ways and dispersals

Air Commodore C C Darley wrote in 1959:

'I used what I believe was the first runway in the Air Force (sic) in January 1915 when with 3 Squadron at Choques near Bethune in France. At the time we were using a ploughed field as an aerodrome and it became very sticky during Christmas 1914. We were flying Bleriots at that time before taking over the Morane Parasol. The runway was a single line of railway sleepers just wide enough to take the undercarriage of a Bleriot and did help enormously. The first paved runways were put down in 1931 at Kohat, being two strips 30 yd wide by 600 yd long. A taxi-way 60 ft wide joined the tarmac at the front of the sheds to the end of one of the runways. Otherwise, one turned round at the end after landing and back-tracked. One could just do that with the aircraft we had at the time — Wapitis with no brakes.'

Early in 1916, an 8 acre area of Northolt aerodrome was covered with cinders to alleviate winter bogging, ash tracks joining it to the hangar aprons. Almost certainly the first proper runway in Britain was built at Cranwell. The single east-west strip had been excavated in 1928 and surfaced with rolled ash, but it was improved a few years later by adding hardcore overlaid with tarmac. The runway was intended originally for experimental long-range flights and in 1939 was lengthened to 1580 yards.

In 1930, Manchester's Barton Airport was claiming to be the first in the UK laid out to 'the American principle with definite runways for landing and take-off. Cinders have been laid to form three runways raised above the level of the unprepared surface as is done in the great majority of cases in the USA'. As we have seen, the method was not new and, as

well as at Northolt, the RFC had used cinders to combat the mud of the French winter.

The very wet winter of 1936/37 was a foretaste of problems to come when the muddy areas adjacent to concrete aprons spread farther and farther on to the landing grounds. In May 1937, the C-in-C Fighter Command asked for runways at certain fighter stations, but higher authority deemed the cost to be prohibitive and quite beyond any figure that they dare to request from the Treasury! Lateral extensions to parking areas were considered and this developed into the provision of a perimeter track when the AOC 11 Group suggested a track all round the aerodrome. He felt that this would ease the bogging problem and help in the maintenance and fuelling of aircraft.

By June 1937, Bomber Command also was beginning to realize that its next generation of aircraft would require hard runways, and that they might be grounded by mud at a critical stage in any future war was more than a possibility. The Air Ministry produced many excuses including the fact that runways would rule out practice bombing on aerodromes and necessitate more bombing ranges, that there would be no natural braking effect as with grass and that they were impossible to camouflage.

There was some optimism that the Courtney Take-Off System would solve all the problems. This consisted of a rail track running in any desired direction, regardless of wind, and an auxiliary power unit to launch a carriage on which the aircraft was mounted. The bizarre scheme was never adopted, however, and it appears that it was mainly a red herring to blunt the attacks of the pro-runway lobby!

Late in 1937, the RAE was given the task of investigating the effect on a grass aerodrome of a taxiing aircraft for which the heaviest aircraft then in service, the Whitley, was selected

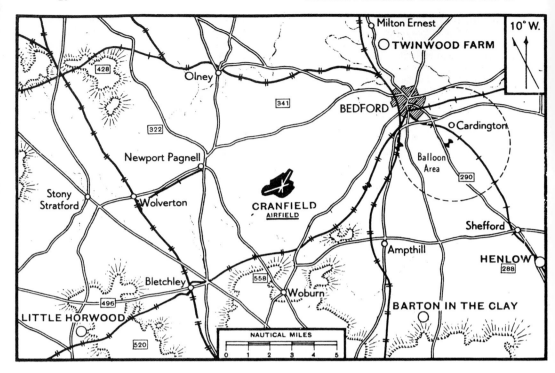

ALL HEIGHTS IN FEET ABOVE MEAN SEA LEVEL

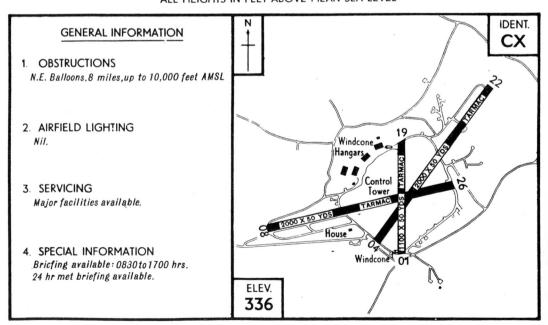

GENERAL INFORMATION

1. OBSTRUCTIONS
N.E. Balloons, 8 miles, up to 10,000 feet AMSL

2. AIRFIELD LIGHTING
Nil.

3. SERVICING
Major facilities available.

4. SPECIAL INFORMATION
Briefing available: 0830 to 1700 hrs.
24 hr met briefing available.

IDENT.
CX

ELEV.
336

One of the first RAF stations with paved runways: Cranfield, Beds, as it was by 1946.

for the trials. It was modified by the fitting of a massive steel beam connecting the standard undercarriage units with special wheels and tyres at each end. Steel weights could be attached to the girder to bring the Whitley's normal take-off weight of 22,000 lb up to 40,000 lbs. Preliminary trials were carried out at Farnborough in December 1937 to measure the depth of the depressions made by the aircraft while moving or standing. It was not, of course, flown while so modified.

No problems were encountered and, temporarily refitted with its normal wheels, the Whitley was flown to nearby Odiham which, although not intended to be a bomber station, was constructed to the same specification. The Whitley bogged down almost immediately when taxied at high weight, although on a higher part of the aerodrome it was taxied successfully, as was a Hawker Demon with its tyre pressure adjusted to give the same characteristics as the Whitley.

The official verdict on the tests was that there should be no difficulty operating bombers up to 40,000 lb weight from properly-prepared grass airfields. It was felt that the poor results at Odiham were due to recent filling of the ground next to the new hardstandings, and that a real bomber of that weight would have twice the power to pull

itself out of the ruts. (The stresses on the undercarriage seem to have been ignored!)

The Whitley test was performed also at Stradishall in March 1938 with mixed results. The fact that both Odiham and Stradishall were among the first RAF stations to be equipped with runways speaks for itself. Events in the Spanish Civil War provided overwhelming evidence that a modern air force could not operate all the year round from grass aerodromes and the Air Ministry could no longer evade the issue. In fairness, however, it would appear that the real villains were the politicians whom the Air Ministry knew were unlikely to provide the necessary money.

Sir Hugh Dowding was saying in November 1938 (PRO AIR 2/2067):

'We must have these runways at almost all fighter stations if we are able to operate fighters by day and night during a wet winter. I have pressed this view on the Air Ministry for the last two years. The initial cost of the runways will of course be high but, apart from their operational necessity, they will pay for themselves hand over fist in 10 years. This eternal tinkering with the drainage of aerodromes will not be necessary. In wet weather only the runways will be used and so the rest

Laying duckboards to combat the mud at Carew Cheriton, Dyfed, during the winter of 1939/40 (Via Fred Adkin).

Odiham during the Royal Review in 1953. It was one of the first RAF stations to be equipped with runways (P.H.T. Green Collection).

of the aerodrome will not become a swamp and can be used again without repair as soon as the weather improves.'

It was not until 28 April 1939 that an Air Ministry conference decided that runways should be laid at the following fighter aerodromes in order of priority: Kenley, Biggin Hill, Church Fenton, Debden, Northolt, Tangmere, Turnhouse and Hendon. However, only those at Northolt and Turnhouse were completed by the time the war began, although the remainder, apart from Hendon, were well under way. Other RAF stations known to have had one or more runways before the Second World War were Catfoss, Benson, Odiham, Stradishall, Aldergrove, Thornaby, Linton-on-Ouse and North Weald. RNAS Gosport had two short tarmac runways built largely for carrier landing practice pre-war. They were abandoned in 1940 and replaced by four much longer grass strips, an almost certainly unique regression!

The early runways were essentially graded Tarmac, usually about 2.5 in thick laid over a subgrade which incorporated brick or stone hardcore. A top-coat of asphalt was added for water-proofing and side drains catered for rainwater run-off. As aircraft weights increased, problems began to occur. At Aldergrove in Northern Ireland, for example, the runways built on peaty subsoil had developed 'waves' by 1941 which subjected undercarriages to severe strain.

Successful Tarmac runways depended, it was

said, on a solid foundation. Where inferior hardcore such as pit ballast was used, the surface was likely to disintegrate. The three runways laid at Hampstead Norris in Berkshire during the summer of 1940 used chalk and ash as hardcore, but soon gave way in a number of places and had to be reconstructed. Certain airfields had Tarmac as well as concrete runways, examples being Snaith with two runways of concrete and one of Tarmac, Wombleton with two of Tarmac and one of concrete and Stratford with two-and-a-half in concrete and half in Tarmac.

This partial use of Tarmac was necessitated by a shortage of cement reducing the output of concrete, which had proved to be the best material for runway construction. Its properties were known and predictable, although the design theory of concrete slabs was still controversial. The standard slab thickness was 6 in, except for hard-standings, perimeter tracks and the ends of runways which were 5 in. Experience soon showed that hard-standings, taxi-tracks and holding areas were subjected to heavier loadings than the normal take-off and landing runs, due to concentrated loads of marshalling aircraft with vibration from running up engines, plus bomb trolleys and heavy vehicular traffic. The thickness was therefore increased to 8 in throughout. The year 1943 was to see a widespread programme of rectification put into effect to strengthen these areas or to prevent further deterioration.

The requirement for speed of construction dominated everything. Supervising officers had to strike a balance between speed, sub-grade strength and concrete thickness in order to complete such a vast programme in so short a time with the materials and labour available. It was necessary to improvise methods of construction, to use materials which would normally be considered unsuitable and to carry on working in weather conditions which would have stopped work of lesser importance. There was no readily-available fund of knowledge of runway bearing strengths and the builders learned as they went along, there being no time for elaborate research. Not surprisingly, a number of failures occurred. What *was* surprising was that so much of the concrete stood up to the demands that were later put on it and that failures were usually found to be the results of poor workmanship or particularly bad materials.

It is not advisable to lay concrete in frosty conditions but this was often done to avoid delays, and while the consequences were not evident for some time, eventually the concrete began to sink and crack. In August 1943, for example, RAF Topcliffe in Yorkshire reported that, owing to the extremely heavy traffic created by the Halifaxes of 1659 HCU, the

condition of the runways and perimeter track was becoming serious despite constant maintenance. The Secretary of State for Air was challenged to explain why aircraft had been written off at certain unnamed aerodromes owing to faulty concrete. His reply in Parliament stated that severe frost was the cause but that only minor damage had been suffered by the aircraft concerned. The problem was perhaps most severe at 8th Air Force bases where there were a number of cases of heavily loaded B-17s breaking through runways and taxi strips.

As a temporary solution to the shortcomings of grass aerodromes, accelerator tracks were laid at a few of them in 1940, including Farnborough, Feltwell and Mildenhall. This was an idea borrowed from the Germans who used them extensively in Northern France and had provided them at airports such as Berlin-Tempelhof since at least 1934. They assisted the take-off of heavily-loaded aircraft which, by the time they ran on to the grass, were already partially airborne. A major problem was the joint between the metalled surface and the grass which soon became muddy even when only used at low speeds.

RAF Oakington near Cambridge was the aerodrome which probably suffered the most from pre-war policy. In March 1941, Harold Balfour, Under-Secretary of State for Air, wrote to Lord Beaverbrook, head of the Ministry of Aircraft Production:

It was the Stirling which brought home the folly of not building runways. This example from 1665 HCU did use a runway but found it too short, and ended up straddling the A49 road at Tilstock, Shropshire! (R.R. Glass).

'I tried today to fly to Oakington but found it impossible to land because the aerodrome was reported unserviceable. A Spitfire pilot the day before had turned over in the mud and killed himself. I had to go to Wyton, itself only just serviceable being badly cut up with no runways. I found that they had to load up the Stirlings at Wyton which are then sent on operations after struggling light off the sodden surface of Oakington.

'My experience of the past was the same. I received an assurance that 'all will be well on the day' and that there were other methods and measures that I, as a layman, would not understand, which would be far more effective than runways. Here we are with the first Stirlings, unable to function normally because of an untracked base.'

In a letter to Beaverbrook in February 1941, 'Bomber' Harris was typically forceful.

'For twenty years everybody on the stations and the squadrons has been screaming for runways without avail. The maximum consolation obtained from Air Ministry on the subject when I was a Group Commander in the days of peace was a long dissertation on the potentialities and promise of 'worm action' towards making our new aerodromes fit for bombers to live on. I am absolutely satisfied that the amount of effort, labour and expense of not having runways is incomparably greater than the effort, labour and expense it would take to install them. Through not having runways our effort will be seriously detracted from in normal winter conditions and reduced very probably to zero in abnormal winter conditions. Every other nation throughout the world has long been convinced of the necessity for runways, but we ourselves have always been apparently just as convinced that our view is right. We alone are the only soldier in step in the entire battalion.' (PRO AIR 19/492).

The runways now being provided at new bomber stations allowed little margin for error in anything but ideal conditions. There were many accidents to returning aircraft when they over-ran the strips, particularly at night. Following trials at RAE in the second half of 1940, it was decided to fit certain bomber airfields with an experimental form of arrestor gear. A much stronger version of that used on aircraft carriers, it consisted of two steel cables 400 ft in length stretched across the runway and supported 6 in above it at 33 ft intervals. The cables were 100 ft apart and connected to hydraulic braking equipment in a pit at the side of the runway.

Twenty airfields were selected initially, including Elsham Wolds, Lakenheath, Linton-on-Ouse, Middleton St George, Swinderby and Waterbeach, most having six sets to guard all three runways. However, no progress was made with modifying Lancasters and Halifaxes to accept a hook and, with an improvement in pilot training and longer runways becoming the norm, the project was officially abandoned in July 1943. Traces of the equipment can be seen at many of the sites to this day.

The steps in lay-out development up to 1941 can be summarized as follows:

May 1939 A typical airfield consisted of four grass strips, one of 1,300 yd by 400 yd and three of 1,000 yd by 200 yd. At that date the first runway programme was initiated. At 12 stations, runways 800 yd by 50 yd were begun along two of the four grass strips and were connected with a perimeter or taxi-track, 50 ft wide, which in most cases followed the airfield boundary so far as the topography allowed. In July 1939 the 800 yd runways at two stations were increased to 1,000 yd.

February 1940 Bomber airfields were designed with three strips of minimum length 1,000 yd as near 60° to each other as possible. New airfields to those requirements were planned for future extension up to a runway 1,400 yd long and two subsidiaries of 1,100 yd.

December 1940 All bomber airfields were constructed with one runway of 1,400 yd and two of 1,100 yd.

January 1941 Increase of bomber airfields to one 1,600 yd runway and two of 1,100 yd, capable of extension to 2,000 yd and 1,400 yd respectively.

March 1941 Fighter stations to have one main runway 1,300 yd long with two subsidiaries of 1,100 yd. Night fighters to have one of 1,400 yd and two of 1,100 yd.

July 1941 All stations to have ideal dimensions of one main runway 2,000 yd long and two subsidiaries 1,400 yd long. Minimum to be 1,600 yd and 1,100 yd respectively.

November 1941 All bomber stations to be extended to the ideal dimensions wherever practicable.

The requirements of 1942 set the ultimate wartime standard for the RAF operational airfield and it was to this standard that construction of new stations and extensions to existing fields followed until the end of the war. It was known

Peplow, Shropshire, in February 1944. The central runway intersection was not the ideal configuration (PRO).

I. PEPL. 24·2·44. // PEPLOW AERODROME
52°48 N. 02°20 W.   SCALE $\frac{1}{6700}$ N

as the Class 'A' Standard and was designed for all contemporary heavy bombers. The fundamental requirements were as follows:

Strips (the area clear of significant obstructions) Three were planned as far as possible at 60° to each other, the main strip of 2000 yd by 400 yd and two subsidiary strips of 1,400 yd by 200 yd. Wherever possible the main strip was aligned in a north-east, southwest direction.

Runways A main of 2,000 yd by 50 yd with subsidiaries of 1,400 yd by 50 yd with 100 yd cleared area at both ends as an overshoot. On subsidiary runways where the differences in levels of the ends of the runways exceeded 20 ft, the runway length was if possible increased by 100 yd for every additional 10 ft in rise. Fillets at runway intersections were provided to enable aircraft after landing to turn on to runways not in use whenever a shorter route to their dispersal was possible than continuing to the end of the runway. Margins to a width of 75 yd on each side of the 50 yd runways were consolidated and prepared to a state suitable for emergency landing and take-off. In most cases, the turf was cultivated to provide normal grass airfield conditions.

Gradients Runways and strips: Maximum longitudinal gradient 1:80. Maximum transverse runways 1:60, maximum transverse margins 1:50.

Perimeter and access tracks Built to a standard 50 ft width. The minimum radius of curve was 150 ft on the centre line when the internal angle between two sections of track or between track and runway was more than 60°. When this angle was 60° or less, the minimum radius of curve was 200 ft on the centre line. To prevent damage to aircraft should they run off the track, an area was cleared each side to a depth of 30 ft. No buildings or other obstructions were erected within 150 ft from the centre of the track. No other track or hardstandings were within 150 ft centre to centre.

The ideal runway configuration was thus an equilateral triangle which would reduce the concentration of target, minimize cross-wind effects and avoid the possibility of a crash blocking all three runways at a central intersection. This was not always possible, however, owing to the size of the land available and other terrain restrictions. Crosby-on-Eden near Carlisle, Elvington in Yorkshire and Peplow in Shropshire, to name but three, were built with a central intersection.

During 1944 there was a requirement for several airfields for special purposes which exceeded the normal Class 'A' Standard. Airfields for very heavy bomber and transport aircraft were planned with a main runway 3,000 yd by 100 yd and subsidiaries 2,000 yd by 100 yd. Strip widths were 400 and 250 yd respectively. On the East Coast, three emergency runways for disabled aircraft were constructed with massive paved strips 3,000 yd long and 250 yd wide.

The possibility of furnishing flying training stations with concrete runways was discussed at some length during 1940. In March, Flying Training Command came to the conclusion that it was not in favour of the provision of runways for the following reasons:

a)   Construction during the summer months would render airfields unserviceable during a most valuable training period.
b)   Those airfields which had good grass surface and were well drained did not require runways.
c)   During night landings, pupils would frequently run off a 50 yd wide runway and in many cases crash on reaching the grass surfaces if it were boggy.
d)   Fifty yd wide runways would be dangerous for night flying.

However, a subsequent report from the CO at Cranfield, a runway airfield allocated temporarily to an SFTS, made it clear that experience during the winter of 1940/41 showed that there were distinct advantages in having runways on a training station. Amongst the facts that he advanced to support this contention were that in the first three months of 1941 nearly all flying was carried out from the runways, only one accident being attributable to aircraft running on to the grassed area. In addition, no difficulty had been experienced by staff or pupils in operating from runways at night.

During the four months commencing November 1940, when attempts were made to use the grass surface, as many as 15 propellors were damaged in one day as a result of mud and stones being flung into them, and several cases of retraction failure were traced to mud clogging the moving parts. In contrast, at no time when runways were in use was there any appreciable damage to propellors beyond normal wear and tear.

As a result of the experiences at Cranfield, previously held opinions were reversed and it was decided to construct hard runways and perimeter tracks at a number of SFTSs and their RLGs. Since operational stations had priority, the programme was limited by scarcity of labour to two concrete runways each at Brize Norton, Hullavington, Shawbury, Tern Hill, Little Rissington and Manby. Kidlington, Southrop and Cranage were provided with two

A training station and today's Inverness Airport, Dalcross was provided with paved runways right from the start because of bad surface conditions (Via V.L. Winterburn).

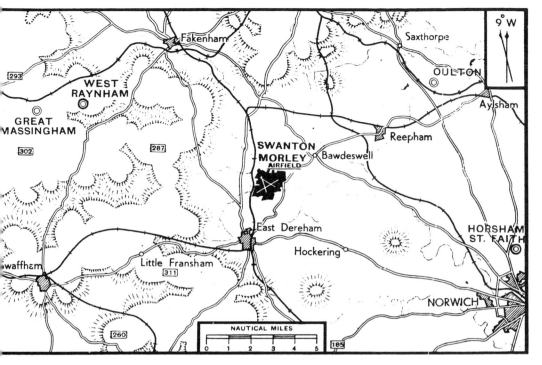

ALL HEIGHTS IN FEET ABOVE MEAN SEA LEVEL

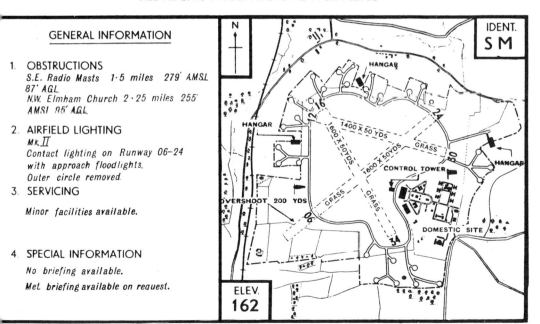

GENERAL INFORMATION

1. OBSTRUCTIONS
   S.E. Radio Masts 1·5 miles 279' A.M.S.L.
   87' AGL
   N.W. Elmham Church 2·25 miles 255'
   AMSL 95' AGL

2. AIRFIELD LIGHTING
   Mk. II
   Contact lighting on Runway 06-24
   with approach floodlights.
   Outer circle removed.

3. SERVICING

   Minor facilities available.

4. SPECIAL INFORMATION

   No briefing available.

   Met briefing available on request.

Some aerodromes remained grass-surfaced throughout the war: Swanton Morley, Norfolk.

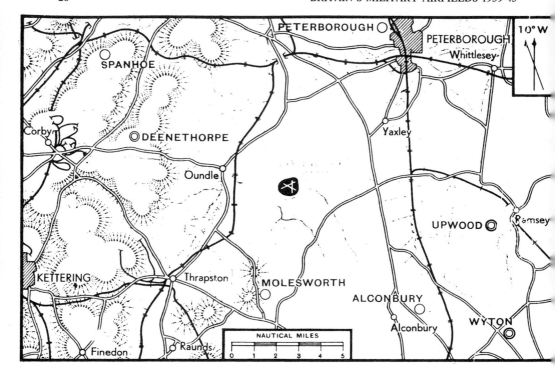

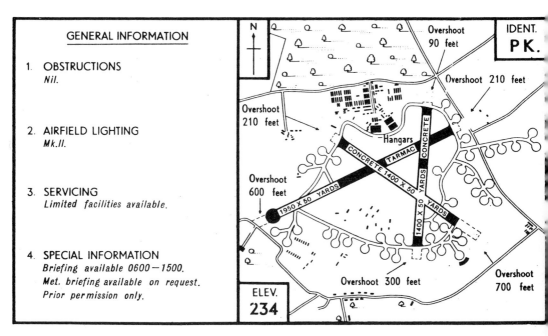

GENERAL INFORMATION

1. OBSTRUCTIONS
   Nil.

2. AIRFIELD LIGHTING
   Mk.II.

3. SERVICING
   Limited facilities available.

4. SPECIAL INFORMATION
   Briefing available 0600–1500.
   Met. briefing available on request.
   Prior permission only.

Polebrook, Northants, extended for Fortress operations.

Newly-delivered B-17s parked on a finger hard-standing at an Ulster airfield, probably Langford Lodge, in March 1944 (P.H.T. Green Collection).

runways of Army Track and the same was done at South Cerney, Chipping Norton and Windrush in Sommerfeld Track. The initial programme was complete by May 1942 and was followed by runway construction at 26 more training aerodromes.

As mentioned briefly above, a pre-war perimeter track was an 18 ft wide roadway around the landing area for support vehicles. When intended for aircraft it was normally 35 ft wide (later increased to 50 ft) and termed a taxi-track. However, the term perimeter track, often abbreviated to peri-track, was soon in universal use to mean either. In February 1939 a track was sanctioned for the perimeters of all fighter stations. Where runways were in existence or under construction and did not join the peri-track, they were to be linked to it by an 18 ft wide extension. These 'bat handles', as they came to be known, were laid at many other aerodromes.

Unfortunately, they proved very difficult to find when taxiing at night off a runway and, by the end of the war, most had been enlarged to runway width as labour became available. Some Commanding Officers did not like these taxi-links in direct extension of the runway centre-line and had them built at an angle to it. Peri-tracks were also supposed to follow the perimeter of the aerodrome for camouflage purposes as the curved line would not be so obvious. The very wet weather of November 1940 played havoc at those grass aerodromes still lacking a peri-track and it was suggested that surrounding public roads should be utilized where possible.

As runways at certain stations were length-ened progressively, so the peri-track was extended to give access. In a number of cases, the bomber OTU aerodrome at Seighford near Stafford being an example, the peri-track was left unaltered to save construction time. The runway extension was merely built with a turning circle at the end. Backtracking was of course necessary, but the increased runway occupancy time was deemed acceptable. At 8th Air Force bomber bases such as Grafton Underwood and Polebrook, however, it was not conducive to the speedy departure of large numbers of aircraft.

Between the wars, service aircraft were kept in hangars as often as possible when not in use. There was no provision for dispersal nor any need for it but, by mid-1938, it was realized that some contingency plans must be made for aircraft dispersal around the airfield boundary so that in war concentrations of aircraft in hangars and on aprons could be avoided. Feltwell in Norfolk was one of the earliest stations to make the necessary arrangements. Gaps were cut in the hedges and ditches bridged to allow access to the neighbouring fields in an emergency. There was some embarrassment at Stradishall when it was discovered that two German subjects had bought houses within the area earmarked for dispersals!

In February 1939 officialdom decreed that all service aerodromes were to disperse their aircraft within the perimeter. Duxford, however, was permitted to utilize the natural camouflage of a strip of woods just beyond its south-west corner. An experimental pit for the protection of aircraft was dug at Feltwell but

Top *Argosy G-APRN over Desborough, Northants, a former bomber OTU station with loop hard-standings and a bomb storage area in the woods to the left* (Roy Bonser Collection).

Above *Spitfire of 609 Squadron taxies along the A343 to an emergency dispersal off Middle Wallop aerodrome, 1940* (Roy Bonser Collection).

it cost considerably more than had been expected. It also encroached on the aerodrome surface and, because it was necessary to extend the walls of the pit to about 11 ft above the ground, the further advantage of reducing obstruction by parked aircraft was nullified.

Soon after the beginning of the war, the problem became one of reconciling effective dispersal with easy access to runways. Temporary hardcore tracks soon became useless and with the advent of more and heavier aircraft and the development of paved runways and peri-tracks, dispersal standings were upgraded to equal the strength of the peri-track. Affording permanent sites for minor overhauls, refuelling and bombing up, the

early standings were circular in shape, of 125 ft diameter and approached by an access track. They were sited irregularly round the peri-track with due regard to inconspicuousness and local ground configuration.

As the size and numbers of aircraft further increased, the scheme became less and less viable owing to the sterilization of long stretches of access track by small numbers of aircraft. The problem was exacerbated by a Bomber Command order issued in the early months of the war which required aircraft to be fully dispersed half an hour before sunrise and not placed in hangars until half an hour after sunset. Only aircraft undergoing repair or major inspection could be retained under cover. A maximum of two squadrons was permitted at each parent station dispersed in groups of three, individual machines to be at least 50 yd apart and groups at least 300 yd apart.

Later developments saw the introduction of the 'frying-pan' type of access track in various diameters up to 125 ft sited immediately off the peri-track, and the 'spectacle' or 'loop' type similarly positioned. The latter type became the standard dispersal on bomber stations by 1943 and consisted normally of groups of four, two being placed opposite to one another on each side of the track. The undesir-

able locked-wheel turns necessary on the frying-pan type were avoided and marshalling heavy bombers for take-off was made much easier. The distance between hard-standings was a minimum of 150 ft edge to edge, and where the ground was unsuitable for a loop type a frying-pan was substituted, the aim being to equip every bomber base with 50 hard-standings.

During February 1942, Fighter Command policy decreed 50 hard-standings at each aerodrome and 25 at satellites. The standard shape was seven-sided, 44 ft wide for single-engined fighters and 62 ft for twins, the designations

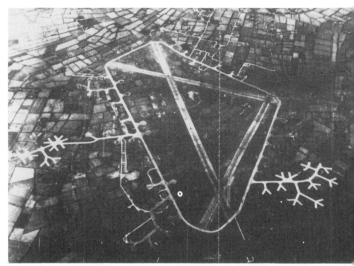

Right *Cluntoe, Northern Ireland. A USAAF training base with the standard 'frying pan' hard-standings of the early war years plus finger dispersals and a star-shaped multiple standing for the open storage of reserve aircraft.*

Below *Loop and frying pan dispersals at Bishops Court, 1944, on the southern corner of the aerodrome. The aircraft are Ansons and a single Halifax. Note the blister hangars, original field boundaries and a farmhouse between runway and peri-track (Via E.A. Cromie).*

Above *Loop dispersals at Ballykelly, Northern Ireland, together with post-war Operational Readiness Platform adjacent to runway.*

Below *Fighter hard-standings off the perimeter track at Rednal, Shropshire, as featured on the cover of* Action Stations *volume 3.*

Bottom *Whirlwind of 263 Squadron in improvized log dispersal at Drem in July 1940 (J. Munro).*

Prentice and Cessna 172 in an old fighter pen at Biggin Hill.

being FCW4621 and FCW4820, respectively. At many OTUs a small hexagonal bay, FCW4474, jutted directly from the peri-track at intervals. Maintenance Units eventually acquired a variety of hard-standings to cater for the open storage of aircraft as the threat of air attack diminished. Chief amongst them were the 'finger' type and the star-shaped 'multiple standing'.

Paved dispersals were almost entirely lacking in Flying Training Command and many local measures were taken to remedy the deficiency using combinations of hardcore, ashes and metal tracking. In January 1944 dispersal regulations were relaxed on aerodromes in the Midlands and north-west and other rear areas so that aircraft could be concentrated to any extent desirable to facilitate maintenance and handling. Marshalling areas for glider operations were a special case and during the spring of 1944 extensive metal tracking was laid at airfields earmarked for airborne units.

A parallel development to hard-standings was the dispersal pen — revetment in Ameri-can terminology — intended to protect parked aircraft from anything other than a direct hit. Walls of sandbags were used at first until a purpose-built pen to a standard E-shaped design became available. It came in two sizes, the Hurricane Pen being 126 ft wide internally and 34 ft in depth, whilst the Blenheim Pen was 175 ft by 42 ft in depth. The names referred merely to typical single and twin-engined fighters of the day.

There was a proposal to provide doors to the pens but calculations showed that they would have to weigh about 4 ton each to be effective. The alternative of putting in earth or concrete traverses in front of the shelter pens would not have been acceptable from an operational point of view. Standard air raid shelters bolted together in sections were built into the walls of the pens, the whole unit being a forerunner of today's Hardened Aircraft Shelters. Experiments were in fact carried out with roofing the pens until Fighter Command ruled that they considered such measures unnecessary.

Chapter 3

Airfield requirements for the Royal Air Force 1940-42

The first wartime programme for airfield requirements was drawn up in August 1940 when the target was 75 more aerodromes and satellites than then existed. Almost immediately this total was increased to 125, of which 104 were actually completed by the end of that year. Many of these new airfields had grass surfaces, but it had long become apparent that year-round flying was only possible from paved runways, except in the case of small trainer types. Henceforth virtually all new sites would have to be provided with runways, which obviously made the construction task even more daunting.

As a general policy it was accepted that all airfields should be interchangeable in function as far as possible, although frequently the limited size and available ground prevented this. The many technical and instructional buildings could not, of course, be applied to all types, but it does explain why some training airfields had bomb dumps or fighter dispersal pens and many operational ones instructional sites. It was the responsibility of the Air Staff to decide the overall numbers of various types of aircraft — bombers, fighters, coastal and so on — and the number of squadrons which could be based on any one aerodrome.

A working plan was soon established, with bombers being concentrated in East Anglia, Lincolnshire and Yorkshire; Coastal Command in the south-west, Scotland and Northern Ireland and Bomber OTUs in the Midlands. Navigation and air gunnery schools were located around the Irish Sea coasts, with various other types of training unit scattered across Britain to the rear of the operational areas.

A special section of Air Ministry Works Directorate was responsible for the detailed planning of accommodation to meet the differing functions and personnel establishments of RAF units. The need for the standardization of the design of stations had been apparent for several years before it became effective, but there were so many factors peculiar to the fighter, bomber and training functions that it was a formidable task. There was a wide disparity in numbers and combinations of officers and other ranks and numbers of multi-engined and single-engined aircraft. There was also the difference between the preparation and briefing for a bombing operation and the constant readiness with the shortest warning for fighter interception of an enemy attack.

Operational stations and OTUs even within the same Command were necessarily organized on different lines. A great measure of success was, however, achieved principally for bomber and coastal units by the design and provision of the standard station to a fixed overall establishment of personnel with dual alternative uses for buildings surplus to one function and deficient in another. The same type of station was readily adaptable for airborne and glider units when the need arose and, in the later stages of the war, was able to handle large numbers of escort fighters and intruders operating against pre-arranged targets rather than *ad hoc* interception.

Within the spectrum of bomber, fighter, transport and training units there were 59 separate and distinct functions during the Second World War. Many airfields catered simultaneously for two or more entirely different units and major alterations, ranging from runway construction or extension to extra domestic accommodation, were carried out at 210 of them as their role was changed. As Bomber Command expanded, some aerodromes were regrouped to form a clutch of three: a parent and two satellites. The satellites in their turn were often upgraded to parent station. Examples of this include Skellingthorpe, Dalton, Kirmington, Warboys,

Cark, Cumbria. Built as a fighter aerodrome but relegated to training like many others in north-west England after the Luftwaffe *turned its attentions towards Russia* (A. Cust).

Kimbolton and Podington. Kimbolton and Podington were transferred to the USAAF for Fortress operations, Kimbolton retaining its satellite-type watch tower until the 1970s when both it and its replacement were demolished. Goxhill in Lincolnshire, however, was built as a bomber field but allocated to the USAAF for fighter training.

All these changing factors and the resulting development tended to upset the original rules of safety distances between airfields. The C-in-C Bomber Command had said in 1941 that he was prepared to operate from aerodromes as little as two miles apart, but heavier aircraft and larger circuit patterns had made the risk too high even in wartime. In the extreme cases of Scampton and Ingham in Lincolnshire and West Raynham and Great Massingham in Norfolk, one of the pair was regarded as useless for operational flying and downgraded accordingly.

With a German invasion still a strong possibility in March 1941, Fighter Command drew up plans for alternative aerodromes in the event of a forced withdrawal from south-east England or the east coast. Squadrons at Biggin Hill would move to Mount Farm near Oxford and those at Northolt to Steeple Morden in Cambridgeshire. Benson was soon substituted for Mount Farm owing to operational demands. Crosby-on-Eden, outside Carlisle, was to be the withdrawal station for Usworth, and Ringway (now Manchester International Airport) that for Kirton-in-Lindsey. North Weald units would go to Heston whose OTU would move to Llandow in South Wales.

In the event of squadrons being bombed out of their stations or satellites, it was arranged that they would move to alternative aerodromes while their own were rapidly repaired. The small landing ground at Caxton Gibbet was earmarked for Duxford but, with Typhoons coming into service here, it was soon replaced by the new bomber field at Bourn. Both Grantham and Shawbury were available to Digby and in Scotland Castletown's aircraft would move to Evanton and Ayr's to West Freugh. Luton was Northolt's alternate aerodrome and was sufficiently equipped to rearm and refuel one fighter squadron in an emergency. It was, however, deemed unsuitable for Spitfires during the winter months and Cranfield would then be used instead.

By December 1941, the Germans had turned their attentions elsewhere but contingency plans were made for the disposition of RAF squadrons should the *Luftwaffe* resume its heavy attacks on Britain. The airfields near the south coast were obviously the most vulnerable and the evacuation of aircraft and their refuelling and rearming parties was planned. Wide dispersal of the day fighter squadrons based to the south and east of London was envisaged.

Martlesham Heath aircraft would move to Great Sampford and Debden; Bradwell Bay's to Castle Camps; Southend's to Fairlop; Gravesend's to Radlett; Manston's to Stapleford Tawney and Hornchurch; Hawkinge's to Lympne and West Malling; Friston's and Shoreham's to Redhill; Ford's to Tangmere, Odiham and White Waltham; Westhampnett's

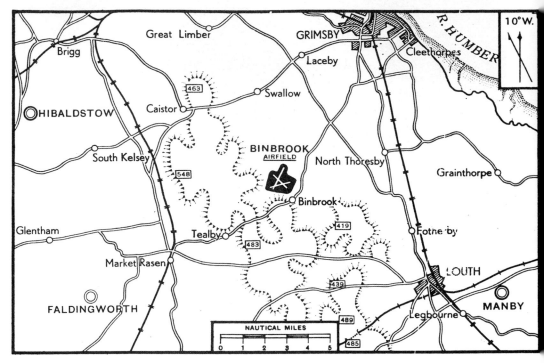

ALL HEIGHTS IN FEET ABOVE MEAN SEA LEVEL

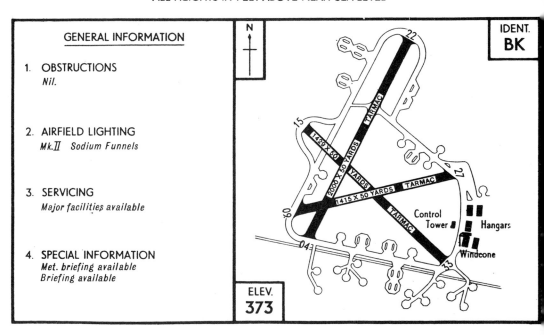

Binbrook, Lincs, one of the last permanent stations built before the war.

Edgehill, Warwickshire, a typical bomber OTU satellite station seen in 1987 (Tony Hooper).

to Farnborough and Merston's to Middle Wallop.

Of the night fighter squadrons, 29 at West Malling would withdraw to Hunsdon, 264 to Aldermaston or another suitable airfield in the Reading area, 219 at Tangmere would go to Middle Wallop and 1 to Farnborough and 23 at Ford would move to Boscombe Down. Refuelling facilities might also be found at such aerodromes as Little Horwood and Wing and servicing could be done at Benson with a satellite at Booker.

Some of the almost equally valuable fighter OTUs turning out replacement pilots were sited in vulnerable positions and were to be moved westwards in the event of an enemy threat. No 52 OTU would leave Debden for Aston Down, 53 OTU Heston for Llandow, 55 OTU Usworth for Crosby and 56 OTU at Sutton Bridge for Hawarden. Some of the moves took place at a later date but only to separate training from operational areas.

As the air war progressed, new requirements appeared. One example was the decision taken in May 1941 that each bomber OTU must have a second satellite. It was noted that the OTU areas in the Midlands were already congested, but it was desirable that the minimum distance between two aerodromes should be five miles and the maximum between parent and satellite 15 miles. Worcestershire, Herefordshire and Shropshire were among the counties scoured for new sites but few were suitable. The result was that most OTUs soldiered on with only one satellite.

In 1942 the original planned ratio of one OTU to support 10 squadrons, making a total of 25, was greatly increased. Under the new requirements, 43 bomber OTUs were deemed necessary in the UK, which involved the retention of flying training aerodromes which would otherwise have been available for other purposes when Flying Training Schools were transferred overseas. Also, many of the Advanced Flying Units could not be relocated in Canada and elsewhere, as part of their func-

tion was to acclimatize crews to flying conditions in Northern Europe.

It was the intention to transfer to the dominions every training school which it was not essential to locate in the UK. Canada, however, was finding it harder to complete new aerodromes on schedule as the sites became progressively more difficult to prepare. The other problem was that, although many airfields were being vacated by training units moving overseas, these were in the main too small for operational use.

It was hoped to carry out Airborne Forces training in Canada, the Middle East and India, since these units could not accept shared aerodromes, particularly when gliders were involved. In the event this training remained within the UK. It was hoped also to move some OTUs to Canada even though this would mean flying or shipping out aircraft from Britain, but this did not happen to any appreciable extent.

The intensity of flying training and the increasing demand for pilots placed a great strain on the facilities at parent stations of both Service and Elementary Flying Training Schools. Relief Landing Grounds were the answer, 24 being brought into use soon after the war began. Early in 1940 a further 24 were being laid out. Because they were needed so urgently, these early RLGs were brought into service with the minimum of preparation work. This meant the selection of a few reasonably level fields, the removal of hedges and the provision of drainage to replace the filled-in ditches.

Little construction work was carried out in the initial stages, three huts only being erected for the Flight Commander's office, timekeeper and crew room, and hutted accommodation for a small defence guard of 12 men. To this was added a petrol installation of 4,000 gallons and, at a few places, a Bellman hangar. At the beginning of 1941 a further development occurred at 11 of the RLGs when the facilities were increased so that in emergency

The arrival of the USAAF in Britain brought with it more demands for airfields. Air Chief Marshal Sir Trafford Leigh-Mallory at an American base. The C-47s belong to the 434th Troop Carrier Group but there are a number of possibilities for the location.

a bomber squadron could operate from each.

The entry of the USA into the war brought with it another major upheaval in airfield planning, although at first it was an indefinite but undoubtedly large commitment. The Air Ministry was already beginning the construction of dozens of aerodromes in East Anglia, ostensibly for its own use, but no doubt with an eye to future USAAF bombing operations. The first reliable forecast for USAAF deployment in the UK was received at the end of March 1942 and allowed for a total of 115 groups to be in place by the end of June 1944. Fortunately, few actually materialized before 1943, which allowed the contractors to finish most of the airfields which were needed for initial operations.

On 30 December 1942, the Air Ministry drew up a Schedule of Airfield Requirements designed to accommodate planned RAF expansion in 1943 and beyond. A few aspects of the Schedule of Requirements bear little resemblance to what actually happened, usually where forecasts of future operations went awry. It was noted that each Fighter Sector had some two or three additional airfields to enable squadrons to be concentrated to meet the scale of attack employed by the Luftwaffe from time to time. For this reason there could be no accurate relationship between the numbers of squadrons and numbers of stations. No provision was made for RAF transport units, although it was stated at that time that a mere six squadrons were planned, needing three aerodromes. It was in fact almost a year before Transport Command, formed in March 1943, received more than a handful of Dakotas.

The December 1942 airfield requirements, although not quite the final word on the subject, equipped the RAF with more than enough bases to pursue the war to its conclusion. The balance went to the USAAF and, combined with the existing allocation and its own construction efforts, the steady expansion of this force never stalled for lack of accommodation. As early as July 1943 a requirement for 12 VHB (Very Heavy Bomber) aerodromes with 3,000 yd runways was envisaged to deploy the B-29 and the Vickers Windsor. A 'most secret' minute in PRO files dated 21 April 1943 contains the intriguing comment 'there may be the possibility of the production of B-29s being undertaken in this country' (AIR 20/2803). There is, unfortunately, no other evidence to support this unlikely scheme. Marham, Sculthorpe and Lakenheath were the first VHB bases and were closed during 1944/45 for reconstruction. Honington, Wyton, Gransden Lodge, Molesworth, Leuchars and Beaulieu were also chosen. Matching and Andrews Field in Essex were possibilities but there were found to be too many agricultural objections.

Many other airfield improvement schemes were necessary as the war went on. Among them were the advanced bases for heavy bombers in north-east Scotland from which to launch operations against Norwegian targets, principally the *Tirpitz*. There was also a series of terminals and staging posts for the USAAF's Transatlantic Ferry and the upgrading of several former RAF bomber satellites for 8th Air Force units. Further details of these and many more can be found in the appropriate volumes of the *Action Stations* series.

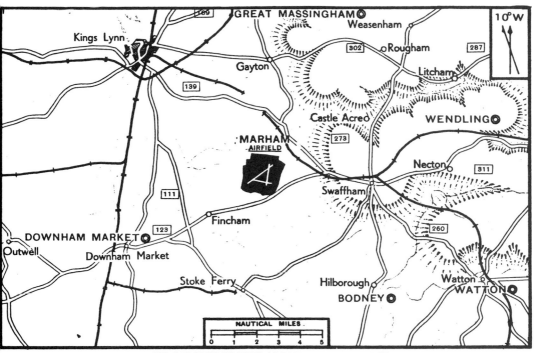

ALL HEIGHTS IN FEET ABOVE MEAN SEA LEVEL

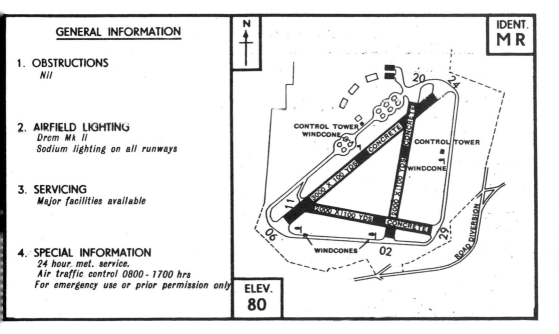

GENERAL INFORMATION

1. OBSTRUCTIONS
Nil

2. AIRFIELD LIGHTING
Drem Mk II
Sodium lighting on all runways

3. SERVICING
Major facilities available

4. SPECIAL INFORMATION
24 hour met. service.
Air traffic control 0800 - 1700 hrs
For emergency use or prior permission only

IDENT.
M R

ELEV.
80

Marham, Norfolk, was upgraded to a Very Heavy Bomber airfield by 1946 with one 3,000 and two 2,000 yd runways.

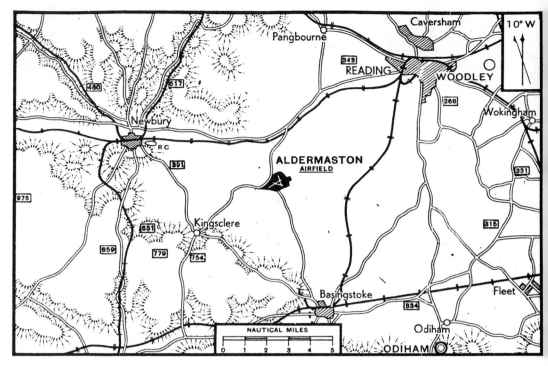

ALL HEIGHTS IN FEET ABOVE MEAN SEA LEVEL

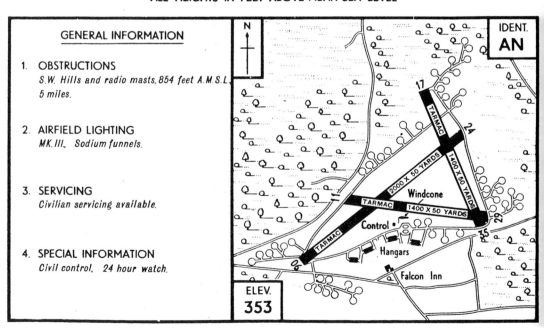

Aldermaston, Berks, planned as a bomber OTU but used by Airborne Forces.

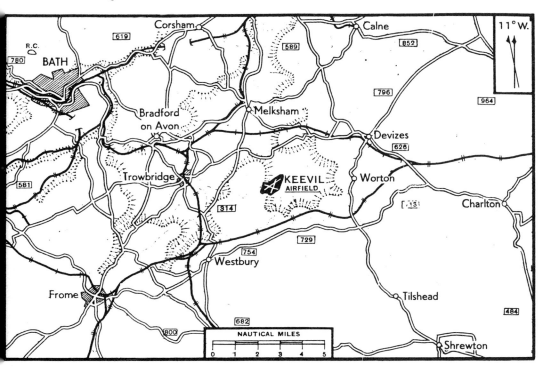

ALL HEIGHTS IN FEET ABOVE MEAN SEA LEVEL

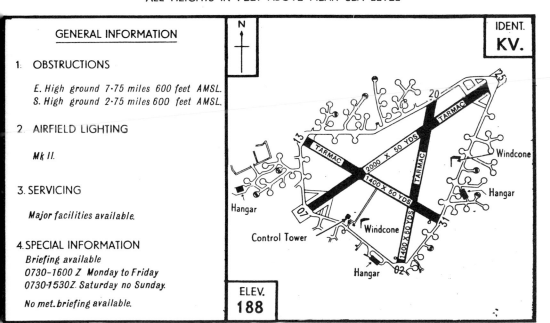

GENERAL INFORMATION

N

IDENT.
KV.

1. OBSTRUCTIONS

   E. High ground 7·75 miles 600 feet AMSL.
   S. High ground 2·75 miles 600 feet AMSL.

2. AIRFIELD LIGHTING

   Mk II.

3. SERVICING

   Major facilities available.

4. SPECIAL INFORMATION
   Briefing available
   0730-1600 Z Monday to Friday
   0730-1530Z Saturday no Sunday.

   No met. briefing available.

ELEV.
188

Keevil, Wilts, planned as a fighter OTU, built as a bomber OTU but used mainly by Airborne Forces.

Built in 1942 for Coastal Command, Banff was relegated to training before finding its forte late in 1944 as a Mosquito Strike Wing HQ (Via Chaz Bowyer).

Schedule of airfield requirements
30 December 1942

Category	Total
RAF Bomber stations (125 heavy and 17 light bomber squadrons)	80
USAAF bomber stations	70
Two Special squadrons and Bomber Development Unit	3
Heavy Conversion Units (scale of approximately one for every seven heavy bomber squadrons)	18
Target towing, gunnery, bombing and beam approach training	12
Bomber OTUs (approximate scale of one for every five heavy and medium bomber squadrons and one for each light bomber squadron)	54
USAAF bomber Combat Crew Replacement Centres	9
Bomber forward airfields for attacks on SW France and Norway	10
RAF Fighter Sector Stations (each to accommodate two squadrons)	32
RAF forward airfields and satellites	77
USAAF fighter stations	4
Fighter OTUs (approximate scale of one for every ten squadrons)	27
Multi-seater fighter OTUs	4

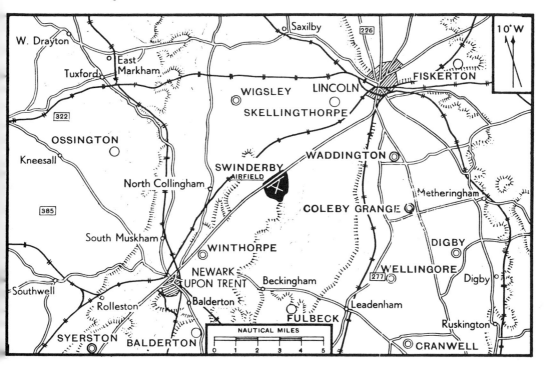

ALL HEIGHTS IN FEET ABOVE MEAN SEA LEVEL

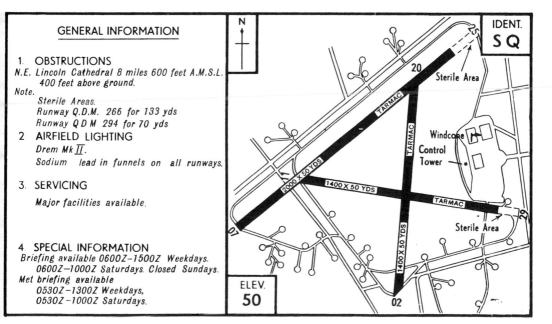

GENERAL INFORMATION

1. OBSTRUCTIONS

N.E. Lincoln Cathedral 8 miles 600 feet A.M.S.L.
    400 feet above ground.

Note.
    Sterile Areas.
    Runway Q.D.M. 266 for 133 yds
    Runway Q D M 294 for 70 yds

2 AIRFIELD LIGHTING
    Drem Mk II.
    Sodium   lead in funnels on all runways.

3. SERVICING
    Major facilities available.

4. SPECIAL INFORMATION
    Briefing available 0600Z–1500Z Weekdays.
       0600Z–1000Z Saturdays. Closed Sundays.
    Met briefing available
       0530Z–1300Z Weekdays,
       0530Z–1000Z Saturdays.

IDENT.
SQ

ELEV.
50

Swinderby, Lincs. The Fosse Way runs parallel with the main runway and a Hampden once made a successful night landing on it in error.

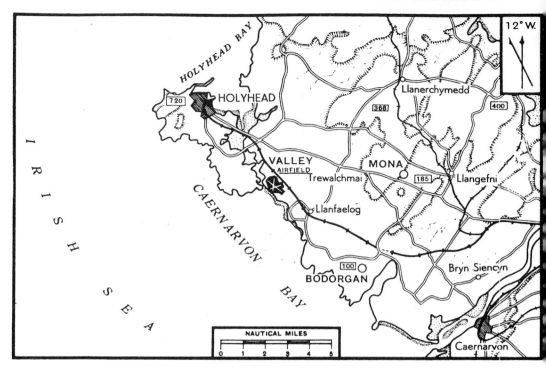

ALL HEIGHTS IN FEET ABOVE MEAN SEA LEVEL

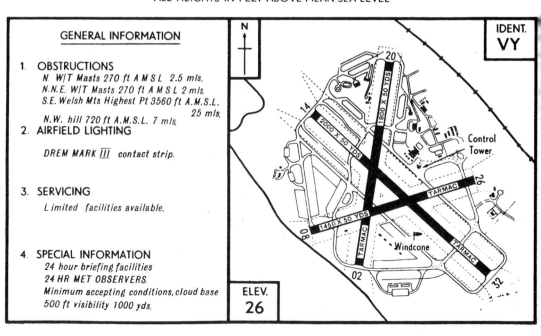

GENERAL INFORMATION

IDENT.
VY

1. **OBSTRUCTIONS**
   N W/T Masts 270 ft A M S L 2.5 mls.
   N.N.E. W/T Masts 270 ft A M S L 2 mls.
   S.E. Welsh Mts Highest Pt 3560 ft A.M.S.L.
                                        25 mls.
   N.W. hill 720 ft A.M.S.L. 7 mls.

2. **AIRFIELD LIGHTING**
   DREM MARK III contact strip.

3. **SERVICING**
   Limited facilities available.

4. **SPECIAL INFORMATION**
   24 hour briefing facilities
   24 HR MET OBSERVERS.
   Minimum accepting conditions, cloud base
   500 ft visibility 1000 yds.

ELEV.
26

Valley, Anglesey, a fighter aerodrome whose weather record was so good that it was developed into a Transatlantic Ferry Terminal for the USAAF.

USAAF fighter Combat Crew Replacement Centres	4
Advanced Landing Grounds in Southern England	27
Coastal Command operational stations	31
Photo Reconnaissance	2
Coastal OTUs	15
PR OTU (37 aircraft)	1
General Reconnaissance School (61 aircraft)	2
Torpedo Development Unit	1
Army Co-op operational stations	19
USAAF observation stations	10
AOP squadrons	3
Army Co-op OTUs	6
Anti-Aircraft Co-op Units	14
Airborne Forces operational stations	7
Glider Exercise Unit (60 aircraft and 60 gliders)	2
Glider training units	7
Glider Instructors School	2
Glider Conversion Unit	1
Parachute Training Unit	2
USAAF Transport Groups	12
Elementary Flying Training Schools	39
Service Flying Training Schools	4
Advanced Flying Units	46
Central Flying School	2
Flying Instructors Schools	11
Air Observer Schools	2
Air Gunners Schools	8
Specialized Schools (Air Navigation School, Central Gunnery School, Air Armament School, Beam Approach School, Beam Approach Development Unit, Airfield Control School)	6
Refresher Flying School	1
Staff Pilot Training Unit	1
Radio and Signals Schools	5
MUs and Aircraft Storage Units	26
USAAF Repair Depots	4
Ferry Reception and Dispatch Units	5
Ferry Unit and two Overseas Aircraft Preparation Flights	3
Experimental Establishments (Royal Aircraft Establishment, Aircraft and Armament Experimental Establishment, Telecommunications Flying Unit and Airborne Forces Experimental Establishment)	4
Communications Flights and Squadrons	5
Total	**740**

Chapter 4

Airfield construction

The Air Ministry's Directorate-General of Works, a technical branch of the Civil Service staffed by civilians, was responsible for supplying aerodromes in accordance with the RAF's operational requirements. The first stage in each case was to give reconnaissance engineers four days to examine and report on a proposed site. They were expected to find out its characteristics, such as flying obstructions, soil type and drainage and also to ascertain if there were any local hardcore and brick supplies. If the site met the basic demands the contractors were invited to tender, having been shown the approximate area on a map but not given much more detail owing to a rather misplaced desire for secrecy. Many construction firms were involved in the work, including Wimpey, Laing, McAlpine and Taylor-Woodrow, and the airfield programme was largely responsible for their subsequent success.

Even in wartime there were numerous objections from landowners and farmers, local authorities and MPs, who invariably suggested another site which they claimed was just as good. Not surprisingly these were always on someone else's land! However, the Air Ministry's sweeping powers of requisition under the Emergency Powers (Defence) Act of 1939 normally overcame any opposition, although minor alterations in lay-out were sometimes made to suit agricultural interests.

Obstructions on the approaches were demolished but local protests were heeded on occasion. For example, the clustered chimney stacks of the ancient Toseland Manor in Huntingdonshire were to be demolished but the proposed runway at nearby Graveley was slightly realigned and they were saved. But at Mullaghmore in Northern Ireland a school and a mill were blown up by Royal Engineers, and a school close to the end of a runway at Bobbington in Staffordshire was also removed.

At the beginning of the programme there was hardly any heavy construction plant available, but it was soon acquired from America in ever-increasing quantities. Through the summer months men and machines worked fantastically-long hours. Time and motion study on site was first seen on the airfields, where every effort was made to cut cycle times

Building a runway 'somewhere in England' 1942 (IWM CH7347).

RAF Aldergrove 13 June 1942 during major re-construction which involved the laying of a completely new runway system to replace the original 4 runway pattern (Via E.A. Cromie).

and increase production. Much Irish labour was attracted to this country and rewards were high, giving rise to some criticism that the men who built the aerodromes earned much more than the pilots who flew from them. The inevitable time-wasting and slackness was also a target and in the case of the Irish it was said that their efficiency depended on the influence of the local priest!

In 1942 a peak labour force of 60,000 men was employed in the UK solely on the task of airfield construction for the RAF and USAAF. Ernest Bevin, then Minister of Labour and National Service, decreed that some 28,000 men due to be called up for the forces were to be left in the building industry until October of that year. He stated also that the country's entire building manpower was to be devoted to the project and that all public and municipal work would have to be postponed. There was friction with Churchill over this as the Prime Minister was most concerned about the effect on civilian morale of facing a further winter living in bomb-damaged houses which had received only temporary repairs. Bevin prevailed, however, and repair work was suspended until 1943.

The metamorphosis of peaceful agricultural land into what was virtually a small town was accomplished in a matter of months. Once the

site had been approved and the blueprint stage passed, an officer, the equivalent of a civilian resident engineer, arrived. Great numbers of workmen were brought in buses or lorries from the nearest towns and convoy after convoy ferried in the material for clearance and construction. As a result of close co-ordination between the Air Ministry and the Railway Executive Committee, aerodromes were usually located near to wayside stations.

It is interesting to note that to a considerable extent the *Luftwaffe* could be said to have contributed to its own downfall, for the wreckage of buildings destroyed in air raids provided a ready-made supply of hardcore, London itself contributing over two million cu yd of material. During 1942, a regular service of six trains a day was run into East Anglia alone, carrying on average 440 tons of rubble, tarmac and cement, the latter being concentrated at a few centres, such as Roudham in Norfolk, for distribution on a daily basis.

First, every tree was removed, roots and all by means of tractors and steel hawsers, hedgerows were wrenched from the ground and any remaining obstructions were blasted out with explosives. Ditches and hollows were filled in and pipes laid to connect with the main system of drainage. The surface was then roughly levelled by mechanical excavators and bulldozers, and workmen reduced the irregularities still further by hauling ploughing discs over the broken earth and using chains and harrows. The final polish came when bladegraders, long straight-edged knives, planed down the earth so that no gradient was more than 1 in 60. Experience had soon shown that it was best to lay the perimeter track first so that lorries bringing material for the runways could avoid becoming stuck in mud, an ever-present hazard.

While all this was going on, some attempt was made to camouflage the work although this was an impossible task, as anyone who has seen a half-built motorway from the air will agree. At Goxhill in Lincolnshire, the raw chalky soil stood out like a sore thumb and vast quantities of soot and coal dust were used to tone it down. The USAAF's 56th Fighter Group was one of the first units to be based at Goxhill and Robert Johnson complains in his book *Thunderbolt* that a layer of coal dust covered everything on the field! It was recommended also that tree-trunks and contractors' plant should be used to obstruct partly-built aerodromes.

The aim was to discourage enemy landings but it sometimes had unfortunate results for our own aircraft. On 16 December 1940, Blenheim V5432 of 236 Squadron became lost in bad weather and hit cables which had been stretched across a new runway, whilst landing at Perranporth in Cornwall. Bad weather was the downfall of another Blenheim, T2273 of 27 MU, which simultaneously became RAF Honiley's first visitor and first accident on 11 October 1940 when it hit a newly-dug drain.

As soon as the runways were laid, grass seed was sown so as to bind the surrounding soil and reduce the inevitable mud. Hangars and other essential buildings were now erected, although at some places, such as High Ercall, the hangars were put up first so as to provide a dry place in which to store cement. Water pipes and telephone lines were laid and as the buildings became habitable, the RAF took over. The first man in uniform to arrive at a new station was the Equipment Officer whose job it was to arrange for the supply of stores. As soon as the NAAFI was installed and a senior Medical Officer certified the camp as fit for use, the permanent staff were posted in.

Finally, the aircraft arrived and the station was in business. Amenities were often very basic to start with. At High Ercall cooking was done originally on field kitchens, whilst there were no roads on the station and no washing facilities, so water for washing was begged from a neighbouring farm and carried to the base in new dustbins, the lids being used as wash basins! Having finished the actual landing ground, contractors usually considered that their main job was done and subsequent work on domestic sites was slow. At Atcham the officers of 131 Squadron found the mud so tiresome that they took matters into their own hands and laid a cinder track to the Mess themselves.

Guy Jefferson witnessed the birth of a bomber base and the following account is adapted from an article he wrote for the Airfield Research Group newsletter in 1980.

'As a young teenager in March 1942, I obtained a job as an office boy with a firm of contractors busily engaged in the building of the bomber airfield at Tholthorpe in North Yorkshire. Although a landing ground had been provided at this location in 1939, when I arrived the grass airfield was in the course of being enlarged by numerous earth-moving machines which were lumbering around in what appeared to be a chaotic fashion, but which nevertheless was well organised and planned by the site agent and his surveyors.

'My employer was Messrs Gerrards Ltd and this firm was responsible for the construction of the perimeter track, this being the first major item to be built, presumably so that it could serve as an access road for other contractors who were to come along later and lay the runways and dispersal points. Anyone who has seen the beginnings of an airfield will be aware of the vast amount of mud and soil churned up in the process. Any vehicle not equipped with caterpillar tracks left the taxi-way at its peril.

'At the same time as the landing area was being developed, other contractors such as Tarmac Ltd were laying down roads to the many dispersed sites. These were located chiefly around the village of Tholthorpe and along the country lane leading south to Flawith. Once these roads were completed, yet another contractor (Russells) arrived and began to erect the buildings, most of which were Nissen huts. High priority was given to the completion of the domestic sites which, when finished, were pressed into use for housing additional workmen as the building of an airfield was an enormous project, even by present day standards. Up to a thousand workmen were involved, the majority of whom seemed to be Irishmen either called Pat or Mick. This domestic side was self-sufficient with cooks, cleaners, nurses etc being employed, all utilizing the facilities recently completed.

'I remember getting slightly involved with this domestic aspect when several hundred steel lockers arrived for use by the workmen. I was given the job of matching the keys which had arrived in one big bunch! By a happy chance the lockers had been dumped on the serviceable grass area of the airfield and whilst I was out there sorting through the keys, from out of the blue an Oxford training aircraft landed and taxied over towards me. This was the first of many unofficial and illegal visits by these aircraft during the summer of 1942 when student pilots and their instructors would land and stop for a cigarette. I suspect that they came from 15 (Pilot) Advanced Flying Unit which was based at Acaster Malbis at that time but I have no proof of this.

'The building of the bomb dump and the burying of the large petrol storage tanks was the next stage in the programme and it was whilst cycling to these sites to collect the time sheets that I had my second exciting experience with aircraft at Tholthorpe because, lo and behold, I came across two Spitfires concealed behind a hedge just outside the perimeter track. These belonged to a Polish squadron and for some reason must have force-landed the previous evening. As there were no RAF personnel yet stationed at the airfield, these aircraft were completely abandoned and I was able to sit in the cockpits, quite a thrill for a fifteen year old!

'Something that intrigued me occurred in the autumn of 1942 when an attempt was made to camouflage the landing area. This was achieved by means of painting in the outline of hedges and trees which had previously been removed. It involved the mixing of a cheap brew of thin dark green paint and applying it via a spray fitted to a tractor in a similar manner to current crop spraying. I think that there was an official plan that should have been followed but on the occasions that I went along for a joy ride with the old tractor driver, he formed his own ideas as to where the hedges should be and put the tractor into full lock and did a complete circle when he felt that there ought to be a tree.

'After the completion of the perimeter track, a new contractor arrived for the laying down of the concrete runways, this being Henry Boot Ltd. This company did not do things by halves and a massive deployment of both men and machines took place. An enormous new machine had just been developed for the laying of concrete, the likes of which had never been seen in this country or, at least, that is what I was told. It resembled the present day machine which lays our motorways, the type where the lorries

bringing in the raw materials reverse onto an integral ramp whilst the whole device goes along at walking pace laying the finished product. This particular machine could lay hundreds of yards of concrete a day and, working seven days a week, it was not long before the three runways were complete.

'Due to it becoming marooned in the centre of the airfield, a completely sound farmhouse and its associated buildings had to be demolished and the enormous bulldozers made short work of it. Having been brought up on a farm, I found this rather distressing, but such is the price of war. The three steel hangars were taking shape by early 1943 and with the airfield virtually completed, most of the workers were transferred to other airfields under construction, thereby releasing the living sites for cleaning up before handover to the RAF.

'The warm spring sunshine was bleaching the new concrete runways brilliant white, not exactly an asset for a military target, and I was somewhat relieved when an attempt was made to tone them down, even though the method used appeared to be unorthodox to say the least. The process consisted of spraying tar on to the surface and, while this was still sticky, wood chippings were applied and then sprayed with matt green paint. The mind boggles at the amount of wood chips necessary for the complete coverage of the runways.

'Close inspection today reveals traces of wood chips on the sections of the runways which still remain. With the runways and many other features completed, it was then only a matter of putting the finishing touches to the verges and applying the dark green matt camouflage to everything that did not move and then waiting for the arrival of service personnel and aircraft. As the skies over the Vale of York were filled constantly with Halifax bombers there were many false alarms when aircraft circled the new airfield, but eventually one entered the circuit and made a perfect touchdown. Thankfully, the concrete held but there was a large cloud of wood chips.

'Soon the first operational night bombing mission had been mounted by the resident Canadian squadron and, although I had been a mere office boy, I felt a certain sense of satisfaction in having played a small part in the building of an operational station. When I finally left Tholthorpe in September 1943 the lanes around the village were filled with airmen wearing the *Canada* brevet on their shoulders. By October I had started working for yet another contractor, this time at Linton-on-Ouse, but that is another story.'

The Air Ministry was sufficiently far-sighted during the early stages of the war expansion programme to select several reputable civil engineering contractors with the sound organization and resources necessary for large scale airfield construction. It was on the foundation of these few contractors that the scheme was based and from which grew a contracting army which in five crowded years turned out over £200 million worth of engineering works. This represented about 800 different contracts spread over 136 firms employing at their peak effort over 130,000 men.

There is insufficient space here to mention more than a handful of the companies involved but the following serve as examples, together with a few of the aerodromes for which they were the main contractor.

Sir Alfred McAlpine — Chalgrove, Fairford, Melton Mowbray.

George Wimpey & Co Ltd — Tarrant Rushton, Dunkeswell, Cheddington.

John Laing & Son Ltd — Merryfield, Bassingbourn, Bovingdon.

J Mowlem & Co Ltd — Market Harborough, Silverstone, North Witham.

Taylor Woodrow Ltd — Little Snoring, North Creake, Chelveston.

Constable, Hart & Co — Framlingham.

Bovis Ltd — Rivenhall, Folkingham.

Richard Costain Ltd — Attlebridge, Bury St Edmunds, Wormingford.

W & C French Ltd — Boxted, Debden, Kimbolton.

Stewart Partners Ltd — Eglinton.

Walker & Slater Ltd — High Ercall.

In July 1943 the Air Ministry justified the granting of a large number of contracts to a certain well-known firm by saying:

'The plain fact is that they are far and away the most efficient of any airfield contractors and are prepared to put in very low prices. Under the circumstances it seems impossible without prejudicing the war effort not to use them to the maximum. The Managing Director has informed me that he is prepared to come out of the war without making any profits, provided in the meantime he has established such a position as to give him the master hand in post-war work.'

The other major force responsible for building airfields was the RAF Airfield Construction Service which was formed in March 1941 as RAF Works Services to carry out the emergency repair of aerodromes damaged by enemy action. It owed its origins to a 1940 organization known as No 1 Works Area (France) which was engaged in aerodrome construction for the RAF in that country until evacuation in mid-June. Its officers were immediately set to work reconnoitring for emergency aerodrome sites in the south and west of England which could replace the main bases if the *Luftwaffe* put them out of action.

The unit was given the job of preparing a number of grass aerodromes and a few with runways within the triangle Hereford, The Lizard and Bournemouth. Its most difficult project was Predannack in Cornwall, an exposed moorland site whose dense china clay was the worst possible foundation. Hardcore was brought in streams of lorries which struggled through the mire and the quarries of Cornwall supplied huge quantities of stone until the airfield was finally completed.

No 1 Works Area (Field) as it had been redesignated formed the nucleus of RAF Works Services. As the RAF began to take the initiative in the air war its function of emergency damage repair largely disappeared, to be replaced by one of active assistance in the construction of new airfields. The structure consisted of two Works Squadrons supported

Badge of 5002 Airfield Construction Squadron.

by Plant Squadrons which operated the heavy engineering equipment. Three Works Squadrons and one Plant Squadron were controlled by a Works Wing.

Early in 1943 the organization was renamed The Airfield Construction Service and under this more appropriate title undertook its first important constructional assignments. These were the improvement of many existing RAF stations, including new hard-standings and runway and taxi-track extensions to support the ever-increasing loads. They were also called upon to build the Advanced Landing Grounds (ALGs), with the help of the Royal Engineers as described in Chapter 13, and later on the network of balloon sites to fly the anti-V1 barrage south of London.

The 20 Airfield Construction Squadrons were located within each of the 20 AMWD Works Areas and the list below gives examples of their activities. Six more were formed in 1944 for overseas service.

5001, 5002, 5003 and 5004/ACS covered East Anglia and the East Midlands. In November 1943, 5001 erected a T2 hangar at Langham and built an access road and apron to a T2 at Little Snoring.

5005 ACS — southern England. Regrading and maintenance at ALGs.

5006 ACS — Yorkshire. Major improvements to Sherburn in Elmet including a 2,000 yd Sommerfeld Track runway. Peri-track extension in Bar and Rod Track at Riccall.

5007 ACS — north-east England. Additions to watch tower at Morpeth, Various jobs at Acklington, Thornaby, Charterhall etc.

5008 ACS — south-west Midlands. Additional hard-standings at Kemble, PSP touchdown area at Brize Norton, repairs to runways and peri-track at Staverton.

5009 ACS — North Wales and north-west England. Replacing Army Track runways at Cranage with PSP, laying 34 miles of drainage at Sleap in 1944 to alleviate flooding.

5010 ACS — Scotland and Western Isles. Construction of additional storey to watch office at Benbecula.

5011 ACS — Scotland and then Southern England. Dismantling and re-erecting blister hangars at Dyce, building new watch office at Sumburgh, construction of 2,000 yd concrete runway at West Malling.

5012 ACS — south-west England. Work at Chivenor, St Eval, Davidstow Moor etc.

5013 ACS — East Anglia. Building 30 Laing huts at Mendlesham in January 1943.

5014 ACS — East Anglia. Erecting B1 hangar at Witchford.

5015 ACS — South Midlands. Laying PSP runways at Kingston Bagpuize.

Badge of 5003 Airfield Construction Squadron.

5016 ACS — South Yorkshire and Lincolnshire. Runway extensions at North Coates and Binbrook, construction of three concrete runways at Finningley.

5017 ACS — South Wales. Laying Sommerfeld Track standings and re-siting three blister hangars at Carew Cheriton, laying underwater cables at Pembroke Dock.

5018 ACS — Scotland. Building 13 torpedo hard-standings and shelters at Leuchars.

5019 ACS — Northern Ireland and Isle of Man. Work at Cluntoe, Bishops Court, Andreas etc.

5020 ACS — soon moved to Azores.

5021 ACS — soon moved to Iceland.

5022-5024 ACS — formed for work on Continent but prior to the move they performed various tasks in Southern England.

5025 ACS — Far East.

5026 ACS — Kent. Building V1 defensive installations.

In the middle of 1942 the first American Engineer Aviation Battalion arrived in Britain and relieved some of the pressure on civilian contractors. To gain experience the battalions were given some minor jobs on certain RAF airfields, such as Lossiemouth where they completed an extension to the north-south runway in November 1942. A number of airfields were constructed simultaneously but the first to be completed by American engineers was

Above *Lysanders of 56 OTU at Kinnell, near Dundee, very much a 'duration-only' site* (P.H.T. Green Collection).

Left *Gosfield, Essex, under construction by US Engineers in 1943* (W. Bonenberger).

Above right *Another short-lived aerodrome — Annan, Dumfriesshire. It looks only half complete but is already in use by 55 OTU* (Via Chris Thomas).

Right *Sparrows of 271 Squadron at an unknown location which has the usual unfinished look of the period* (Via Zdenek Hurt).

at Great Saling in Essex, later to be named Andrews Field in honour of Lieutenant General Frank M Andrews the first US Theatre Commander who had been killed in an air crash in Iceland.

Work started in July 1942 and for seven months nobody engaged on the project had more than four days leave. The job continued overnight with the aid of shaded lights which could be extinguished immediately in the event of an air raid and in three months the main runway had been completed. Two more runways and a perimeter track were laid and all the necessary buildings which amounted to over 500 separate units were erected. On 21 April 1943, after one-and-a-half million man-hours had been spent on its construction, Andrews Field was handed over for operational use.

Also in Essex, the 819th EAB built Gosfield which was later to be used by a 9th Air Force A-20 group. Their experience as told in the unit history was typical. For many months the men were given a steady diet of 'ram, lamb, sheep and goat, mud, leaky tents, rain and

nightly air raid alerts.' Fourteen of the fields planned for American ocupation were built exclusively by EABs. They included Harrington in Northamptonshire, Willingale, Great Dunmow and Raydon in Essex and Eye and Debach in Suffolk. The US Engineers at first scorned the use of hardcore subgrades, preferring to lay the concrete directly on to the ground after the latter had been tamped and rolled. However, English clay has an unfortunate characteristic in that it loses all its bearing strength when wet. This resulted in some accidents when heavy bombers broke through the surface and operations had to be suspended while repairs were effected.

When the USAAF Air Transport Command's London Terminal was transferred to Bovingdon during September 1944, the lack of a proper parking apron was a severe handicap to efficient operation. No personnel could be spared to build one, however, until the US Navy expressed an interest in the development of Bovingdon as it, too, was using the field for transport flights. A detachment of *Seabees* from the 97th Naval Construction Battalion

duly arrived in November 1944 and built two large aprons. This was probably the same unit which carried out work at the USN's Liberator patrol base at Dunkeswell in Devon.

The British Army had in the meantime gained considerable experience in airfield construction during the war in the Western Desert and in 1942 the War Office decided to form Airfield Construction Groups, Royal Engineers. They were normal engineer or pioneer units which had been given special training in airfield construction. However, the total of five ACGs formed initially during the summer of 1942 was inadequate for all the work involved in the preparation for the Invasion and resources had to be pooled with RAF Works Squadrons and Canadian Engineers. It was Canadian troops who were largely responsible for the construction of Dunsfold in Surrey, a plaque in front of the control tower commemorating the fact. The Royal Engineers played a major part in the building of RAF Port Ellen on the Isle of Islay during 1942, there being an acute shortage of civilian labour on the islands. The Royal Marines, too, had

engineering units which were used to a limited extent for the maintenance of certain naval air stations.

The overall rate of airfield construction reached its peak in 1942 when 125 new aerodromes came into use, an average of one every three days. Thereafter there was a steady decline until the end of hostilities. In 1945 some doubt was expressed as to whether the three runway lay-out had been essential. In practice the subsidiary runways were seldom used at night bomber stations, and in order to secure early use of a new site, it was usual for the main runway to be completed first and put into operation. A second was then provided and the RAF appeared to fly quite happily from two runways when they had only two. Therefore, with hindsight, it was thought by many that a two or even single runway configuration might have been adopted universally, resulting in a very great saving of labour and materials. Certain economies were in fact made at several training fields. At Charterhall in Berwickshire, for example, two runways were built but only a short stretch of the planned third strip was laid. Fordoun in the Aberdeen area was designed to have three runways but only two were constructed.

Between 1939 and 1945, 444 airfields were constructed in the UK. At one time nearly a third of Britain's total construction labour force was engaged in the work. Apart from the labour involved in building its runways and taxi-tracks, a Class A airfield was likely to consume 20 miles of drain, 6 miles of water main, 4 miles of sewer, 10 miles of roadway and four and a half million bricks.

Airfield names

It was not difficult to find names for aerodromes in the early days, as they were merely called after the nearest village to the site. As they were relatively few, problems of confusion over similar names rarely occurred, although Shotwick was renamed Sealand to differentiate it from Scopwick in Lincolnshire. However, the orgy of airfield building during the Second World War required a certain amount of care in the choice of a suitable name for each. The basic principle was still to use that of a neighbouring village, but if this had a phonetic resemblance to an airfield title already in existence, that of another local village was adopted. For example, Conington compromised Honington so that airfield was called after Glatton, a village some distance away. Sites under construction often bore names entirely different from their eventual ones, Clays of Allen in North-East Scotland, for example, became Fearn.

RAF stations were sometimes named after geographical features such as Shepherds Grove (after a neighbouring wood), Akeman Street (the Roman road of this name ran across the aerodrome), Hells Mouth and Needs Oar Point (both were coastal features.) Many an obscure farm was perpetuated in aviation history, Mount Farm, Blakehill Farm, Twinwood Farm and Babdown Farm being just a few of them. Leicester East was something of an anomaly being designed to set it apart from the other three aerodromes around the city, Rearsby, Ratcliffe and Braunstone. It remains active but the 'East' was dropped about eight years ago in favour of Leicester Airport, the other three having closed long before.

Some very quaint titles were bestowed upon the bases from which the latest in twentieth century machinery was to operate. How about Little Snoring, Hinton-in-the-Hedges, Bogs O'Mayne, Findo Gask and Halfpenny Green? Moreton-in-Marsh was the inspiration for 'Much Binding in the Marsh' in a well-known radio programme of the day. If the pre-war Aerodrome Improvement Board had had its way the delightful Middle Wallop would have been renamed 'Haydown'!

The first American-built aerodrome was called Andrews Field in honour of Lieutenant General Frank M Andrews, first commander of the 8th Air Force who was killed in a flying accident in Iceland. The use of *Field* as a suffix was a common American practice but the only other usage in England of which I am aware was the fighter training base near Shrewsbury sometimes referred to as Atcham Field. USAAF stations were allotted numbers as an aid to administration and these were used extensively in official documents and records. Ground stations which might be merely an office in a British city were numbered in the same sequence.

The RAF also employed numerical designations in certain circumstances: for example Bomber Command No 62 Base comprised an HQ at Linton-on-Ouse and sub-stations at East Moor and Tholthorpe. For an explanation of the system see *Action Stations 4*. The non-geographical numbered airfields used by Fighter Command for the Invasion are detailed in Chapter 14. There was also a short-lived method during 1940/41 of designating certain fighter airfields by the Sector grid letter and a number, an example being Collyweston in Northamptonshire, designated 'K3' as it was the third aerodrome in a clutch. Royal Naval Air Stations were named in the same manner as ships and more details will be found in Chapter 15.

A few aerodromes were renamed when it was discovered that their names were too similar to those of others, causing misdirection of stores and personnel. Bobbington became Halfpenny Green, reputedly because USAAF crews were confusing it with Bovingdon, but no documentary evidence can be found to support this story. One wit said that it reflected the de-valuation of the pound! Rhosneigr and Heneglwys became Valley and Mona, repectively, probably to make pronunciation easier for the average Englishman!

Local people stubbornly continued to refer to aerodromes by the name of the nearest village and often still do, which can cause problems when asking directions to a disused site. Calveley in Cheshire is known in the area as Wardle, while Tilstock in Shropshire, originally known by the RAF as Whitchurch Heath, is always referred to locally as Prees Heath.

A further consideration is the nicknames given to aerodromes by their RAF and USAAF occupants. Most are fairly obvious and show a loathing of the mud, rain and rural isolation of so many temporary wartime airfields. I imagine that practically every station had one but most are long-forgotten. Amongst them were 'The Duckpond' (Duxford), 'Goat-hill' (Goxhill), 'Little Horrible' (Little Horwood, 'Mudford Magna' (Ludford Magna), 'Prangtoft' (Sandtoft) and 'Clamp Hill' (Hullavington). The one for High Ercall is unprintable! Molesworth's Living sites rejoiced in the name of 'Pneumonia Hill' and a small wooded hill perilously close to RAF Elgin earned the name 'Gremlins' Roost'.

Inevitably, the correct pronunciation of some of the airfield names was not obvious and I append a list of those which commonly give trouble:

Burscough	Bursco
Calveley	Carverley
Debach	Debitch or Debbidge
Deopham Green	Deefham Green
Fordoun	Fordoon

Halfpenny Green	As spelt during the war, but now universally known as Ha'penny Green
Hawarden	Harden
Kingston Bagpuize	Bagpuze
Kinnell	Accent on the second syllable
Kirkwall/ Grimsetter	Grimzetter
Llandwrog	Thlandoorog
Maghaberry	M'Gabbery
Poulton	Poolton
Seighford	Sighf'd
Shipdham	Ship-dum
Sleap	Slape
Tatenhill	Tate-enhill

Chapter 5

Miscellany: strip aerodromes, emergency landing grounds and other specialized sites

Strategic demands resulted in the construction of a number of airfields at locations which would never have been considered in peacetime except, perhaps, as rudimentary grass strips. The Battle of the Atlantic, for example, left a series of fine aerodromes which now serve the population of the Scottish Islands. In Northern Ireland, too, no expense was spared to convert stretches of boggy countryside into Coastal Command and support bases, Belfast owing its Aldergrove Airport to a wartime Aircraft Storage Unit.

As early as 1936, the Air Council was studying the feasibility of so-called strip aerodromes on sites restricted by the terrain to a single runway. A fixed metal screen would enable aircraft to land irrespective of the wind direction. In retrospect it can be seen also as yet another ploy to avoid building more than one hard runway at existing service aerodromes. RAF Manby, still under construction at that time, was chosen for the experimental landing screen which was similar to the metal slatted screens used to shelter the entrances to airship hangars, but measuring 1,600 ft long and 50 ft high. A Westland Wallace from North Coates was loaned for the trials.

Preliminary tests during the winter of 1937/38 showed that a Wallace could be landed and taken off safely by an experienced pilot in a 27 mph wind at 60° to the screen. A Harrow, Whitley, Battle and Blenheim were also operated successfully until the screen was dismantled in March 1938 to enable Manby to be opened for normal use. The Royal Navy was interested in building a screened landing ground in the Plymouth area where, in their words, 'a full size aerodrome site is almost impossible to find'. (They had even suggested draining part of Plymouth Sound at Trevill to build one.) Gibraltar had another strategic requirement for a screen and in January 1940 the original structure, extended to 3,000 ft, was re-erected at Rollestone on Salisbury Plain. CFS then tested it with a Tutor, Master and Hurricane.

Wellington 1c Z1111 of 311 Squadron taxying downhill at Dale, a bleak clifftop site in south-west Wales (Via Zdenek Hurt).

Gliding at the former RAF Connel, near Oban. The two tarmac runways are only 12 degrees apart in alignment so that they could be fitted into the small space available.

By mid-1940 the idea of a screen had been dropped, but the strip aerodrome concept remained very much alive. It was now envisaged that two or three concrete runways could be laid at a conventionally unsuitable but strategically vital, site regardless of the ground between the strips. These would be orientated with the prevailing winds and joined by taxi-tracks. The first strip aerodrome was built at Scatsta in Shetland for the defence of the nearby flying boat base at Sullom Voe. It was literally carved out of the landscape; the shorter of the two runways started at the base of an 800 ft hill, climbed another hill and descended to the sea. Some 13 ft of peat had to be taken out during its construction and the main contractor for the aerodrome was the Shetland County Council, using hired plant and a high percentage of local labour.

To help protect shipping off north-west Scotland, the naval ports at Lochewe and other places, the aluminium factory at Fort William and Coastal Command bases in the Hebrides, a forward fighter aerodrome was requested near Oban. The Aerodromes Board carried out a reconnaissance in January and February 1941 and came up with three possible sites; the civil aerodrome at Connel, a narrow strip of grassland at Corran, nine miles south-west of Fort William, and a similar cramped area at Crinnan in Argyllshire. A search for a landing ground on the island of Barra produced only one possibility, which was not pursued.

The Connel site was at first condemned as unacceptable until it was found that two runways only 12° different in alignment could be fitted in to the available land. When completed it was never used operationally and served

mainly as an ELG. Today it makes an attractive gliding site and a convenient small airport for Oban. Another pleasant little site which owes its existence to hasty wartime decisions is St Angelo, now Enniskillen Airport. Close to the border with Eire, it was originally an SLG for the MU at Aldergrove, two runways being built on the poorly-drained land in an L-shape necessitated by the small hills which surround it. Owing to the shortage of aerodromes in Ulster, it was taken over as a Fighter Sector Station.

Some of the airfields constructed on sandy soil in the Western Isles and elsewhere in Britain used the wet sand mix method for their runways whereby sand was mixed with hydrated lime and a special grade of bitumen. Since this surface was easy to repair it was used for the enormous crash strips at Carnaby, Woodbridge and Manston. Known offically as Emergency Landing Grounds, the single runway at each was 3,000 yd long by 250 yd wide, allowing three parallel lanes so that if one were blocked by a crashed or damaged aircraft, there was still room for other aircraft to get down. In the words of an airfield controller of the time, 'There is enough room for even a brakeless Mosquito to change its mind!'

The first of the crash strips had come into being at RAF Wittering in 1943, where a 4,500 yd grass runway linked it to the neighbouring aerodrome at Collyweston. It was, however, too far inland, and thus an incomplete answer to the problem of battle-damaged aircraft crash-landing back at base and blocking runways or rolling off the end, often with fatal results. Manston in Kent had already seen many an emergency landing and was a natural choice for the first ELG site, with two others at Woodbridge, near Ipswich, and Carnaby, near Scarborough, both close to the coast. All had the single strip aligned east-west so that a disabled aircraft could make a straight-in

approach from the sea and land downwind if
necessary.

The term ELG was employed also for
rudimentary sites throughout the country
which could be used by aircraft in an emergency. They were normally to be found in the
vicinity of a proper airfield and were intended
also as a bolt-hole if the latter were severely
bombed. ELGs had first been nominated on
six sites during 1934/35 in the London area
for the use of night fighters in the event of
engine failure, where flares were lit when
required, the sites being Wormwood Scrubs,
Hackney Marsh, Plumstead Common, Bry-
mon Hill, Streatham Common and Clapham
Common. On 20 June 1940 action was taken
to instruct station commanders throughout the
RAF to search for at least one ELG near their
aerodrome. They were told that no possibility
should be excluded and that golf courses, parks
and race courses were amongst the most likely
locations.

An attempt was made in the summer of 1941
to find suitable stretches of road in the vicinity of bomber stations to act as emergency
strips. There were found to be too many
problems, however, as apart from the likelihood of heavy bombers swinging off the
paved surface while landing or taking off, the
priority movement of military vehicles on
main roads would be hindered. It was suggested that the scheme might be more suited
to fighter aircraft, but it does not appear to
have been adopted.

No complete list of ELGs seems to have survived and since they had no facilities there is
little evidence of them today. I have looked at
Haroldston West in south-west Wales, but the
only clue to its former use is the unusually
large field. The reader is referred to *Action
Stations Volume 10* for a very good investigation of the ELG at Sway in Hampshire. Other
known ELGs include the following:

Blidworth, Notts (became SLG)
Bray Court, Berks
Burford, Glos (ELG for Little Rissington)
Chattis Hill, Wilts (ELG for Middle Wallop)
Cold Kirby, Yorks (same site as Sutton Bank?)
Great Shefford, Wilts
Hatties Plantation, Morayshire
Kirkpatrick, Dumfriesshire (became RLG)
Oatlands Hill, Wilts (became satellite for Old
  Sarum)
Pyrford Court, Surrey (ELG for Vickers,
  Weybridge)
Tadcaster, Yorks (former WW 1 aerodrome)
Waltham St Lawrence, Berks
Winterbourne Stoke, Wilts
Wolvey, Warks.

There is a further class of landing ground
which defies comprehensive coverage; this was
the 'Cub strip' used by US Army units which
operated light aircraft for liaison and artillery
spotting. The Piper Cub had the ability to land
and take off with a very short run, so practically any stretch of level grass in the vicinity
of an army camp was adequate. Cricket fields
and parks are known to have been used and
there were no less than six sites within the

St Angelo airfield from the south, taken in 1984 (Ernie Cromie).

Stornoway in July 1944. A somewhat cramped Coastal Command site built on a pre-war civil strip which itself had shared the land with a golf course (P.H.T. Green Collection).

Bristol city boundary alone. Other known strips include those at Swanwick in Derbyshire, Porthcawl and Abergavenny in South Wales and Kington in Herefordshire.

Almost as ephemeral but better documented were the sites used by ATC gliding schools. When first set up in 1942 they were confined in the main to playing fields and other convenient unobstructed areas, their operations being incompatible with busy RAF stations. Later many were transferred to redundant airfields and a full list of their operating locations can be found in Ray Sturtivant's article *Cadets With Wings* in *Aviation News* Volume 11 No 24.

Finally, it is not generally known that the *Luftwaffe* had a clutch of landing grounds prepared for them in Norfolk during 1940! At least that is what I am led to believe from an

obscure file in PRO (AIR 2/4557). In May 1940 some observant soul noticed that there were seven separate locations each with one or two distinctive red-painted barns. Hedges had been removed and, according to officers from RAF Watton, all had the aspect of specially prepared landing grounds, being almost bare of crops and rolled hard. The positions were Sporle, Baighton, Cantley, Halvergate, Paston, Guestwick, and South Repps.

Further investigations revealed that all the sites were owned by the same property company, the directors of whom were aliens, registered as Dutch. A plan was formulated to take them over simultaneously so that they could be obstructed and camouflaged and the local population questioned. Tantalizingly, I can find no further evidence that the situation was ever resolved.

Chapter 6

The airfields that never were

The Aerodrome Board's staff had reported on nearly 4,000 possible airfield sites in Britain by September 1939. In each locality an average of nine sites were inspected for every one accepted. The list of proposed locations is too long to reproduce here and is of academic interest only. Shropshire's contribution included Condover, Cressage, Uckington, Uffington, Rudington, Wrockwardine, Moreton, Monkmoor and High Ercall. Two of these names will be instantly recognizable to the airfield enthusiast as they actually came into existence. Monkmoor, however, although formerly a First World War aerodrome on the outskirts of Shrewsbury, was never reinstated.

The method of finding sites was simple. First, the 1 in Ordnance Survey map was studied and all flat areas which were free from obstructions inside circles of about 1,100 yd radius were marked off. Areas below 50 ft above sea level were generally ignored and those over 650 ft were eliminated because of problems with hill fog. The marked areas were then walked field by field and the maximum landing and take-off distances estimated. Any obstructions were noted and, if available, a geological map was used to ascertain the nature of the subsoil. Relatively few of the likely sites were actually laid out as aerodromes before the war, but the results of the survey were filed away for future reference.

The Fleet Air Arm had its own requirements for aerodromes and there was liaison between the Admiralty and the Aerodromes Board. The latter suggested sites which fitted in with naval plans, one of the first being at Kilrenny in Fife which was needed as a relief aerodrome for Donibristle, together with another site further up the coast at Crail. The 10 affected tenants at Kilrenny were no doubt relieved when the old First World War field at Crail was revived and the Kilrenny plan abandoned.

In November 1938 the FAA was allocated a number of locations for development. They included Fifehead Magdalen in Somerset which presumably became RNAS Henstridge, Yeovilton, Ibsley, Holmsley South and Hartford Bridge Flats. The option on the last three was not taken up and they were subsequently built for the RAF. Names which vanished into obscurity were Maiston Magna, South Ripley and Frimston Down.

Despite the enormous scope, some of the airfields which were built for the RAF were extremely poor choices. Most of them date from mid-1940 when the war situation was so bad that some of the previously laid-down standards for gradients and obstructions were disregarded so that an aerodrome might be ready for use within months. Better a poor site available almost immediately than a first class one ready later. Fairwood Common (now Swansea Airport) was a typical example, being reported as dangerous by some of its Commanding Officers owing to excessive slopes and changes in gradient.

In March 1942 Cheddington in Buckinghamshire was declared to be unsuitable for OTU flying and could only be used as a satellite because of adjacent high ground. The same could be said of Wellesbourne Mountford, although it was destined to remain a parent OTU station. One of the most potentially lethal was Wombleton in Yorkshire, intended to be a bomber base but which was so close to the North York Moors that a fully-loaded Halifax could not climb out safely from certain runways. For this reason it never aspired to become more than a training airfield. Templeton, near Haverfordwest was another oddity. Why *did* they build an airfield with a hill in the middle of the triangle formed by the three runways?

Cottam was another Yorkshire aerodrome whose proximity to high ground proved unacceptable. It was planned and built as a bom-

Templeton's runways seen from the hill in the middle of this rather unsuitable Welsh aerodrome.

ber station but no squadrons ever operated from it, and it was eventually allocated to 91 MU for use as a bomb dump. Some equally unsuitable spots were rejected, however, such as Laugharne in Carmarthenshire (shades of Dylan Thomas!) whose soil was so wet that there was no foundation for buildings, and Witherslack in Westmorland. The precise position of the last-named is uncertain but it would have certainly been in a very hilly area.

Early in the war it was suggested that because of its generally poor weather and industrial smoke, Usworth near Sunderland should be abandoned in favour of Woolsington. Instead the airfield was active until the 1980s, Woolsington being barely used until developed as Newcastle Airport. West Raynham in Norfolk was considered unsuitable for modern aircraft in 1940, the tops of the hangars being invisible from the opposite side of the aerodrome! The RAF made do with it, however, and it remained active with some development until 1975.

The airfield construction programme reached its height in 1941/42 when bomber bases for the USAAF were the main priority. Towards the end of 1942 it was found that progress in airfield building was failing to meet the target owing to poor weather and shortages of labour, equipment and materials. Roger Freeman observes in his book *Mighty Eighth War Manual:*

'In December the Air Ministry, in consultation with the RAF and USAAF, reviewed the whole airfield building programme. A decision was taken to postpone all planned airfields where work had not actually started. As a result 8th Bomber Command stations that at that time had not progressed beyond surveying, planning and notice of land requisition were indefinitely postponed. They were Finedon in 1st Division Area, Crowfield in 3rd Division Area, Beaumont in 4th Division Area, and High Roding, Ingatestone, Maldon, Cold Norton and Southminster in the 5th Division Area. Some of these planned airfields, having been given USAAF Station Numbers, persisted in 8th Air Force directives until the end of hostilities, making Beaumont and Cold Norton a mystery to the uninitiated as only farmland was to be found at these Essex villages.'

Beedon, Brightwalton and Hawthorn Hill were part of a string of airfields across Berkshire intended for USAAF transport or observation units. Another site was Massington which I cannot find on the map but I suspect that it was in the same county. Hawthorn Hill, had it been built, would have made a better site for London's main airport after the war, being located just to the south-west of Windsor. A further clutch of airfields for transport or observation aircraft was planned around Salisbury Plain. The sites were Cricklade, Market Lavington and Ogbourne. Other unbuilt airfields for the same role were Tresham in Gloucestershire and Quarley Down and Rotherwick, both in Hampshire.

The observation role was a short-lived one in the 8th Air Force and most of the units soon departed to North Africa to join the newly-formed 12th Air Force. The *Bolero Plan* for the deployment of aircraft to the 8th included eight transport groups, requiring 12 airfields in what was expected to be the US Army area in south-west England. Few of the troop car-

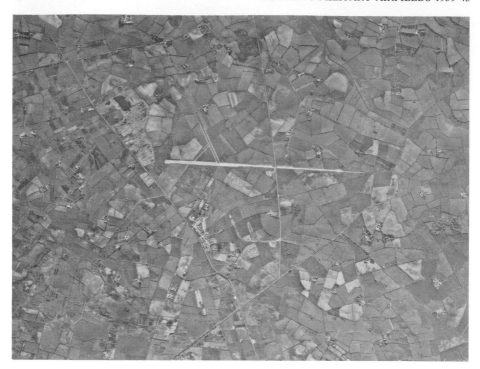

rier groups appeared until the autumn of 1943 and most of their designated airfields — Blakehill Farm, Broadwell, Fairford and Down Ampney among them — were allocated to RAF transport squadrons.

To support its operational bases in East Anglia, USAAF was given several aerodromes in Northern Ireland to serve as Combat Crew Replacement Centres, roughly the equivalent of an RAF OTU. However, because the buildup of the 8th Air Force was very much slower than expected, some of the airfields were taken over for RAF use when ready for occupation. Construction of another at Kells Point in County Tyrone was never begun but the site at Millisle on the Ards Peninsula is a story in itself. It was well advanced when further work was abandoned, £58,000 having been spent, which was quite a large sum in those days.

The evidence of this venture can be seen when one drives along a country road two miles west of Millisle village. A long ribbon of concrete crosses the road at right angles, part of a runway that was two-thirds completed. About half of another was laid, together with a stretch of perimeter track which ends abruptly in the middle of a field. Most of the technical site was built and is now used for light industry. It was fortunate that local farms and cottages had not yet been

The never-to-be-completed Millisle aerodrome in Northern Ireland. The partially-built runway is aligned roughly north-south with the incomplete technical site, including a base for a T2 hangar, to the north-west (Via E.A. Cromie).

demolished but some of them now sit alongside a motorway-width road! The sight is quite astonishing and one is tempted to say that it could only happen in Ireland!

A bleak spot in Yorkshire known as Huggate Wold was surveyed and earmarked as a heavy bomber base. However, the plan was dropped in favour of the development of a more suitable alternative at Full Sutton, a few miles to the west. Perhaps because Huggate had already been requisitioned, it was later used for exercises in the laying of steel mesh runways in preparation for the invasion of Europe. This occurred in the autumn of 1943 and two squadrons of Mustangs were present for a few days to try out the temporary strips. Huggate then reverted to farmland.

Some airfields were obviously in an advanced state of planning when objections were raised by existing stations in the same district, hence this entry in the Operations Record Book for No 7 Group on 28 April 1942:

'Visit to Culworth, proposed site for an OTU parent near Moreton Pinkney, Northants with a gentleman from 8 Works Area. It was decided that subject to alterations to the alignment of one runway, the site was agreed. However, in view of the fact that the aerodrome will be midway between Chipping Warden and Silverstone, recommended that it should be re-sited farther to the north.'

There was a serious clash of interest between the requirements of farming and food production and the need for more airfields. The correspondence between Air Ministry and the Ministry of Agriculture and Fisheries, some of which has survived in the Public Record Office is long and sometimes acrimonious. The Air Ministry often gave in to valid objections but could be obdurate where operational necessity demanded. The recurring theme was that with a strong air force we could import food but we could never import airfields. To illustrate the conflict of opinions, I now quote the text of a letter from the Ministry of Agriculture and Fisheries to Sir Archibald Sinclair, Secretary of State for Air, and the subsequent reply:

'I wrote to you about the recent decisions to acquire sites for aerodromes at Grove and Castle Donington. The proposed site at Grove [in Berkshire] comprises 272 acres of first quality milk-producing land. The Aerodromes Board has, I understand, been unable to find any possible alternative in an area which has already been very throughly explored and exploited. As the site is badly needed as an integral part of the plan for bomber OTUs and their satellites in this part of the country, I am prepared in the circumstances not to press my objections to its acquisition.

'I am not too happy about Castle Donington, however. Here, some 465 acres of highly productive land are affected and no fewer than 308 are arable or under crops for this harvest. We have now been informed that it is the only possible site for a satellite for the operational station which is being located at Wymeswold and authority has been given for its acquisition. The Wymeswold site itself is one to which, in view of your urgent requirements, we raise no objection as less than two thirds are under the plough and the land is not of the very highest quality. We know, however, that Castle Donington is under consideration for its satellite and can be acquiescent in Wymeswold's acquisition conditional on

a site other than Castle Donington being found for the satellite. As we were originally informed that Castle Donington was required as a bomber aerodrome, we had no reason for supposing that there was any connection between it and Wymeswold.'

Sinclair's explanation was as follows:

'At that time there were four sites under consideration in this area — Wymeswold, Castle Donington, Ragdale and Derby — from which we hoped to get two pairs of aerodromes. Ragdale proved to be undesirable but not impossible from the construction point of view. The Derby site which is being used as an EFTS has also had to be ruled out as a potential bomber site owing to a demand for greater EFTS capacity.

'We are therefore left with Wymeswold and Castle Donington as a pair. Of the two, the former appeared the more satisfactory parent. Castle Donington therefore became the satellite. Please do not think that because Castle Donington is to become a satellite, precious agricultural land is being thrown away on something which is not important. The difference between parent station and satellite is now small, the only difference being that the former has technical and domestic accommodation, the latter domestic only. A site may perhaps be provisionally selected as a bomber satellite and may, during the course of negotiations later be diverted to some other use. Coincidentally, the function of Wymeswold which was planned as a bomber airfield has now had to be changed to a bomber OTU.

'To return now to Ragdale where there are two possible sites, of which Ragdale I is an Emergency Landing Ground which we wished to extend to full size last summer but were unable to do so because of an old-established army range and no local alternative could be found. Ragdale II was provisionally selected in January this year. Either Ragdale I or Ragdale II will be required as a second satellite for Wymeswold. If the army cannot find an alternative range we shall have to take Ragdale II as well as Castle Donington.'

Neither of the Ragdale sites was developed but if the decision to build Castle Donington had not been upheld, the present day East Midlands Airport would have been established somewhere else. EMA would likely have been built on a 'green field site', to use the current jargon, as few other locations in the East Midlands had as much potential.

As we have seen above, agriculture was not the only barrier to the development of some sites. Other services might already be in occupation or too close for harmonious working. In November 1942 the Air Ministry wrote to the War Office in these words:

'We are having difficulty in obtaining the one aerodrome site we need to complete No 8 (US) Bomber Group. The site which we should like to obtain is one at Finedon, Northants. It is excellently suited to the purpose and there are no agricultural objections. The only difficulty is that it impinges slightly on one of your tank training sites. Therefore, if we cannot have Finedon the only alternative is Buckden, to which there are very strong agricultural objections.

The army's prior claim was upheld, however, and Finedon never did materialize, nor did Buckden.

Meanwhile, the Admiralty, which had no definite programme of further airfield requirements up to 1942, now found itself needing more locations for training purposes. It was observed privately that, as they were rather late in the field, most of the suitable sites had been taken up by the RAF. As a temporary solution certain aerodromes were handed over to the Navy and lodger facilities were granted at others. In September 1942 the Admiralty commented somewhat acidly that one site at Rhyl in North Wales on offer 'appears suitable in every way subject to agreement as to ranges. Unlikely the station could be completed before September 1943 at the earliest. It is virtually certain that there are local snags in connection with the construction of the site, otherwise it would never have been offered to us'.

The project at Rhyl and an adjoining one at Myn-Rhos, also for the FAA, were eventually discarded when both were found hazardous for night flying because of nearby hills. A possible location for a Torpedo-Bomber-Reconnaissance armament practice station at Abergele in the same Welsh coastal area was suggested in the summer of 1943 when the FAA urgently needed new stations.

As part of the same expansion programme, the Admiralty planned a number of airfields in the north-west. Midge Hall near Leyland in Lancashire was to replace Eglinton in Northern Ireland as a fighter practice station; Cuddington and Grafton Hall in Cheshire would form preliminary fighter training wings after completion of armament training at Midge Hall; and Guilden Sutton near Chester

was to be employed for the disembarkation of aircraft from carriers in the Mersey. Unfortunately, this neat little scheme was firmly quashed by the Ministry of Agriculture and Fisheries who objected in the strongest possible terms to the loss of this valuable land at such a late stage of the war. The FAA was then forced to meet its commitments by expanding existing airfields.

The Admiralty had encountered the same problem the previous year when a site at Piercebridge in County Durham to which they had turned their attention, was described as the best square mile of farmland in the country. (This phrase was a standard ploy used by all farming interests!) Bomber Command wanted it, too, for an operational base but they also were disappointed. The continued demands for more naval aerodromes were countered by a statement:

'The Air Council have constantly done their utmost to make up for the shortage of naval aerodromes. They feel they are bound, however, to record that as responsibility for planning ahead to meet naval needs has not rested with them they are unable to accept any obligation to meet these needs or the sacrifice of any requirement in the RAF programme which they regard as essential.'

As the war drew to a close, the future of transatlantic air services looked promising so several grandiose schemes for airports were put forward by local councils. Most were little more than artist's impressions with a great deal of licence but the one based on RAF Squires Gate at Blackpool was actually planned in some detail. It was to have a 5,000 yd runway and two 4,000 yd subsidiaries, and inside the triangle formed by them there were to be three more strips of about 2,000 yd each for continental and feeder services.

As if this were not enough, a four mile diameter lagoon for flying boats was proposed in the Ribble Estuary, its administrative buildings connected to the new terminal by a road and rail tunnel under the river! In the words of the planners, 'The chief idea is that passengers arriving, say, from West Africa by flying boat, can be transferred to the New York airliner in a matter of perhaps 20 minutes complete with baggage.' Needless to say, it never happened, nor did the scheme to build an enormous runway on top of an extended pier at Rhyl!

Marginally more realistic was the search for a huge tract of English countryside for conversion into a reasonable facsimile of the Muroc test centre in California, which was later to become Edwards Air Force Base. The

Penrhos, North Wales, was condemned as dangerous by the pre-war Airfield Improvement Board unless the hill in the background to this photo of a 312 Squadron Hurricane was levelled. Needless to say, this mammoth task was never attempted! (Via Zdenek Hurt).

planning for what was to be a national aeronautical research establishment began as early as the summer of 1944. The existing Royal Aircraft Establishment at Farnborough was incapable of expansion to the *five mile* runway thought necessary for the testing of future high speed aircraft so a number of potential locations were investigated.

The suggestions centred around existing airfields whose runways could definitely be extended to 5,000 yd and probably to 8,000 yd. They included the grass aerodrome at Weston-on-the-Green in Oxfordshire, Pembrey in South Wales, Squires Gate, Middleton St George, Silloth in Cumberland, Fulbeck in Lincolnshire, and Breighton and Elvington in Yorkshire. An 8,000 yd strip at each of the latter three was thought to be quite feasible.

The final choice was the amalgamation of three airfields, Thurleigh, Twinwood Farm and Little Staughton, with a giant five-mile-long concrete runway linking Thurleigh and Little Staughton, a taxi-track joining it to Twinwood on which support and hangarage facilities were to be built. No doubt the Council for the Protection of Rural England would, quite rightly, have had something to say about this, but it never materialized. The RAE Bedford site was based on Thurleigh, however, but it never reached anywhere near the proportions envisaged.

It seems that London's Heathrow Airport would never have been approved if drastic wartime powers and regulations had not been employed to push it through. Lord Balfour of Inchrye, Under-Secretary of State for Air from 1938 to 1944, wrote in his book *Wings Over Westminister* how he urged that the Fairey Aviation Company's small aerodrome at Heathrow should be expanded for the long-range transport of troops and supplies to the Far East for the final assault on Japan. He and his supporters knew that there were other airfields in the Home Counties which could be made to do the job just as well, but what they really wanted was the basis of a great civil airport for post-war London. Agricultural and housing objections were summarily overruled and we all know the result of what some say was the most disastrous planning blunder ever!

The controversy of the last two decades over the siting of London's third airport is outside the scope of this book but it has left one permanent mark in the form of a memorial plaque at Wing, once a bomber OTU airfield near Cublington in Bedfordshire. The final word on the subject of the airfields that never were appears in the inscription:

'This spinney was planted in 1972 by the Buckinghamshire County Council in gratitude to all those who supported the campaign against the recommendation that London's third airport should be at Cublington. Parish Councils, organizations, societies and many individuals contributed towards the cost of the spinney. This point is the centre of the area proposed for the airport. Midmost Unmitigated England.'

Proposed airfield sites

This list is not claimed to be comprehensive. It has been compiled from many sources and I have been told on good authority that most of the official records on the subject have been destroyed. Further information from readers would be welcomed. Local enquiries around the projected site would probably establish how advanced the plans were and whether the tenants were ever informed of them.

Location	Remarks
Abergele, Denbighs	Planned RNAS for TBR practice.
Antrim, NI	Planned for a bomber OTU but not built, presumably because of agricultural objections.
Appleton Wiske, N Yorks	Possible RAF bomber base, development overcome by farming interests.
Ardglass, NI	Provisional bomber OTU site, but Bishops Court built instead.
Assington, Suffolk	Possible 8th AF bomber base but plans dropped by August 1942.
Astley, Warwicks	Provisionally selected as RLG for Honiley.
Aston Upthorpe, Oxon	Suggested satellite for Harwell.
Ballymoney, Co Antrim	Intended for OTU?
Barnsley Wold, Glos	Planned USAAF transport or observation base but not built.
Beaumont, Essex	Immediately north of village. Tentatively offered to 8th AF as bomber base 10 August 1942. Confirmed September 1942. Indefinitely postponed 16 December 1942 USAAF Station 148.
Beedon, Berks	Planned USAAF transport or observation base but not built.
Bright Walton, Berks	Planned USAAF transport or observation base but not built.
Buckden, Cambs	Possible 8th AF bomber base but not proceeded with owing to agricultural objections.
Bulphan, Essex	Site surveyed as possible 8th AF bomber base.
Burnham, Essex	Site surveyed as possible 8th AF bomber base.
Caerlaverock, Dumfriesshire	Proposed satellite of Robgill (qv).
Calmsden, Glos	Originally 12 SLG. Not used. Intended for 5 MU, Kemble.
Cannock Chase, Staffs	Proposed expansion aerodrome on former Army camp site.
Castle Hedingham, Suffolk	Under consideration in 1941 but not built.
Catfirth, Shetland	Possible fighter base for Shetland defence but rejected.
Cold Norton, Essex	1½ miles west of village. Tentatively allocated 8th AF as bomber base. Confirmed September 1942. Construction

	indefinitely postponed 14 December 1942. Took in First World War Stow Maries aerodrome site. USAAF Station 163.
Copston Magna, Warks	Expansion site for a medium bomber station but not proceeded with.
Corran, Argyllshire	Possible forward fighter base.
Cricklade, Wilts	Planned USAAF transport or observation base but not built.
Crinan, Argyllshire	Possible forward fighter base.
Crowfield, Suffolk	Immediately north-east of village. Tentatively allocated 8th AF as bomber base 10 August 1942. Confirmed October 1942. Construction indefinitely postponed 14 December 1942.
Cruden Bay, Aberdeenshire	Planned RNAS.
Cuddington, Cheshire	Planned RNAS for fighter training.
Culworth, Northants	Proposed site for OTU parent station but too near existing aerodromes so not proceeded with.
Dapple Heath, Staffs	Provisionally selected as RLG for Meir.
Dunstable, Beds	Proposed expansion site for medium bombers.
Essendine, Rutland	Possible RAF bomber base but too many agricultural objections.
Eyton, Shropshire	Possible satellite for Rednal but not built.
Finedon, Northants	Planned 8th AF bomber base but site overlapped a tank training area which War Department refused to give up.
Fressingfield, Suffolk	Possible 8th AF bomber base but plans dropped by August 1942.
Frimston Down,	Suggested site for RNAS but not proceeded with.
Grafton Hall, Cheshire	Planned RNAS for fighter training.
Grimsthorpe, Lincs	Possible RAF bomber base, but too many agricultural objections.
Guilden Sutton, Cheshire	Planned RNAS for aircraft disembarking from carriers in Mersey.
Handsacre, Staffs	Provisionally accepted as satellite for Perton in January 1941 but not built.
Hawthorn Hill, Berks	Planned USAAF transport or observation base but not built.
Helsby, Cheshire	Required by FAA in 1942 but loss of agricultural land unacceptable.
High Roding, Essex	One mile north-east of village. Tentatively allocated 8th AF as bomber base 10 August 1942. Confirmed September 1942. Warning of land requisition served. Construction indefinitely postponed 6 December 1942. USAAF Station 177.
Hillborough, Norfolk	Suggested satellite for Watton.

Huggate Wold, Yorks	OS 106/860570. Surveyed as heavy bomber base but found unsuitable. Used for temporary runway exercises October 1943 with Mustangs.
Ingatestone, Essex	One mile south-west of village. Tentatively allocated 8th AF as bomber base 10 August 1942. Confirmed September 1942. Warning of land requisition served. Construction indefinitely postponed 16 December 1942.
Kayshill, Ayrshire	Intended as SLG for Prestwick and under preparation in November 1941. Abandoned.
Kells Point, Co Tyrone	Planned as USAAF CCRC but not built.
Kilrenny, Fife	Planned as RLG for Donibristle but dropped in favour of Crail.
Kirkandrews, Cumbria	Project for FAA fighter school.
Laugharne, Carmarthenshire	Turned down by AM Works Dept. Too wet, no foundations for buildings.
Lisnaskea, Co Fermanagh	Planned satellite for St Angelo.
Litfoss, Yorks	Provisionally selected as satellite for Catfoss.
Little Clacton, Essex	Possible 8th AF bomber base but plans dropped by August 1942.
Longhurst, Northumberland	Proposed satellite for Morpeth.
Macaroni Down, Glos	Originally 13 SLG. Intended for 5 MU, Kemble. Said to have been completed but not used. Too close to RAF Southrop?
Maidenhead, Berks	Planned as an 8th AF bomber CCRC but not built.
Maiston Magna	Suggested site for RNAS but not proceeded with.
Maldon, Essex	Allocated 8th AF 10 August 1942 as bomber base. Confirmed September 1942. Warning of land requisition served October 1942. Construction indefinitely postponed 16 December 1942.
Malpas, Cheshire	Possible satellite for Rednal, but turned down by AM Works Dept.
Market Lavington, Wilts	Planned USAAF transport or observation base, but not built.
Maudesley, Lancashire	Proposed site for Coastal OTU.
Mawbray, Cumberland	Planned as a satellite for Silloth. Still pending in January 1943 but not built.
Midge Hall, Lancashire	Planned RNAS for armament training.
Millisle, Co Down	Intended to be USAAF CCRC, but abandoned when partly completed.
Myn-Rhos, Denbighs	Planned RNAS for fighter training.
North Stoke, Avon	Planned USAAF transport or observation base but not built.

Ogbourne, Wilts	Planned USAAF transport or observation base but not built.
Quarley Down, Hampshire	Planned USAAF transport or observation base but not built.
Piercebridge, Co Durham	Admiralty showed interest, but required for Bomber Command operational station. Not built owing to farming objections.
Ragdale, Leics	Planned as second satellite for Wymeswold but objections from WD because part of site was an old-established range.
Rhyl, Flints	Planned RNAS for fighter training.
Robgill, Dumfriesshire	Project for fighter OTU.
Rose Valley, Morayshire	Existing bombing range planned for re-development as satellite for Kinloss or Lossiemouth.
Rotherwick, Hampshire	Planned USAAF transport or observation base but not built.
Shipton Moyne, Glos	Proposed development of existing Down Farm (23 SLG) as USAAF bomber base. Strong objections from Ministry of Aircraft Production — plan dropped November 1942.
Sinderby, Yorks	Suggested satellite for Dishforth.
Snarestone, Leics	Required for an FAA Advanced Flying Unit, but too many agricultural objections.
Southgrove, Wilts	No 47 SLG. Intended for 25 MU, Wroughton, but not used. A concrete road appears to be the only evidence today.
Southminster, Essex	1¼ miles north-west of village. Tentatively allocated 8th AF as bomber base August 1942. Confirmed September 1942. Construction indefinitely postponed December 1942. USAAF Station 173.
South Ripley, Hants	Suggested site for RNAS, but not proceeded with. The site was probably utilized as Bisterne ALG.
Stony Stratford, Bucks	Proposed site for bomber OTU.
Strensall, Yorks	Possible RAF bomber base, but too many agricultural objections. Also part of an existing bombing range.
Tresham, Avon	Planned USAAF transport or observation base, but not built.
Weeley, Essex	Possible 8th AF bomber base but plans dropped by August 1942.
Wharles, Lancashire	Provisionally selected as satellite for Squires Gate.
Witherslack, Westmorland	Surrounded by hilly terrain.
Yardley Gobion, Northants	Proposed expansion base for medium bombers.

Chapter 7

Watch towers, hangars, ancillary buildings and installations

The watch tower or watch office, in American terminology the control tower, is undoubtedly the most evocative building when it survives on derelict airfields. It is no coincidence that the Runnymede Memorial to missing Commonwealth aircrew is dominated by a symbolic watch tower. This building was the nerve centre of every wartime aerodrome, rivalled only by the operations block, and it is fortunate that so many still stand today.

Prior to 1939 control of air traffic was non-existent within the RAF, but there was a requirement for a so-called Duty Pilot to book aircraft in and out. In the early days a hut in the apron area or, at places like Duxford and Leuchars, on the corner of a hangar roof, served as his office. When the Expansion stations were built a special building was designed which anticipated some measure of future airfield control. The watch office was in fact situated on the first floor with the Duty Pilot's room below. An 'FTS Type' watch office incorporating the Chief Flying Instructor's office was provided at Flying Training Schools, examples still in existence including those at Shawbury and South Cerney.

Some stations constructed immediately before the war were supplied merely with a single storey hut, a bay window being the sole concession to field of view. Some fighter satellite aerodromes built in 1940/41, such as Fearn, Llandwrog and Condover, had a small block-shaped building of one storey, its doorway protected by a blast wall. Parent stations were given a two-storey building with an internal stairway built on the rear elevation, the Air Ministry drawing number being 518/40. Many are still in use today with appropriate modifications, example being Bournemouth/Hurn Airport, Carlisle Airport, Hawarden and Wick.

By 1942 many of the fighter stations and their satellites had become redundant and were relegated to training. Whilst the 518/40 tower was more than adequate to cope with the demands of a vastly increased flying pro-

Watch office on the corner of a hangar roof at North Coates forms the background to this photo of Fairey IIIFs (Roy Bonser Collection).

Top left *Expansion Period watch office at Cosford* (Roy Bonser).

Top right *Modified version at Bassingbourn with an extra storey added to each section.*

Above *Rudimentary watch office of the type built at many fighter satellite aerodromes in 1940/41. This example was at Llandwrog, now Caernarfon Airport.*

Below *518/40 Type parent station tower seen at Rednal, Shropshire.*

Top left *12779/41 tower at Deenethorpe, Northants, a former 8th Air Force B-17 base.*

Top right *Up-graded satellite tower at Montford Bridge, Shropshire.*

Above left *13726/41 tower at Condover near Shrewsbury. The original satellite watch office can be seen in the background on the right.*

Above right *13726/41 tower at Finmere, Bucks. Note the small windows which were easier to black out but hardly conducive to a good view of the airfield.*

Below *Watch office at Seighford, Staffs, with attached crew and operations rooms.*

gramme, the buildings at the satellites were far to small. The answer was either to build a new tower or add an observation room to the roof of the existing watch office, or perhaps build it on top of an extension to one of the side elevations. The result has misled historians, including myself, into believing that this was an entirely different type of tower rather than an adaptation. Credit is due to Paul Francis of the Airfield Research Group for uncovering the facts of the situation. Good examples of the modification can be seen at Montford Bridge in Shropshire and Kinnell near Dundee, while a building where an observation room was merely added to the roof still stands at Matlask in Norfolk.

In an apparent attempt to standardize Flying Control buildings at the numerous operational aerodromes being built in 1941/42, the 12779/41 type came into being. With its six windows on the front elevation, it has become the most familiar of all these building types. The window sizes varied and some were even bricked up to half their original depth to make them easier to black out. With some detail differences the building was redesignated 343/43, Broadwell in Oxfordshire being one of many survivors. A number of airfields built in the mid-war period and planned as bomber operational and OTU satellites were equipped with a tower similar in layout to the 12779/41 but slightly smaller and with four windows at the front. To drawing number 13726/41, it was also built at some Training Command stations such as Windrush, Long Newnton and Chipping Norton.

Above *Royal Navy pattern tower at Dale, Dyfed, 1945 with workmen making the finishing touches (FAA Museum).*

Below *Three storey late war pattern tower at Dumfries.*

Skeletal USAAF tower at Warton, Lancs, beside the original building (G. Gosney).

A further variation on the control theme was the combined watch office/crew room/ops room, developed by altering and adding to the original hut-type watch office mentioned above. The reconstruction usually took place in several phases to meet changing requirements and examples can be found at Seighford, Stratford and Long Marston. Probably unique in Britain was the tall USAAF pattern temporary tower built at Warton when the view from the existing building proved inadequate for handling the large numbers of aircraft movements. It was dismantled in the early 1950s and an entirely new control tower was built at a later date.

As the war drew to a close. A few airfields, including Farnborough, Gaydon and, of all places, Findo Gask, were provided with a three-storey building evidently inspired by the Fleet Air Arm's standard tower. Heathrow Airport had one on its northern perimeter but it was certainly demolished by 1983. Post-war RAF towers were generally adaptations of wartime buildings, a glasshouse being added to the roofs of most. The VCR (Visual Control Room in civil parlance) now incorporated angled windows to eliminate reflections. This was not a new idea, however, as Gatwick's control tower had this feature well before the war. Prestwick was another early airfield with an angled glass tower, as was Langford Lodge in Northern Ireland.

Mary Lee Settle's memorable account of her WAAF experiences, *All the Brave Promises*, sums up the atmosphere of the watch office in which she spent so many hours: 'It was built like a functional Puritan square, jutting up blindly, covered with brown and green undulations of camouflage, impotent against its unnatural shape.

Hangars

An important clue to the origins and use of a particular airfield is provided by hangars, or sheds as they were known in earlier days. The word hangar, by the way, is yet another aeronautical term borrowed from the French and originally meant a covered space for a carriage.

When it formed in May 1912, the Royal Flying Corps possessed a standard form of permanent hangar; a large wooden shed with gabled front and sliding doors to accommodate up to three BE type aircraft. Later some of the wood was replaced by galvanized iron and several of these structures can still be seen today, including a row of them at Montrose. A larger permanent hangar became necessary as the RFC expanded, the result being the 1956 General Service Shed. The 1917 pattern GS shed was slightly larger and is often termed the Belfast because of the Belfast wooden truss method of supporting the roof. Three double blocks form the basis of the RAF Museum at Hendon.

Canvas hangars were used in the field, particularly on the Western Front, the first main type being the Royal Aircraft Factory hangar designed in 1913 but soon superseded by the lighter and more portable RE7 type. The well-known timber framed Bessonneau, supplied in large numbers from 1916, was the next development and many were brought out of storage for emergency use in the Second World War. The ultimate in canvas hangars was the Hervieu series introduced in 1917, some with 130 ft spans to accommodate Handley Page V/1500s.

Special hangar erection parties were trained in transportation of the structures in convoys

Top left *This is probably an RE7 hangar with the rare Nieuport Triplane at Coudekerque, Belgium, 1917.*

Top right *A 1916 General Service shed seen at Yatesbury, Wilts, in 1983.*

Above *Bessonneaux in two sizes seen at North Coates, Lincs,* circa *1930* (Roy Bonser Collection).

of lorries and their subsequent assembly and dismantling. In winter when the canvas doors froze Bessonneaux were cursed by all, but they played a vital part in protecting the flimsy aircraft of those days.

One of the earliest inter-war hangars designed in steel construction was the Type 'F' Flight Shed, with side-opening doors, examples of which were supplied to almost all the Armament Training Stations of the Expansion period. The Hinaidi was a 1920s contemporary but few aerodromes had them, apart

from Madley in Herefordshire and Chivenor. The Hinaidis at the latter have been reclad during an extensive modernization programme.

The 'A' Type of 1924 design was for a time the biggest permanent GS hangar, with a clear span of 120 ft, a length of 250 ft and doors at both ends. When the RAF was expanding and the need for housing larger types of aircraft was anticipated, it was decided that a new standard hangar was required with a span of 150 ft and length of 300 ft. The answer was

Top *Bessonneaux were still in use at training aerodromes in the Second World War. This example was at Carew Cheriton, Dyfed, for the use of the Coastal Patrol Flight's Tiger and Hornet Moths* (Via F.J. Adkin).

Above *Dilapidated 'F' Type hangar at Pembrey, South Wales.*

Below *Four Hinaidis, distinguishable by their high roofs, and four Bellmans at Chivenor, circa 1965* (W.J. Taylor).

Top *'A' Type hangar at Netheravon* (K.S. West).

Above *'C' Type undergoing demolition at Burtonwood in 1986.*

the 'C' type, many of which have served the RAF well for more than 50 years.

In common with many contemporary buildings for the RAF, the 'C' Type incorporated a number of cunning features. The brickwork was intended to soften its massive dimensions and the large windows to dissipate the blast from a bomb penetrating the roof. For camouflage and to further reduce the dominant effect on the surrounding countryside, trees were normally planted alongside. The doors were constructed with metal plates on both faces so when required they could be filled with gravel to a height of 20 ft to absorb bomb splinters.

The height of 35 ft was known to be excessive, but owing to the likelihood of a change of function at any station this was accepted. 'C' Types were built in varying lengths up to a maximum of 12 bays, the width being standard. The two roof designs, Gabled and Hipped, differed in that the latter had the

ends of the roof gables slanted rather than vertical. Annexes along each side contained offices for squadron and flight commanders, crew and locker rooms, map and briefing rooms, armouries, workshops and stores.

The 'C' Type had a major drawback; it was demanding in both materials and workmanship and its construction was very time-consuming. The solution in 1939 was a simpler building of the same dimensions, allowing it to be built rapidly on the many airfields under construction at that time. The steel firm Sir William Arrol & Co Ltd was responsible for producing the 'J' and 'K' Types as they were to be known. Outwardly indistinguishable, both were chiefly of metal construction with curved roofs of steel plate. The 'C' itself was subjected to the demands of utility and a version called the 'Cl' was produced, making extensive use of asbestos sheeting in place of the brickwork.

The designations 'J' and 'K' may refer to the

'K' Type at High Ercall, Shropshire.

types of office and stores accommodation in the annexes along each side, the 'J' being intended for operational stations and the 'K' for aircraft storage. At High Ercall in Shropshire a 'J' and a 'K' stand side-by-side, both having a defensive pill-box built in at each end, an interesting local modification. A total of 11 'J' Types and 33 'K's were erected in Aircraft Storage Units and, apart from those at operational stations, several bomber OTUs possessed one example each. They included Wellesbourne Mountford, Honeybourne and Chipping Warden. A few USAAF bases inherited them from the RAF, examples being Molesworth, Polebrook, Chelveston and Goxhill, most surviving to this day.

To provide for the storage of reserve aircraft, 24 ASUs were built in various parts of Britian. For dispersal and concealment, each was planned so as to take advantage of the natural features of the district. Some of these depots, such as Kemble and Wroughton, were self-contained with their own landing ground but the majority shared it with an FTS or OTU. An ASU normally comprised an HQ site with one 'C' Type for the dismantling or erecting of aircraft and two 'D' Type Sheds for storage of fully assembled machines. In addition there were four to six sub-sites located well away from the landing ground containing two or three hangars of the Lamella, 'E' or 'L' Type and screened by wooded areas where possible.

The 'D' Type shed was of reinforced concrete and, like the 'C', was the creation of the Design Branch of the Directorate General of Works. The Lamella, ironically, was of German origin designed by Junkers, Dessau in 1930. The name was coined from *Lamellendach*, literally *segmented roof*, and the British rights were acquired by the Horsley Bridge

and Engineering Co. The first in this country was built at Heston, another following at Usworth where it can still be seen.

Horsley produced a special Lamella for the Air Ministry intended solely for the storage of aircraft with wings removed. The curved roof was formed of ⅞ in steel sheet on which was laid 2 in of concrete. For concealment from the air and to give protection against incendiary bombs, 9 in of earth and turf covered the roof. The 'E' Type shed was identical in size to the Lamella but instead of being steel framed was constructed of reinforced concrete. In 1939 when aircraft production was outpacing storage space, a further design of similar shape and size, the 'L' Type, was produced by the Tees-Side Co. A total of 28 Lamellas, 107 'L's and 46 'E's were built.

Under peacetime conditions, it had been general policy to provide hangar accommodation for all a unit's aircraft, except when first-line squadrons were detached to Armament Training Stations for annual exercises. It was thought that this would give groundcrew some experience of maintaining aircraft in the open. With dispersal now the keynote, a small hangar known as the Blister was produced by Messrs C. Miskins & Sons in 1939, a prototype being erected at Biggin Hill in January 1940. Three types were supplied; the 'standard' Blister of wooden arched rib construction clad with corrugated iron and with a span of 45 ft, the 'Over' Blister of steel and 65 ft in span and the 'Extra Over' Blister, also of steel but 69 ft wide. All types were 45 ft long and had canvas curtains at each end made convex by means of struts which virtually eliminated tell-tale shadows. In practice the curtains were often omitted and some Blisters were bricked up at one end. They were easily doubled in

Top *'D' Type on former 24 Maintenance Unit site, Tern Hill.*

Above *'L' Type at Sealand, Clwyd, with its turf covering removed.*

Below *Over Blister Hangar at Little Sutton RLG, Cheshire.*

Left *A1 hangar designed by Ministry of Aircraft Production and once used by Lockheed at Speke, Liverpool, for aircraft assembly.*

Right   *Callender-Hamilton hangar at Atcham, near Shrewsbury, once a USAAF fighter training station (A.S.C. Lumsden).*

Below right *Piper Super Cub with Bellman hangars at Wycombe Air Park, the former RAF Booker.*

length and a further advantage was that they required no floor or foundation, the structure being sufficiently flexible to adjust to fairly uneven ground. In 1942 Dorman Long designed a 90 ft span Blister but this was not apparently used in any quantity.

Over 3,000 Blister hangars were supplied to the RAF, at least 100 being destined for the BEF in France until the Capitulation, when they were diverted to UK aerodromes. Production of the wooden variety was soon abandoned — it seems that airmen were always chopping off bits of the framework to feed hut stoves! In March 1942 all standard Blisters were moved from fighter stations to those of Flying Training Command, whose mainly wooden aircraft did not take kindly to constant exposure to the elements. Many of the steel type survive at disused aerodromes all over the country. They can be found also at farms and industrial sites many miles away from airfields, as can other kinds of transportable hangars.

In March 1939, Fighter Command had requested shelter tents for a single Spitfire or Hurricane at dispersal points on a basis of 12 per squadron. Despite promises to the contrary they were never forthcoming, but the Lamson Engineering Co did design a canvas and steel tube portable hangar for fighters and built two prototypes. Another experimental design never adopted was the Stewart and Lloyd Camouflage Hangar in lightweight steel with canvas doors. It spanned 115 feet and was intended to house a single four-engined bomber or two large twins. Another steel-framed hangar, but of American manufacture and known as the Butler Combat Hangar, was erected at several airfields by USAAF engineer troops. The RAF had a smaller equivalent, the

Merton, with a tubular steel framework, canvas clad with its entrance closed by winch-operated curtains.

A further specialized building was the Robin Type B and its larger counterpart the Super Robin which are described in Chapter 17. It was a Ministry of Aircraft Production design, as were the A1 and B1. The former was erected at many contractors' airfields but the B1 proved so successful that it was adopted also by the RAF for major servicing at many Bomber Command operational and OTU stations.

The TFB which I assume stood for Transportable Flying Boat, was a 1942 design built at a number of marine bases including Sullom Voe. Capable of housing up to two Sunderlands for maintenance, it was 114 ft wide by 240 ft long. Some marine stations were equipped with open-fronted shelters resembling boat houses into which aircraft could be pushed nose-first, and these were referred to officially as Flying Boat Pens.

Returning to the pre-war period, the requirement for a transportable hangar to augment the accommodation at ever-expanding RAF stations was met by two designs, the Callender-Hamilton and the Bellman. The former was designed by Callender's Cable and Construction Co in conjunction with Painter Bros Ltd of Hereford. Eight were erected at several RAF aerodromes in 1938, more being supplied later at such aerodromes as Atcham, Barrow and East Fortune. Examples survive at all three, readily identifiable by their distinctive lattice door guides.

The Bellman was to become the most common steel hangar until superseded by the T-series from 1940 onwards. About 400 Bellmans appeared on British aerodromes during the period 1938-40 but it soon became obso-

lete as a standard war shed with the increase in aircraft sizes. Thus it was that the Air Ministry, in collaboration with the Tees-Side Bridge and Engineering Works developed a more adequate type known as the 'T'. It was produced in three main sizes; the T1 of 95 ft span, the T2 of 115 ft and the T3 of 66 ft. The usual length was 240 ft but the number of bays could be varied to meet local requirements. The technical accommodation normally annexed to the permanent pre-war hangars now consisted of adjacent hutting.

Another Bellman product was a pre-war balloon shed to meet the requirements of the newly-formed Balloon Command. It was replaced in 1939 by a much larger building

over 62 ft high engineered by British Steel Contruction Ltd. Examples can be seen at several former Balloon Centres including Pucklechurch near Bristol, Titchfield, Hants and Bishopriggs, Glasgow. To digress slightly, the two enormous airship sheds at Cardington near Bedford are the last survivors of a considerable number of similar buildings erected at various locations from before the First World War onwards.

The Admiralty had its own requirements for hangarage, but unfortunately they are not as well documented as those of the Air Ministry and there is still controversy over their exact nomenclature. To house small aircraft with folded wings the Tees-Side Bridge and En-

Above *'T2' (left) and 'B1' at Seighford, Staffs.*

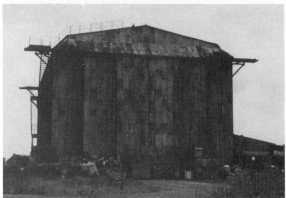

Left *Bellman Balloon Shed at Pawlett, Somerset, in support of barrage balloon cable cutting experiments by RAE.*

gineering Co produced the Admiralty Type 'S' Shed in 1940. Two years later a second 'S' Type appeared with sloping sides, apparently very similar to the Mainhill or Mains hangar. These small buildings were supplied in large numbers to Royal Naval Air stations, some having 20 or more scattered around their perimeters.

For major servicing, the Pentad was designed in 1943, being similar in concept to the T2 but with sloping side walls. A naval version of the Blister hangar was known as the Fromson a larger variant being the Fromson-Massillon. FAA documents refer also to other types, such as the Aircraft Repair Shed (ARS), Squadron Hangar and Bellman Naval Hangar. One must not forget the so-called Dutch Barn sheltering a single aircraft, many being erected at Worthy Down in 1940. The Alframe was designed and manufactured around 1944 by the British Alcan Aluminium Co Ltd for MONABs (Mobile Operational Naval Air Bases.) Covered with light alloy sheeting, examples can be seen at Yeovilton and the Portland helicopter base.

Since the war several new hangar types have appeared, including the Alaframa of 1956 which is similar in shape to the current Hardened Aircraft Shelter, the Gaydon, the Ballykelly Cantilever, and the Brize Norton Cantilever. The last two are peculiar to the airfields after which they were named, but the Gaydon at the V-Bomber training base of that name was also built elsewhere, including Valley and Coningsby. It was obviously adapted from the pre-war 'J' Type but much enlarged. Several USAF bases were provided with a Butler Hangar, a product of the American firm which designed the temporary hangar mentioned above. Among the airfields at which Butlers can be seen are Bruntingthorpe and Blackbushe, the US Navy using the one at the last-named.

There are rumours of wartime underground hangars in the UK and indeed Diagrid Structures Ltd designed a reinforced concrete hangar which in 1936 was claimed to be bomb proof when built underground. There is, however, no evidence that they were ever adopted by the RAF but the RNAS *did* try underground structures at Manston in 1918 and spent large sums of money on the excavations. They were

Above   Pentad   at   RNAS Hinstock, Shropshire.

Right *Oxfords packed into a 'VR' hangar at Dalcross in September 1952. This large type of building was uncommon but a survivor forms the basis of the freight shed at Manchester Airport* (Ray Hendry).

little more than hangars built in large pits with a ramp access and one of the depressions can be seen to this day.

Technical and domestic buildings

It was evident at the inception of the Expansion Programme that, particularly with domestic accommodation and certain technical and instructional buildings at operational stations and FTSs, buildings of similar purpose, planning and size would be required at most of them. As a result, it was decided that the policy of standardization or 'type' design should be applied to the fullest extent possible. Bearing in mind the generally rural locations of aerodromes, a simple Georgian style of architecture was chosen as likely to blend most readily into the surrounding countryside in most parts of England.

A further refinement was the careful selection of facing bricks and roofing tiles so as to be appropriate to the district. At Hullavington the planners went so far as to specify stone facing to conform with the traditions of the Cotswold country. Late in the Expansion period, however, shortages of bricklayers and the desire for better bomb protection brought a change from brick to concrete construction generally for the technical buildings at some stations. The messes and barrack blocks of those years were extremely comfortable and well-appointed and it is no wonder that such permanent stations as Bassingbourn and Duxford were to be so highly prized by the USAAF compared with the hutted camps that so many of them were forced to endure. In the technical areas, Station Armouries, Main Stores and Station Workshops were all standard designs. Additional specialized buildings included parachute stores, petrol tanker sheds, fire tender garages and night flying equipment stores, all of which had been of an improvised and inefficient nature.

Planning in 1935 required that certain units, being of a more or less temporary nature, would be housed in non-permanent buildings. Two forms of hutting were devised, the first known as 'B' Type to have a life of about five years, the second, 'A' Type, to last for 10 to 15 years. In principle the construction of both

Above *An elegant Officers' Mess building of the Expansion Period now falling into disrepair at Pembroke Dock, Dyfed.*

Left *Station water tower at High Ercall. The wartime equivalent was a stark framework devoid of the softening effect of the brick facing.*

Above right *Typical Air Ministry timber hut of the immediate pre-war period, seen at Sleap, Shropshire.*

Right *Camouflage-painted Nissen huts on a dispersed living site at an unidentified aerodrome. The positioning is typically haphazard to render them less conspicuous from the air (Via Z. Hurt).*

was the same, but the latter was given a better finish and external weather boarding of Canadian cedar. That some are still in good condition 50 years later is a measure of their quality.

In the early months of the war it was decided that for new stations and major extensions to existing ones, accommodation should be dispersed to minimize the effects of air attack. Beginning with the removal from the main building area of vital structures such as operations blocks and Station Sick Quarters, the scheme developed through various stages so that it soon became policy to disperse living sites in defined groups in the vicinity of the airfield, taking advantage where possible of natural features such as woods for concealment.

Domestic accommodation was at first subdivided into groups of buildings whereby each group housed 150 personnel of all ranks and

was situated approximately 800 yd from the main technical area and 800 yd one from another. Experience soon showed that the distances involved resulted in a disproportionate loss of administrative and operational efficiency. Through a compromise, it ultimately became general policy that in the layout of a station the accommodation should be dispersed so that the technical buildings were subdivided into a main area containing two hangars and the principal workshops, stores, armouries etc and two sub-sites containing one hangar and minor ancillary buildings. Each group was sited between the ends of runways and relative to the dispersed aircraft it served.

The living sites were now placed at a minimum distance from the technical site of 200 yd with the same interval between each. At the outbreak of the war, planning of quarters was based on temporary scales of 120 sq

ft per officer, 70 sq ft per sergeant and 45 sq ft per corporal or airman. These figures were invariably reduced, however, owing to station strengths being substantially above the establishment for which they were planned. In 1942 huts were calculated to house larger numbers of personnel so that the scale was reduced to 96 sq ft for officers, 58 for sergeants and 38 for airmen. The same areas were applied in general to WAAF personnel. A further austerity reduction was effected in July 1943 when the unfortunate airmen were allowed only 32 sq ft!'

Communal buildings, such as dining rooms, institutes, officers' and sergeants' messes, remained substantially static throughout the war period and, broadly, involved a 25 per cent reduction in pre-war provision in the main rooms. On the other hand, very considerable economies were effected in planning by the omission or scaling down of certain ancillary rooms and the deletion of all unessential space in halls and corridors. Further austerity measures were taken in 1943 by the reduction of seating capacity in dining rooms and in mess rooms for officers and sergeants to 50 per cent of establishment, necessitating two sittings for meals.

In the initial provision made for WAAF personnel early in 1940, separate dining rooms, institutes and officers' and sergeants' messes were provided. It became policy, however, in 1942 that WAAFs should share RAF buildings of those types and thereafter separate WAAF communal buildings were omitted and corresponding areas of new RAF accommodation appropriately increased. At Calveley, Cheshire, for example, only the foundation for the NAAFI on the WAAF site was completed and this can still be seen today.

Top *Orlit hut at Great Ashfield, Suffolk* (P. Francis).

Above *Nashcrete hut at Brayton Park SLG, Cumbria* (P. Francis).

Left *Marston Shed at Holme-on-Spalding Moor, Yorks* (P. Francis).

There were many standard designs for domestic buildings and in most cases contingency plans were prepared for the same buildings in two or more forms of construction. They were devoid of elaboration in their design and provided only for the bare necessities of their purpose. Under wartime conditions it was often the case that the excess of strength over the establishment for which they were planned led to long periods of serious over crowding.

The requirement for technical buildings remained reasonably static from the early days of the war, apart from successive additions dictated by the increasing numbers and changing types of aircraft. Considerable advances were made, however, in the accommodation provided for aircrew. They were now given facilities on a squadron basis which included rest and briefing rooms. Workshops and stores were built in composite blocks of hutting of normal spans, but in the larger base stations two or more Romney or Iris huts would be included.

It was the policy for station motor transport to be parked in the open and it was only for maintenance and for drivers' rest rooms that buildings were provided. Considerable growth in the establishment of MT, however, necessitated an increase in the provision of repair facilities and that was met normally by the erection of Marston shedding. General purpose huts were provided at dispersal points

Handcraft Hut at Sleap, Shropshire, originally used for the storage of night flying equipment.

for groundcrew shelters and minor workshops. Similarly, minor stores, workshops and armouries were erected at the subsidiary technical sites around the airfield.

The majority of technical buildings were simple and functional and went under the broad groupings of workshops, stores, armouries, operational support and offices. Within these groups were buildings for many varied purposes, including photographic blocks, aircraft equipment stores, bomb sight stores, gas defence stores, night flying equipment stores, pigeon lofts, radar workshops, engine repair shops, stand-by set houses and W/T transmitting and receiving stations.

The multiplicity of wartime types of hutting resulted from fluctuations in the supply of materials. At no time during the war years was there a sufficiency of one basic material to justify long term adoption of any particular type. Timber construction would be replaced by steel which in turn would be ousted by composite construction of asbestos, timber and bitumen sheeting, then by concrete, 4½ in brick, back to steel and so on.

At the beginning of the war, the standard Air Ministry prefabricated hut was the 'B' Type, the wooden building described above. However, the demands for hutting were now reaching such a phenomenal scale that new wooden types known as 'X', 'Y' and 'Z' had to be designed and produced. Inferior in quality but more economic in timber, they were quicker to fabricate and adequate for their wartime purpose.

By 1940 the timber shortage was so acute that alternative types using less or no timber were developed. They included the Ministry of Supply Timber Hut, the Thorne Hut in timber, the Laing Hut (light timber, plasterboard and felt) and the Maycrete Hut in concrete. The First War Nissen hut (designed by Colonel P. Nissen) was revived and from 1941 large numbers were produced in spans of 16, 24 and 30 ft.

Further restrictions in the supply of materials forced research into the fabrication of buildings using neither steel nor timber. The Air Ministry designed an all-concrete hut but for various reasons it never entered service. A well-known asbestos firm manufactured a very useful building — the Handcraft Hut — which was virtually a Nissen in asbestos cement sheeting. Late in 1942, the Inter-Departmental Committee on Hutting became the sole arbiter on design and supply of all types was centred on the Ministry of Works. The following types were standardized as the alternatives available:

For ordinary accommodation
Nissen 16 and 24 ft span. Only to be used where essential. Ministry of Works Hall Plasterboard. BCF all concrete. Orlit all concrete. Curved Asbestos Cement. Seco 19 ft span in multiples of 12 ft lengths. Tarran. (This type was in fact never used by the RAF.)

For workshops, stores, garages etc
WO shedding 36 ft 6 in span in multiples of 12 ft lengths. Iris or Romney 35 ft span (semicircular) in multiples of 8 ft lengths. WO shedding or Marston 45 ft span in multiples of 25 ft lengths.

Since most RAF stations were steadily developed during their operational life, the result was that nearly all of them had acquired several types of hutting by the time the war ended. A brief description of the various types of huts erected at RAF stations is given below, the dates in brackets showing the periods during which they were made.

AM Type 'A' 18 ft and 28 ft span. Stout timber frame, covered externally with cedar weather boarding to walls and corrugated asbestos sheets to roof, lined internally with fibre or plasterboard. Wood floor. (1935-39)

AM Type 'B' 18 ft and 28 span. Stout timber frame, covered externally with fibre or plasterboard. Wood floor. (1935-39)

AM Types 'X' 'Y' and 'Z' 18 ft span. As Type 'B' but wholly prefabricated and of dif-

Fairly rare BCF concrete hut near Dale aerodrome, Dyfed.

ferent lengths. (1 September 1939-31 December 1940)

MoS Timber 16 ft × 54 ft. Timber frame, covered weather boarding to walls, boarded and felt roofs, unlined, concrete floors. (1 January-30 June 1941)

MoS Thorbex 18 ft × 60 ft. Light timber frame, covered felted plasterboard, lined plasterboard, concrete floor (cant sided). (1 January-31 July 1941)

Mos Maycrete 16 ft × 54 ft. Reinforced concrete posts, Maycrete slab walls, boarded and felt roofs, lined plasterboard, concrete floor. (1 April-31 July 1941)

AM Laing Type 18 ft × 60 ft. Light timber frame, covered felted plasterboard and corrugated asbestos sheets, lined plasterboard, concrete floor. (1 January 1941-30 April 1942)

WO Nissen 16 ft × 36 ft. Steel ribs, timber purlins, covered and lined with corrugated steel sheeting, concrete floor. (Commenced construction 1 March 1941)
WO Nissen 24 ft span in multiples of 6 ft lengths. Steel ribs timber purlins, covered corrugated steel, lined plasterboard, concrete floor. (Commenced construction 1 August 1941)

WO Iris and Romney 35 ft span in multiples of 8 ft lengths. Light steel tubular ribs, light steel purlins covered corrugated steel sheets, unlined, concrete floor (for workshops, stores, etc). (Commenced construction 1 August 1941)

MoS Plasterboard 18 ft × 60 ft. Light timber frame, covered felted plasterboard, lined plasterboard, concrete floor. (1 October-31 December 1941)

AM Nissen 30 ft span in multiples of 6 ft lengths, steel ribs, timber purlins, covered corrugated steel, lined fibre board, concrete floor (for very large messes, institutes etc). (1 December 1941-30 November 1943)

AM Plyfelt Covered 18 ft × 60 ft. Very light timber frame, covered and lined with plyfelt, concrete floor. (1 January-30 April 1942)

AM Revised Laing 18 ft × 60 ft. Very light timber frame, covered light corrugated steel, lined hardboard or plyfelt, concrete floor. (1 May 1942-30 June 1943)

Handcraft 18 ft × 36 ft. No framing, shaped asbestos cement troughing sheets externally, flat asbestos cement sheets internally, concrete floor. (Commenced construction 1 May 1942)

Curved Asbestos 17 ft 6 in × 36 ft. No framing, curved corrugated asbestos cement sheets externally, flexible asbestos cement sheets on battens internally, concrete floor. (Commenced construction 1 May 1942)

HoW Hall Plasterboard 18 ft × 65 ft. Light timber framing, covered felted plasterboard, lined plasterboard, concrete floor. (1 July 1942-28 February 1943)

MoW B/C/F 18 ft 6 in × 65 ft. Reinforced concrete framing, paving slabs external wall, breeze slab internal wall, breeze slab felt covered roof, concrete floor. (1 August 1942-30 June 1943)

MoW Orlit 18 ft 6 in × 60 ft. Reinforced concrete framing, pre-cast concrete slab walls outer and inner face, pre-cast concrete roof covered felt, concrete floor. (1 August 1942-30 June 1943)

Top *De-contamination Centre at Skeabrae, Orkney* (Julian C. Temple).
Above *Operations Block on dispersed site at Talbenny, Dyfed.*
Below *Parachute store at Speke, Liverpool, refurbished but recently burned down.*

MoW Seco 19 ft × 24 ft. Span in multiples of 12 ft lengths, hollow plywood columns and beams, asbestos cement, wood wool, cement and timber composite wall and roof panels, roof felted, concrete floor. (Commenced construction 1 August 1942)

WO and Marston 35 ft × 45 ft. Very light steel framing, covered corrugated steel, unlined, concrete floor (for workshops, garages and stores).

Certain buildings were of a distinctive design and many surviving examples can be seen. Perhaps the most readily identifiable is the parachute store and the gymnasium, sometimes serving also as a church or cinema in certain configurations, is another obvious structure. The windowless gas decontamination centre is often to be found, its massive construction being somewhat similar to that of the operations block, which was generally dispersed well away from the aerodrome. There were several designs, including one that was virtually bomb-proof, being built around a box of steel girders topped by a slab of concrete several feet thick.

A close study of site plans will reveal various other buildings common to most airfields, such as the speech broadcasting building, standby set house and fire tender shed. Instructional buildings and defence works are a study in themselves and details will be found in Chapters 8 and 9, respectively. An interesting point revealed during the research for this chapter was that the 8th Air Force came so near to abandoning daylight operations after severe losses in 1943 that it was requesting night flying equipment stores to be built at each of its bomber bases.

Fuel installations

Up to the mid-1930s, the aviation petrol storage installations at RAF stations consisted of groups of 12,000 gallon tanks in open catchment pits, the total capacity not exceeding 48,000 gallons. Around 1935 this practice came under review and at the same time the mobile tanker or bowser system of refuelling aircraft became standard in the RAF. The policy regarding storage capacity at operational stations laid down that enough petrol for six weeks of intensive operations should be held in tankage units not exceeding 72,000 gallons each. The holdings varied from 48,000 to 216,000 gallons and up to three installations were provided at each airfield, usually sited remotely from each other. The basic unit of storage was the 12,000 gallon tank, 9 ft in diameter and 30 ft long. The tank and pumphouse were protected by reinforced concrete, mounded with earth and turfed. Lubricating oil was also stored to a ratio of five per cent of the total petrol storage per station.

The speed of wartime airfield construction forced a reduction in the pre-war protective measures described above. The concrete casing of the tanks was omitted and they were merely positioned on a concrete raft and backfilled, a skin of clay or similar material being applied to the tank shell as a proof against corrosion. Where sub-soil water was present, the tanks were installed above ground surrounded by a brick wall and mounded with earth. A road circuiting the installation was able to handle a large number of tankers both offloading and filling without congestion. The usual provision on operational bomber stations was two 72,000 gallon units but there were several emergency methods of increasing these stocks to meet the needs of the bombing campaign.

In 1940 it had become obvious that the distribution of fuel, both commercial and aviation, was in danger of breaking down owing to the already overburdened railway system and the vulnerable sea access to the Thames and east coast ports. In 1941 the Ministry of Fuel and Power decided to construct a pipeline to carry aviation and motor fuel throughout the country and to expedite the turn-round of tankers unloading at the west coast ports. The unprecedented demand for fuel in 1943 for the RAF and 8th USAAF stations in East Anglia was met by pipelines linking the national system with the main distribution depots and, where possible, directly supplying airfields.

This was done by laying spur pipelines from the main to feed fuel into about 24 British and American stations which were sited not more than five miles from its route. Well before the war the Air Council had organized a system of reserve storage for aviation fuel with associated distribution depots to augment the existing oil company depots. It is outside the scope of this book to go into more detail on this subject, but disused quarries at Buxton in Derbyshire and Much Wenlock in Shropshire were adapted, the tanks at the former holding up to 40,000 tons of fuel.

Chapter 8

Instructional sites and synthetic training

Flight simulators are an essential part of conversion to today's complicated civil and military aircraft, but the concept is far from new. Ground training devices to economize on aircraft hours and fuel have been around since well before the Second World War and by 1945 some very sophisticated pieces of apparatus were in service. These synthetic trainers, as they were then known, were used not only for the training of pilots but also for all other members of a crew. Many of them required specialized buildings, and numerous examples survive today.

Perhaps the earliest example of ground trainers were the so-called Penguins, retired aircraft with cut-down wings to render impossible anything other than short ground hops. During the first part of the First World War, before the advent of proper two-seat trainers, they enabled new pilots to gain some idea of the feel of an aircraft before going solo.

Pre-dating the synthetic bombing trainers of later years, the RNAS Bomb-Dropping Mirror and Course Recorder was introduced at Luce Bay, near Stranraer, in August 1916. By the use of the apparatus, ground observers could measure accurately the success or degree of error and also calculate the ground speed of an airship in flight.

The early inventions were, strictly speaking, semi-synthetic as actual flying was involved, rather than a totally static, ground-based operation. However, the world's first electro-mechanical flight simulator was invented in 1920 by an American, Edward Albert Link. Soon to be known as the Link Trainer, it was a very basic representation of an aircraft with cockpit controls and flight instruments. A sort of 'bellows' action at the base of the cockpit gave the impression of movement and a pilot could go 'under the hood' for instrument flying practice.

Similar but much less sophisticated was the Reid Pilot Testing Apparatus, produced by Reid and Sigrist Ltd and adopted by the RAF in 1930. It was intended to determine the aptitude of a prospective pilot. I an unaware how long they were in use, but have seen no mention of them in wartime manuals.

With instrument flying still in its infancy, what the RAF really needed was a synthetic device for the training of bomb-aimers. In 1925 the Air Ministry's Laboratory at Imperial College designed the AML Bombing Teacher which taught the use of the Course Setting Bomb Sight. It was later manufactured in quantity by Vickers-Armstrong Ltd as the Vickers Bygrave Bombing Teacher.

The building in which it was housed consisted of two storeys, the ground floor being marked in white paint with an 18 ft diameter circle. A steel ladder connected the ground floor to the 3 ft wide landing which represented the aircraft. This was fitted with a bomb sight and navigation equipment for the pupil and also a seat and rudder bar for the 'pilot'.

A second ladder led to the projection floor from which a powerful lamp projected a 12 ft square aerial mosaic by means of a 10 m square transparency. This represented an area of about 900 square miles, with about four square miles being visible at any given time, just as it would have appeared from a height of 8,000 ft. Means were provided to cause the image to move towards the bomb aiming platform from the various directions, thus simulating the effects of wind on the course of the aircraft. When the pupil had calculated the speed and direction of wind and sighted on the target, he threw a switch which represented the bomb release.

The length of time for the hypothetical bomb to reach the ground was measured automatically and at the appropriate moment the movement of the 'ground' was stopped. Painted on the floor was a 'fixed trail point' which marked

Double Bombing Teacher building at Tilstock, a former bomber OTU in Shropshire.

the spot on which a correctly aimed bomb should drop. Any error was readily apparent because of the difference in the position of the 'target' and this fixed trail point.

Another pre-war invention was the Freiston Deflection Teacher which used a model aeroplane controlled by an operator in the firing shelter on the standard 25 yd range. It was designed to instruct pilots in the use of the ring and bead sight.

The ground training of air gunners was not neglected either and there was much experimentation between the wars. The early attempts involved curved walls on to which a spot of light could be thrown at which the gunner could aim. This equipment was known as the Spotlight Trainer and was manufactured by a firm called Nash and Thompson. At the invitation of the Air Ministry, the spotlight idea was developed by the National Institute of Industrial Psychology (NIIP), a non-profit making scientific body. Before the Second World War they had designed a car-driving simulator and had tried unsuccessfully to apply the principle to pilot training.

The NIIP devised a scheme using a hemispherical screen standing on its edge, resembling a 20 ft diameter radar dish. A steel framework tower stood in front of the screen on which was mounted a Frazer-Nash power turret and projector. The first one was installed at RAF West Freugh and on 16 December 1940 this Turret Gun Sighting Trainer (TGST) was officially adopted by the Air Ministry.

A later design called the Standard Free Gunnery Trainer (SFGT) was very similar to the TGST but allowed use of the electrically-operated Boulton-Paul Type C turret. No guns were fitted, of course, just a light projector to indicate the aiming point to the instructor.

Films of various types of attacking aircraft were employed, engine noise and gunfire from loudspeakers making the exercise extremely realistic.

The Gunnery Trainers were housed in specially-designed buildings, many of which survive today. However, the only one known to retain its original target screen is at Sleap in Shropshire. Unfortunately, this combined 'AML Bombing Teacher and Turret Trainer' stands in a thicket and is difficult to photograph, especially when the trees are in leaf. Roofless and forgotten, it is nevertheless an impressive sight with its massive target screen. Later SFGTs were fitted inside blister hangars with an upright plasterboard screen. This alternative was cheaper and easier to erect and was to be found at Penrhos and Peplow, to name but two locations.

Air gunners were sometimes trained in the Dome Teacher, a peculiar-looking building about 25 ft tall, examples having survived at a number of locations around Britain. It was intended originally for the training of ground anti-aircraft gunners. Sound effects prepared them psychologically for real battle conditions and they were taught deflection shooting and shown how little time there was to engage a fast-flying aircraft. As with the air gunnery trainers, films were projected on to curved walls.

An associated aid was the Tracer Trainer which consisted of a pneumatic gun firing a stream of small ball-bearings in a spotlight beam at a fast moving metal target. The light on the small steel balls gave the effect of tracer ammunition.

Mr H. Anton of Crawley, Sussex, recalls being sent on a course at RAF Coningsby in 1944, which included a few days on the Dome Teacher. He writes:

'One sat or stood at a ground installation of a light machine gun while a film of an aircraft or batch of aircraft was projected on to the circular walls. They would flash overhead or peel off to one side, the design of the dome allowing this to appear realistic.

'As the operator followed the aircraft using his gun sights, he would open fire when he thought the plane was in range and cease to fire as it receded. To assist the instructor to assess your performance, a lighted ring sight would be projected on to the wall, enabling him to see whether you were allowing enough deflection or not. An instrument at his side showed the range at which the pupil opened or ceased fire.

'The film had a sound track which gave

Above *The only known surviving target screen in the combined AML Bombing Teacher and Turret Trainer at Sleap in Shropshire. Summer foliage made it difficult to photograph.*

Above right *Combined Bombing Teacher and Turret Trainer neatly converted into a house at Darley Moor, Derbyshire.*

Right *Dome Trainer at Pembrey, South Wales, with MGB for scale.*

forth machine gun or cannon fire, or bomb explosions, whilst when you opened fire, speakers fitted on the gun installation emitted a deafening noise of gunfire. This gave a realism which you encountered when you went on live firing exercises at the end of the course.'

At some places, Dome Teacher buildings were used also for practice in astro-navigation. The movement of the 'stars' was controlled by a clockwork mechanism. One other use for the Dome was definitely down-to-earth: after the war, one built at Butlin's Holiday Camp at Filey was converted into an amusement arcade for slot machines. It was finally demolished in the mid-1970s.

Somewhat more rudimentary training was given to air gunners by means of a turret mounted on a trailer and towed around inside a hangar by a tractor or Bedford 3-tonner. The gunner would practice sighting on a moving spot of light played on the walls. The USAAF in Britain borrowed the idea but aircraft in the aerodrome circuit were used as targets. At some RAF Air Gunners Schools, turrets were fixed to trolleys and pulled around a small railway track.

Although synthetic training methods gave individual airmen a good grounding in the skills of their trade, they neglected to instruct crews as a single unit in the performance of their duties under simulated operational conditions. This shortcoming was readily apparent during the first months of the war and 'Bomber' Harris, then AOC of 5 Group proposed to solve it by methods which became the blueprint for the later Bomber Command Operational Training Units and Heavy Conversion Units.

He planned his own group training organization at Finningley, which would produce a complete scenario of synthetic procedures for pilots, navigators, air gunners and wireless operators. New crews would train under an instructor, first individually, then as complete crews. He emphasized that they would be put through this training over and over again, until they were really proficient in their duties and thus have some hope of being able to perform as a team in the air under the stress of operational conditions.

Harris acquired three fuselages from written-off aircraft (probably Wellingtons) to represent a formation on ops, For instructional convenience each was broken apart into nose, middle and tail, each section being occupied by the appropriate members of the crew, except that the pilot would sit in a Link Trainer. Intercom, wireless, navigational and other equipment was made to operate realistically so that the crews could be sent off on a synthetic operational flight.

Blind take-offs and landings would be included and special situations created, such as icing, tactical problems, aircraft and ship recognition, emergency landings and so on. Accurate courses would have to be steered and navigators would have their information fed to them at the tempo normally experienced in operational flying, including the run-up to the target, aiming and release of bombs. Similarly, the wireless operators and gunners would have to perform their tasks, the latter even receiving surprise attacks from model German fighters.

Harris wrote, 'The individuals, and finally the whole crews, will be put through this "hoop" time and time again, *ad nauseam* if necessary, until they are procedure perfect.'

RAF Abingdon was the second station to take up the dummy fuselage scheme but meanwhile, Wing Commander Gordon Iles at the Coastal Command OTU at Silloth was developing the idea into something that was the direct forerunner of today's flight simulators. Known as the Silloth Trainer, it was a complete Hudson fuselage which employed electrical and pneumatic apparatus to simulate instrument readings, effects of control movements and engine sound as experienced in actual flight. The use of an air bellows to move the fuselage no doubt stemmed from Iles's pre-war experience as an organist! The Silloth simulated flight much more accurately than the very basic Link Trainer and was more truly representative of a large operational aircraft.

It was noted at the time that it was not possible, without complicated cinematographical effects and the utilization of considerable space, to provide any accurate simulation of scenic effects during flight. However, it was felt that this was not really necessary for the type of training envisaged, the needs of all members of the crew, apart from the air gunners, being catered for.

The design was easily adaptable to all types of operational RAF aircraft and there was no shortage of fuselages salvaged from crashes. By September 1942, for example, a Beaufighter fuselage was installed in a hangar at 54 OTU, Charter Hall, Wellingtons at the OTUs at Wellesbourne Mountford and Westcott, a Havoc at 51 OTU, Cranfield and even the FAA at Crail acquired a Beaufighter.

The Silloth Trainers were often set up in the Gunnery and Crew Procedure Centre, often referred to as the Airmanship Hall and found on most Bomber OTU instructional sites. Where there was no fuselage available, there were facilities for crew training as Murray Peden describes in this extract from his classic *A Thousand Shall Fall*.

> 'The "Grope" was basically an exercise that simulated the navigational and other problems a crew could expect to encounter on an operation. It was carried out in a large gymnasium-like building that was divided at the back into half-a-dozen twin-level studios, each housing one crew. The pilot and bomb aimer were ensconced in an open area on the higher level, and the remainder of the crew in the ground level portion of the "aircraft".

Crew Procedure Centre or 'Airmanship Hall' at Chipping Warden in which Murray Peden's crew were put through their paces.

Dummy ops room building, in fact a Laing Hut on a brick base, at Rednal, once 61 OTU.

'While the exercise was going on, simulated engine noise necessitated the use of intercom between the different crew positions. The multitudinous problems we encountered on our simulated raid — on Bremen — were mainly of the variety we had encountered on earlier classroom problems, but an additional complication was introduced by the fact that the large wall clock that governed all our actions travelled at one and one-half times normal speed. This kept everyone nipping about like road runners in an attempt to keep abreast of developments. To project a six-minute alteration of course, the navigator actually had to do the necessary calculations in four minutes, and new drift readings and other corrected information kept streaming in at a dizzy pace.'

Dinghy drill was also practised in the Procedure Centre before initiation into the miseries of wet dinghy drill. When one was available, this was performed at the local swimming pool. Crews were blindfolded to simulate night conditions and thrown into the pool with a whistle each and an inflated rubber dinghy which had been deliberately turned upside down. With difficulty the dinghy was located and righted and, by blowing their whistles, the crew assembled and climbed aboard.

Although the problems of bomber crew synthetic training were solved, the needs of the fighter OTUs were still not being met. It fell to local enterprise at unit level to come up with answers. At 57 OTU the Hawarden Trainer was designed with the object of simulating as faithfully as possible the full procedure of an operational flight from a state of readiness in the crew room to filling out a combat report at the end. Amongst other things, it taught cockpit drill and the value of keeping a good look-out.

The Hawarden Trainer consisted of the centre portion of a written-off Spitfire fuselage mounted on trestles facing the end of the hut, with the pilot's head about 60 ft from the end. The end of a hut, the ceiling, sidewalls and a screen behind the pilot were painted with a realistic cloudscape. Behind the screened fuselage was a 'sector controller' whose sole means of communication with the pilot was by intercom.

A 1:48th scale Me 110 could be moved around by means of rails and wires and a six volt electric motor bought from Woolworths! This gave the illusion that the static fuselage was gaining on it. It all sounds alarmingly crude but it proved a very effective training aid, so much so that it soon became part of the official OTU course at Hawarden. Various modifications and improvements were made at other fighter OTUs, 61 calling theirs the Rednal Trainer.

Peculiar to fighter OTUs were dummy operations rooms, just like the real thing but in cheaply-constructed buildings, rather than the normal elaborate reinforced concrete structures which were often underground. The one at Eshott in Northumberland has been partly demolished but an identical building at Rednal is intact, the controller's dais and many small rooms for intercom and other equipment being easily recognizable.

The night fighter OTUs had their own requirements which were supplied by the Hunt Trainer. Briefly, this consisted of an aircraft model reflected in a movable mirror which could be adjusted to a given range. The lighting was arranged so that the night sky was simulated, varying from no moon to full moon. Stars and moving white clouds could be staged to mimic the effect of contrast. The aircraft model was attached to an electric motor and could be moved so that it could be seen from all angles.

The equipment was considered to be a practical demonstration of night vision in an aircraft complete with the effects of dirty Perspex, cloud contrast and the distraction of overbright cockpit lights. The latter were fitted to the partition immediately in front of the pupil. Coupled with four hours of this synthetic training, the OTU trainees were also given five hours of night aircraft recognition as part of the course, using slides.

Torpedo dropping was another specialized operational task. The FAA at RNAS Crail in Fifeshire built their own Torpedo Attack Teacher. A large dish, similar to the one used in the TGST described earlier, was painted with a horizon line and clouds which are still to be seen there today. A Barracuda cockpit — alas long gone — was mounted in front of it and dummy torpedo attacks could be made on shipping targets projected on to the huge dish.

Another complaint during the early war period was that one of the chief weaknesses of aircrew was their inability to map-read under all conditions. This was further complicated by the fact that Empire-trained crews were unfamiliar with the unique topography of this country and therefore could only be instructed effectively within the UK.

In order to come up with some solutions, the Navigation Training Synthetic Development Unit (NTSDU) was formed at Woodley Aerodrome, near Reading on 7 May 1941. The life of this unit was expected to be six months, during which it was hoped that map reading, D/R navigation and astro-navigation training devices could be created. Woodley was already occupied by the Phillips and Powis factory building Miles Masters and it was arranged that they would provide skilled labour where necessary for fabricating the apparatus.

The first line of investigation was the AML Teacher, but it was soon apparent that this could not easily be adapted for navigational purposes. After some experimentation, the Air Navigation Instructor was perfected. It occupied a large empty building which was well blacked-out. Inside at one end were tiers of cubicles, each holding a pupil, up to a total of 25, this being the largest navigation class at that time. The cubicles were fitted with a table, chair and a drift sight.

It was designed so that an almost unbroken view of the floor was obtained. A picture of the ground was projected on to it by means of moving transparencies at a predetermined speed and direction. The ground appeared to move in towards the cubicles, providing the track and ground speed remained good. A

gallery running round the remaining three sides of the building allowed map reading practice to be carried out even when an exercise proper was in progress.

The coloured ground slides represented a scale of 1:25,000, the most convenient to cover the whole of the British Isles. Even then, 2,000 of them had to be handpainted and this task was farmed out to a number of art schools. Once the tedious job was done, however, lantern slides, films and transparencies could be produced *ad infinitum*.

The NTSDU also devised, amongst other things, a screen for synthetic night flying, of which more later, a Ship Recognition Trainer, and an engine noise simulator, the latter being simply a gramophone with an appropriate record. Experimental flying was done first at Upwood and later at Upper Heyford. The unit was also assisted by the Empire Central Flying School Research Flight at Hullavington.

The training of Flight Engineers was supported by several simulators of a technical nature. One of them was invented by the Training Aids Development Unit (TADU) at Cardington and taught engine handling. It displayed normal engine instrument readings and showed the relationship between various combinations of boost and RPM. Fuel consumed was expressed both as gallons per hour and air miles per gallon.

The other specialist in the crew was the Wireless Operator and at his disposal were a variety of synthetic aids. Unavoidably, the somewhat abstruse theory of radio had to be explained with the help of a blackboard and, frequently, an overdose of higher mathematics. However good the lecturer might be, the chances were that the trainee would find it difficult to associate the descriptions with the actual working, or failure to work, of airborne equipment, especially when he was encased in an oxygen mask, dressed like a Polar explorer and, not improbably, having various forms of unpleasantness thrown at him.

The answer to this was the Harwell Box, designed early in 1940 at the RAF station of that name. It is best described as a sort of torture chamber in which a wireless operator did his final ground training. It consisted of a small box comparable with the accommodation which he would find in an aircraft, fitted with all the appropriate radio equipment. Signals were fed down a line, simulating the actual reception conditons, and a system of beacons was provided so that he could obtain bearings.

Whilst he was going through whatever drill was being laid down by the instructor, a loudspeaker very close to his left ear produced a continuous roar of desynchronized engine noise. To unnerve him even more the speaker periodically emitted bursts of machine gun fire. One model of the Box included a method of swinging the whole cabinet about so as to add the risk of airsickness to the troubles of the unfortunate pupil! Course failures were considerably reduced and it was soon in widespread use at the Radio Schools, as many as 40 Boxes being connected on one circuit for simultaneous exercises.

The Link Trainer mentioned briefly earlier was widely used in wartime, having been found the most economical and efficient method of teaching the basics of instrument flying and beam approaches. It was manufactured under licence in Britain by Singer-Link-Miles. The Central Link Training School was formed at Borehamwood, Herts on 5 August 1940 to give a four-week course to instructors. Links were used well into the 1950s until replaced by the new generation of flight simulators.

At RAF Bridgnorth in 1946 there were two adaptations of the standard Link inside a Dome Teacher building used for aptitude tests on aircrew candidates. There was no blind-flying hood and the usual stub wings jutting out each side were joined to an upper wing by vee struts. The wings were painted yellow and the effect was of a sawn-off Tiger Moth.

It remains to describe one other synthetic procedure, more accurately semi-synthetic as real flying was involved. This was the Day-Night Scheme invented at a time when it was vitally necessary to continue night flying training through the longer and safer daylight hours. It was possible also to modify the conditions to suit the stage of training reached by a pupil and his particular capabilities.

There were four different day-night flying arrangements in use: (1) The Single-Stage (Flarepath) Scheme, for which the pupil wore special goggles and was only able to see the sodium lamp flarepath and his sodium-lit instruments; (2) the Two-Stage (Flarepath) or Two-Stage Brown Scheme, in which all but the light from the flarepath and instruments were cut off in two stages for the pupil; (3) the Two-Stage Blue Scheme, in which the aircraft was fitted with pale blue screens and the trainee wore amber goggles, and (4) the Two-Stage Amber Scheme, in which the colour positions were reversed. Schemes 3 and 4 were reserved solely for instrument flying and night navigation training.

The later stages for day-night simulation were developed by the NTSDU at Woodley on a crashed Magister fuselage and flight-tested at Upper Heyford in an Oxford. At the end of 1942 all development and supervision work was handed over to ECFS so that day-night methods could be standardized at all the different training units.

Without boring the reader with too many technical details, the schemes exploited the properties of various combinations of coloured filters. The Single-Stage (Flarepath) Scheme was the one most often used. By means of a special filter, all the colours in the spectrum, except that emitted by a sodium lamp, were unable to pass through, yet this particular light could be seen through the filter in almost its natural brilliance. If the pupil wore goggles in which this special filter was fitted and if the instrument panel and controls could be lit by a sodium-vapour lamp, he would see only those instruments and controls and the sodium flarepath. Consequently, he would, in effect, be flying in pitch-black outside conditions, relieved only by the flarepath lights. The instructor, meanwhile, was able to see out quite normally and thus monitor the student's progress and look out for other aircraft.

The normal arrangement of the sodium flarepath consisted of eight lamp units, six of them facing the direction of approach with duplicates at each end turned at right angles to the others to give the pupil an indication of the position of the flarepath while making a circuit. Since the normal-coloured angle of approach indicator lights could not be seen through his filtered goggles, special arrangements had to be made to give him the necessary approach angle guidance.

A sodium lamp at the approach end of the runway was fitted with a series of shutters which could be set in motion mechanically to give signals which can best be described as 'quick dot' or 'slow dash' at the wish of the operator. The latter watched the approaching aircraft through a grid wire sighting device which told him whether it was above or below the correct approach line. If it was below the line, he signalled quick dots and if above, slow dashes.

Day-night flying was usually practised at a relief landing ground. 5 (Pilot) Advanced Flying Unit at Tern Hill, for example, used nearby Chetwynd. Such is modern technology that the whole thing can now be achieved by a pair of liquid crystal goggles whose opacity is controlled electronically. They can simulate any visibility from two miles down to zero, either by day or by night. The pilot is still able to read his instruments and his instructor's view is not obscured by hoods or tinted Perspex.

Synthetic training was normally concentrated on a purpose-built Instructional Site at RAF training aerodromes, usually found for convenience between the technical and dispersed living sites. At 58 OTU's satellite at Balado Brigade in Scotland, it was nicknamed 'Synthetic City'. Changing operational re-

Top *Main training block at Milfield, Northumberland, once the Day Fighter Leaders' School.*

Above left *Totally renovated Turret Trainer used for offices at the former RAF Tilstock Instructional Site.*

Above right *Double Turret Trainer at Silverstone, Northants.*

quirements meant that a number of airfields had Instructional Sites which were hardly used, while others had them added or improvized at a later date.

The sites found at former fighter OTUs are not very distinctive, most of the training aids being housed in ordinary huts, modified where necessary. Rednal had its Dummy Operations Room and huts for Link Trainer, armament, signals and intelligence, all of which are now used for farming purposes. Calveley in Cheshire was built originally as an operational fighter station, but when it was relegated to advanced fighter training, accommodation for the training section was added alongside the approach road to the camp. Some fighter OTUs had a Fisher Front Gun Trainer, but I have so far been unable to discover how this worked.

Instructional Sites at bomber OTUs, in contrast, are readily indentifiable. One of the best preserved is at Tilstock in Shropshire but,

although all the original buildings are intact, there is no evidence of their previous use. They include the Crew Procedure Centre, a Bombing Teacher, SFGT and lecture rooms. At Silverstone the Procedure Centre is used by an agricultural firm, whose address is painted on the sides of their vehicles as 'Airmanship Hall, Silverstone', thereby maintaining a link with the past. The rest of the site, which includes a rare triple Bombing Teacher, is derelict.

Looking around these malodorous buildings, which are often buried deep in farmyard manure, it is hard to imagine that they were designed for a deadly purpose and that many of the aircrew who trained here so enthusiastically eventually flew off to their deaths over Germany. In use, they must have produced a horrendous racket of amplified gunfire and engine noise. Now, it can all be reproduced by computers with unlimited potential in realistic simulation, but here was where it all began.

Chapter 9

Airfield defences and camouflage

Airfield defence works form a study in themselves, but little has ever been written on the subject, perhaps because it is so hard to find any information in offical records. Henry Wills' book *Pillboxes* is fascinating but the subject matter is confined mainly to defence works aimed at resisting invasion, with less emphasis on the more specialized applications on and around RAF airfields.

With their far-flung perimeters surrounded by fields, hedgerows and woods, aerodromes are not easily defended, but before the Second World War the RAF paid little attention to the problem. In February 1939 it was, however, noted that a new policy of dispersing aircraft around and sometimes beyond the perimeter would make defence far more difficult. Even at this late stage, preparations for the active defence of RAF stations were confined to the provision of a limited number of light machine-gun posts for anti-aircraft use. Certain operational stations were scheduled to have additional guns of higher calibre — two-pounder and 3 in — but no further works were constructed for them.

The capitulation of France and the sudden threat of invasion in the summer of 1940 forced rapid action. Large scale projects for the defence of airfields against air and ground attack were initiated, consisting chiefly of pill-boxes and rifle pits and very extensive wire entanglements. The less technical work — trench digging and the like — was usually undertaken by the defence personnel, but anything of a more elaborate nature had to be done by the Air Ministry's Directorate of Works, an organization which was already stretched with building new airfields and improving existing ones.

Because of the infinite variations in the topography of aerodromes, it was found impracticable to standardize the design of defence works and the types and sizes were many. The procedure adopted in the case of existing airfields was for the local military authority, usually acting through the local defence commander, who was the defence adviser to the station commander, to plan the defences and provide designs for the structural works.

These designs were, more often than not, in the form of sketches and the Air Ministry Works Area headquarters then prepared detailed drawings from which the contractor could work. Virtually all of the Army's senior officers would have had personal experience of the Western Front in the First World War and this is reflected in some of the designs. The Germans in that war seem to have pioneered pillbox construction, the British generally preferring elaborate dug-outs. Many of the pillboxes still to be found at airfields built in 1940 are of massive construction, one on the officers' mess site at Lichfield being a good example.

Whoever was responsible for airfield defence works in Northern Ireland did a particularly good job, for there are designs at many locations in this area which cannot be found anywhere else in Britain. The pleasant little airfield of St Angelo, now Enniskillen Airport, was extremely well-protected, with some interesting pillboxes connected by concrete zigzag trenches about 6 ft deep with a parapet for rifle firing. Full advantage has been taken of the hillocks surrounding the airfield site. Newtownards also has some unusual defence structures which were built by a Field Company of the Royal Engineers.

Much confusion, delay and unnecessary work resulted from the continual changes in the defence plans during 1940 and early 1941. Many were unavoidable, resulting from altered tactical conceptions, knowledge of new weapons, both our own and those likely to be used by the enemy, and the availability of defence personnel. On 13 July 1940, the

General Staff headquarters of Army Southern Command issued a set of notes so that all personnel would understand the sequence of events that might be expected at aerodromes if an invasion occurred. The aim was to eliminate the surprise element and thus prepare the defending troops.

'Large scale attacks on aerodromes will probably take the following form: (1) Attack made at dawn. (2) Me 110s arrive first to draw off our fighters. (3) Soon afterwards, very low flying bombers attack. Bombs are dropped on the perimeter of the aerodrome and aerodrome defences. (4) More heavy fighters then attack the defences with front cannon and machine-guns. At the same time: (5) Complete companies of parachute troops are dropped at three points around the aerodrome about 1,000 to 1,500 yards away. (6) Parachute troops form up in 12 to 15 minutes and storm the aerodrome with machine-guns, hand grenades and, perhaps, two-inch mortars. (7) About ten minutes after this attack has started, Ju 52s and large troop carriers land on the aerodrome at about six a minute. These troops have machine-guns and probably two-inch and three-inch mortars and guns and also motor cycles. (8) Fighters then land whilst a fighter umbrella is maintained over the aerodrome until attempted capture is complete. (9) Should any high bombing take place, do not let the whistling bomb scare you. It is no more dangerous than any other bomb.'

Churchill himself said in June 1940:

'Every man in RAF uniform ought to be armed with something — a rifle, a tommy gun, a pistol, a pike or mace, and everyone, without exception, should do at least one hour's drill and practice every day. Each airman should have his place in the defence scheme. It must be understood by all ranks that they are expected to fight and die in the defence of their airfields. Every building which fits in with the scheme of defence should be prepared so that each has to be conquered one by one by the enemy's parachute or glider troops. In two or three hours the Army will arrive ... Every airfield should be a stronghold of fighting air-ground men and not the abode of uniformed civilians in the prime of life protected by detachments of soldiers.'

The 'Pandah Scheme' enabled an airfield under attack to radio for help to a central control using a coded call-sign. Details to be passed were approximate enemy strength, type (such as infantry, armoured cars or tanks or parachutists) and direction of approach. Army units could then be rushed to the scene. The RAF Regiment had yet to be formed but in the autumn of 1940 the new trade of ground gunner was created solely for airfield defence. By October 1940, there were some 35,000 ground gunners in the RAF. Light AA defence remained the responsibility of the Royal Artillery with Bofors guns, supported by RAF gunners with light machine-guns.

Secretly, the Air Staff calculated that fewer than 5,000 parachutists temporarily paralysing the air defences at seven vital aerdromes in south-east England might pave the way for bomber raids and troop carrier landings in overwhelming force. With the German occupation of Norway, the Scottish airfields suddenly become vulnerable too. At Montrose in June 1940, for example, nine pillboxes were hastily built at strategic points on the perimeter, each designed to hold 10 riflemen and one Lewis gunner. To support them, nine smaller machine-gun posts were constructed from which fire could be brought to bear on the landing ground. Fifty airmen were selected as 'para-shots' — marksmen who could pick off descending parachutists.

The capture of Crete, admittedly at great cost in highly-trained men, was achieved by parachute and glider troops in May 1941. This cast a new light on the likely conduct of an airborne assault on Britain and the Government ordered that a committee be convened to examine ways of improving airfield defences. The idea of trying to defend an aerodrome by holding a series of posts strung round the perimeter was abandoned. Many pillboxes became ammunition stores or dummies to draw enemy fire, and slit trenches, camouflage and concealment became the order of the day. Instead of small, isolated posts, defended localities were established, each held by a flight, while mobile reserves were created or increased with the task of counter-attacking the enemy if he penetrated between the defended localities.

The haphazard provision and design of defence works was improved on instructions from General Headquarters Home Forces and the issue of plans and layouts of typical works which, with appropriate local modifications, were gradually adopted. For new stations, built in 1941, a fresh procedure was introduced, to the effect that as soon as a site had been provisionally accepted, details were forwarded to GHQ Home Forces by the Air Ministry. Simultaneously, copies were sent to the RAF Command concerned. The comments and proposals of both the Army and the RAF on

Airfield defence squad at Hawarden, Clwyd, with adapted Fordson 15 cwt truck in 1941 (E.R. Salkeld).

the defence and operational requirements were then sent to the Air Ministry for consideration. When the site was finally accepted, a conference was held on the spot with all interested parties present, at which the final layout of runways, defence sites and localities and accommodation was settled. Such was its importance that the location of defences was afforded a priority second only to the runway layout and above the requirements for accommodation.

The exact siting of the defence posts within the areas previously agreed was determined immediately the contractors had cleared the site sufficiently to enable this to be done. The local military commander then liaised with the superintending engineer who prepared detailed plans for the main contractor to execute the work. It was thus ensured that the defences were completed simultaneously with the opening of the station.

To guard against the probability of landing on the airfield itself, defence which was already upwards and outwards now had to turn inwards as well. Basic principles laid down in 1941 were as follows:

'Defence must consist of small groups of posts, each group forming a locality. These defended localities must be well concealed, aided by dummies and wired all round. Aerodrome perimeters must have an all-round barrier of obstacles covered by fire from defended localities.

'Pillboxes and field defences should be constructed of concrete laid out so as to form a system of defences around the perimeter. Each shall be designed to cover the aerodrome surface and the external approaches to the aerodrome with light machine gun or rifle fire. The localities should, as far as possible, be mutually supporting and self-contained, each with a supply of small arms ammunition and water.'

Mobile defence was furnished by a number of improvized vehicles. For example, in June 1940, RAF Shawbury had a Morris six-wheel lorry on which were mounted two 'dustbin' turrets with machine guns on Scarff Ring mountings. It was parked near the watch office and could be deployed instantly against enemy troop landings. Armoured cars, known as *Armadillos*, equipped with a 1.5-pounder gun and machine-guns, were hastily issued to many RAF stations. When they were not available, the smaller *Beaverette* was often supplied instead.

On muddy airfields, heavy gun mountings on lorries were found to be virtually useless, but at Abingdon American Dodge trucks were used as mobile defence units, running on wire netting laid as a track round the airfield. They were armed with ancient French guns, relics of an earlier war. It is said that the sight of the unit in action was very impressive and received commendations from the War Office and Air Ministry, but the crews were sworn to secrecy about the fact that the guns had not a single round of ammunition!

Gunners were trained at No 1 Ground Defence Gunnery School which had formed at North Coates, Lincolnshire in December

1939 and moved to Ronaldsway on the Isle of Man during March 1940. The rudimentary course lasted 10 days and classroom instruction on the various guns in use was backed by practical experience in firing at towed targets. Harts, Wallaces and Lysanders were used, the school being absorbed by the RAF Regiment in March 1943. Thereafter, all tuition was synthetic using a Dome Trainer in nearby Douglas.

By the end of 1940, weapon and ammunition supply had improved somewhat. A typical aerodrome, Christchurch near Bournemouth, was armed with four Bofors, 24 Lewis guns, a single 1.5-pounder gun, an *Armadillo*, one Vickers gun, 148 rifles and 463 hand grenades. To man them there were 140 airmen and 27 Royal Engineers. There were still some very unsuitable weapons in use, however, Edzell in Scotland being covered by two 4½ in howitzers emplaced in the hills to the north!

Serious gaps in the defences still existed, an officer visiting the satellite landing ground at Townsend in Wiltshire on 26 May 1941 reporting:

'I found a magnificent airfield capable of receiving troop-carrying aircraft. Approximately 15 valuable operational machines were dispersed around the perimeter. The guard consisted of two patrolling airmen from Hullavington with a machine-gun post manned during daytime only by three men from the Bristol Flying School based at Yatesbury aerodrome. One of the guards told me they only had 100 rounds of rifle ammunition amongst the six men.'

As we now know, the invasion expected in 1940 never came, but it was still a very real possibility. Indeed, an alert of imminent invasion was issued on 8 September, the record book for RAF Towyn on the Welsh coast, reading: 'A Magister flew down from Penrhos to pass on the message "Invasion Alert No 1". Airmen on leave were recalled and secret and confidential documents were removed and prepared for immediate destruction by fire.'

By the summer of 1941, a scale of defence had been agreed upon, depending on an airfield's strategic importance. Class 1 was represented by all stations, relief landing grounds and satellites within 20 miles of selected seaports. They were to be provided with pillboxes around the perimeter, not less than half a mile apart and designed to cover the airfield. A second series of pillboxes would be sited to command the external approaches to the aerodrome and such aircraft dispersal points as could reasonably be included in the perimeter defence. The pillboxes were to make the maximum use of natural cover for concealment, the dummy pillboxes being rather more prominent. Rifle pits with overhead cover were to be dug around hangars and station buildings.

Class 2 aerodromes were those not strategically placed but having a responsibility to repel seaborne attacks with bombers and fighters. Here there was a 25 per cent reduction in pillboxes for inward defence. This class also embraced sites thought liable to air or small scale parachute attack for no particular tactical reason as a diversion or nuisance. For Class 3 aerodromes, a single ring of pillboxes with all-round fire capability was considered sufficient, but at some only barbed wire was provided.

Wire was a simple and deadly means of defence against troops, as experience in the First World War had proved. Dannert Concertina wire was most often used on aerodromes and rusting coils of it still lie in wait for the unwary airfield investigator. It was strung on screw pickets about 5 ft long, similar to those used for tying down parked aircraft, but much longer. Many of them can still be found on old airfields.

When a Dannert Concertina was extended to 50 ft, it had an approximate diameter of three feet and this was adopted as the standard span. The most effective defence was provided by three concertinas in parallel and the Army deemed that an average party of an NCO and seven men with stores already dumped at the beginning of the job, should be able to lay 50 yards of triple wire in 15 minutes in normal ground by day. This military wire had longer, more unevenly spaced barbs than the normal variety.

The so-called disappearing pillbox, more properly known as the Pickett-Hamilton Retractable Fort, provided an element of surprise against an attacker and was at first seen as the answer to the problem of airfield defence. It has been described in some detail elsewhere, so suffice it to say that it was a concrete cylinder with firing slots, mounted inside another pipe and raised or lowered by either hydraulic, pneumatic or mechanical means. The crew of two would enter by a hatch in the roof and when retracted it was flush with the aerodrome surface and able to bear the weight of a taxiing aircraft.

By June 1941, a total of 170 had been installed at 59 airfields and, when it was finally realized that they were virtually useless, 335 had been emplaced all over Britain. These curiosities continue to come to light at regular intervals and there must be many more still awaiting discovery.

The theory of having two or three retractable pillboxes in the middle of an aerodrome

Above left *Pickett-Hamilton Fort in raised position. Note the entry hatch in the roof* (IWM CH17891).

Above right *Mushroom pill-box at Twinwood Farm, Bedfordshire.*

was good but the practical aspects left much to be desired, even if shrouded in artificial smoke as suggested. It would have been difficult to man them until our own flying operations had ceased and the crews would then have had to carry ammunition across open ground with no cover. There was also a considerable risk of their hitting, or being hit by, their own perimeter defences.

The other major problem was water seepage and at many places continuous pumping was necessary. By 1942, Bomber Command considered retractable pillboxes useless and recommended that they should not be installed at any more of its stations. In March 1942 the official view was that the weapons and personnel available could be deployed to better advantage but the forts were, nevertheless, to be maintained in working order.

An even more imaginative device which actually achieved limited success was the Parachute and Cable (PAC) which protected a few aerodromes in 1940. The Kenley installation brought down a Do 17 on 18 August during a low-level attack. It consisted of a system of rockets arranged in line and attached to light steel cables carrying parachutes. They were discharged electrically into the path of hostile aircraft and rose to about 600 ft. The parachutes then opened automatically and the dangling cables formed a brief but deadly obstacle. The impact of an aircraft would cause a second parachute to open at the bottom of the cable and, it was hoped, drag the aircraft to the ground.

In November 1941 the Committee on Airfield Defence recommended that the RAF should have its own defence force under Air Ministry control. Thus, the RAF Regiment was formed from all existing RAF ground defence squadrons and flights on 1 February

1942 and soon relieved the Army of its unwanted responsibility for defending RAF installations in the UK. These defence forces varied in strength from 90 to 280 at different airfields and necessitated the construction of living and messing accommodation, usually on a separate dispersed site.

The knowledge that each German parachute regiment was equipped with several 2 cm anti-tank guns resulted in a recommendation that pillboxes should have walls at least 3 ft 6 in thick with the number of loopholes limited to two. They should house only light machine-guns, the riflemen being stationed in slit trenches sited to protect the pillboxes' blind spots.

The walls of most airfield pillboxes remained, however, much thinner than this, but a further directive resulted in the provision of domed pillboxes with all-round fire being discontinued at airfields. To the design of the F. C. Construction Co Ltd they had a cantilevered concrete roof and there was a similar type known as the Oakington Mushroom Pillbox, although it was thought that their roofs might be lifted by the blast of a near miss. Also, the domed roofs were difficult to construct compared with the simple concrete slab type.

The War Office's Directorate of Fortifications designed a number of pillboxes and full details of most of them are to be found in Henry Wills's book. One of the most common types was hexagonal, and these are to be found on and around many airfields. Some have provision for an AA position on the flat roof, giving an elevated all-round view.

The defence of an airfield was co-ordinated by the Battle Headquarters, a purpose-built strongpoint which, after some development, was standardized as the 11008/41 design for operational stations and a smaller building for

Above *Battle Headquarters at Dale, Dyfed, overlooking the cliffs.*

Left *Battle Headquarters at Baginton, now Coventry Airport.*

satellites and training fields, the 3329/41. There was, however, no hard and fast rule on this as many obscure satellites like Findo Gask in Scotland had a 11008/41 type.

In common with other defence works, they were not included in the original plans for a new airfield but sited by agreement with the local army authority, taking into account terrain and camouflage. If possible, they were built on high ground, often in a hedgeline for concealment or close to farm buildings with which, from a distance, they would blend innocuously. A few, however, were emplaced close to the watch tower.

The 11008/41 type was dominated by a 6 ft square observation post 3 ft above the ground on average, with a 360° view through a horizontal slot. The rest of the building was normally underground, how far depending upon sub-surface water, but earth banks were added if it projected too much. The sunken portion of the Battle headquarters was reached by a stairway at one end, the observation cupola having its own escape hatch. The whole measured approximately 21 ft by 8 ft, and contained an office, sleeping accommodation and latrine. The personnel included a runner for use if telephone communication was broken.

Massively built from reinforced concrete, most of these buildings have survived simply because they are so difficult to demolish and also because they are usually so unobtrusive. Unfortunately, they tend to fill with water, preventing exploration, and even the dry ones require a good torch, assuming the farmer has not blocked them with debris to keep livestock out.

Regular exercises were held at aerodromes to test the efficiency of the defences and reveal any weaknesses which attackers might be able to exploit. An extract from a typical report on a two-day exercise at RAF Long Kesh in Northern Ireland, written by an Army Lieutenant-Colonel, shows how the results would be analyzed:

'January 3-4 Exercise *Bella* for defence of RAF Long Kesh. Number of personnel required to effectively defend station is 1,000. The Battle headquarters is not sufficiently large, at least two more rooms are required to accommodate 12 to 14. The Battle HQ and all Flight Commanders' posts must be supplied with heat and telephone, also, four-inch ducts are required for heat, light, telephone and tannoy. Arrangements must be made to drain all localities, in fact the whole aerodrome requires draining. The north and north-west sides of the aerodrome are unprotected and give the enemy covered approach to the aerodrome, bomb stores and Short and Harland. The north-east corner is blind and requires pillboxes. Newport Bridge, main line of approach for counter-attacking troops, and the technical area require pillboxes. The transmitting and direction finding station is outside the defensive area and cannot be defended by the RAF. Can arrangements be made for the Home Guard to defend? There is no defence work at Maghaberry (the nearby satellite) except for defensive localities in varying stages of completion. There are no Home Guard localities. All work done by civilian contract is very slow and requires constant Royal Engineers supervision.'

Apart from direct parachute or glider landings, the defenders had to face a third possibility, that of an invasion necessitating withdrawal and denial of airfield facilities to the enemy. Stocks of petrol held at airfields would have been of great value to the *Luftwaffe*, as without them fuel would have to be brought across the Channel or else aircraft would have to operate from French bases. Plans were made for the destruction of petrol stocks, but it was found that in the case of the protected underground type of installation on pre-war RAF stations it was relatively easy to destroy the pumping gear and chamber, albeit difficult to guarantee burning of the petrol.

It was not until the end of 1941 that a standard procedure was agreed in joint discussions and experiments by General Headquarters Home Forces, Air Ministry and Imperial Chemical Industries. It consisted of a 42 in diameter concrete pipe sunk adjacent to the end of each 12,000 gallon cylinder tank. The pipes were continued to the level of the tank bottom and from here small charge chambers were driven to the face of the steel tanks. This work was carried out on all existing fuel installations and incorporated in plans for new ones.

To demolish the installation, a chain reaction was initiated with a set of explosive charges. A cutting charge of high explosive laid against the tank ripped it open and simultaneously a separate charge blew a crater into which the petrol flowed. A fougasse — the military engineering term for a small mine — with a delay fuse, went off a few seconds later and ignited the fuel running into the crater.

Happily, it was never necessary to utilize these preparations but an opportunity to test their effectiveness presented itself at Waddington, where an accidental explosion had partially destroyed one of the main installations. A trial was organized with a locally-based company of Royal Engineers, utilizing the full cutting charge on one tank, a small scale cratering charge and a fougasse. The experiment was a complete success, despite bad weather and the absence of properly waterproofed shafts.

Early in 1942, the general principle that only fuel stocks would be subject to systematic demolition was extended to the destruction of airfield surfaces at certain locations on the east and south coasts. The two main methods to be used were the Canadian Pipe Mine System and the Mole Plough. The former consisted of a series of steel pipes thrust-bored beneath a runway and filled with explosive. When fired, a crater 12 to 15 ft wide by 4 to 5 ft deep was blown across the width of the runway.

The second method employed a device known quaintly as the 'Gatwick Sausage', but you will not find it on airport restaurant menus! It was a thin sausage of explosive, the skin of which comprized tough, but flexible, rubber, 1.5 in diameter. It was made in 50 ft lengths and could be coiled like a hawser, though it was preferable to store it in lengths.

In an emergency, each length was tied behind a standard agricultural mole plough and drawn into the ground behind the mole to a depth of between 18 in and 2 ft. Although it could sometimes be pulled through existing cable and drainage ducts, it was generally impossible to use it under hard runways and a further disadvantage was that it was liable to deteriorate if left in the ground. Detonation resulted in a trench 3 or 4 ft deep and 6 ft in width with a wide scattering of earth and stones.

More than 20 airfields were equipped with pipe mines and I suspect that some are still in place! Locations included Hurn, Roborough, Exeter and Westhampnett (Goodwood). On 22 December 1941, trials were held at Winkfield Row aerodrome in Berkshire, at which it was found that a site could be broken up in a single day with one mole plough and eight men, using previously prepared charges. Further tests with pipe mines were done variously at Odiham, Hartfordbridge Flats, Farnborough and Gatwick.

The plough method was obviously the most effective for grass aerodromes, but pipe mines were often used as well. It was suggested as an alternative that conventional mines would provide a quick and easy means of temporary denial. Approximately 250 were required to cover an area of 1,000 sq yd, a trained party taking about two hours to implement this.

Left *Blast shelter beside the control tower at Tain, Scotland.*

Right *Magister R1918 of 312 Squadron at Martlesham Heath in August 1941 with fighter pen blast wall and tannoy to left* (Via Zdenek Hurt).

Bulldozers were considered efficient for destroying airfield surfaces but very slow indeed. Other long-term methods included mustard gas or weedkiller which would kill the grass, but in dry weather would not put the airfield out of operation. Wire mesh runways could be dealt with by ripping out portions of the tracking and leaving the tangled remains on the strip. To harass clearing parties after the RAF's withdrawal, booby traps were to be laid and, when available, small spikes similar to the anti-cavalry caltrops of earlier wars were to be scattered to puncture aircraft tyres.

Since the summer of 1940 when the threat of airborne invasion first arose, it had become essential to obstruct as many open spaces as possible on which enemy transports or gliders could land undamaged. The number of such areas was, of course, incalculable. Many of them were blocked by the Army but initially all of those within five miles of an RAF airfield and, later those within one mile only were the responsibility of the RAF to obstruct. In the early days, derelict cars and lorries were used, later to be replaced or supplemented by other means when the vehicles were needed for their scrap metal content. On the Tain Ranges in north-east Scotland, barbed wire was stretched along the ground, intermingled with a dozen old tractors and lorries. A common method was the digging of trenches in an area 200 to 300 yd square, but it was dangerous to cattle, hindered cultivation and was thus generally restricted to ground of no agricultural value.

Stone or concrete cairns were frequently placed so that no clear run for an aircraft of more than 250 yd was possible. Stout poles served the same purpose, sometimes strung with wire such as surplus balloon cable. Many of them can be seen to this day on the smooth top of Manton Hill, Dartmoor. Often the poles were replaced by scaffolding tripods, a method which was particularly useful on aerodromes that were temporarily out of use, because they could be removed at short notice.

An important aspect of minimizing casualties in the event of an air raid was to give prior warning of attack to personnel who could be almost anywhere on the vast area of an average airfield. The attack alarm system was first introduced on RAF stations in 1936, utilizing the electrically-operated sirens originally intended for the fire alarm system. In line with the Ministry of Home Security's public air raid alarm system, the RAF later adopted the signals 'Alert', a wailing tone and 'Raiders Passed', a steady note better known as the 'All Clear'.

Pre-war non-dispersed stations were equipped with one or two sirens, depending on size. The usual practice was to place one on the roof of a hangar and another in the barracks area, perhaps on the NAAFI or boiler-house chimney or on the water tower. To give maximum coverage, the siting was carefully arranged with due regard to the direction of the prevailing wind, ground contours and the screening effect of buildings.

At early wartime airfields and some pre-war hutted camps, only one siren was provided, normally being installed on a post next to the guard house or on the guard house chimney if it were structurally possible. Standard procedure was for the attack alarm to be controlled from the station operations block but when this building was dispersed away from the airfield, the sirens could be activated from the guard house on receipt of telephone orders from operations. The possibility of confusion with the general public warning system when a town or village lay in the vicinity of an RAF station was reduced by two extra siren signals. These were 'Imminent Danger' (short blasts) and 'Imminent Danger Passed', (a sort of cuckoo note).

Air raid shelters of numerous types were provided normally for small numbers of airmen who would be working in buildings sited close to them. At the beginning of the war they consisted mainly of rudimentary covered slit trenches, but these were soon superseded by

pre-cast concrete shelters of the Stanton type, each holding 25 to 50 men. Concrete sections were bolted together to form the required length and then covered with earth for splinter protection.

Special types of sleeping shelter housing 18 or 33 men, heated and ventilated, were built at dispersal points at fighter stations for the use of pilots at readiness. In the technical building areas, traversed blast walls were built above ground so that the need to take shelter could be delayed as long as possible, thus minimizing the disruption of work. There were standard sizes giving effective blast protection to 10, 20 or 50 men.

Blast protection was also provided for aircraft in so-called fighter pens, each holding two aircraft and E-shaped in plan view. The more elaborate constructions incorporated Stanton shelters, and some well-preserved examples can be found at Kingscliffe in Northamptonshire amongst other places. Sandbags were used for the same purpose and at Drem, near Edinburgh, at least one small log stockade protected the aircraft. The possibility of gas attack was taken very seriously, although fortunately it never occurred. Despite the fact that work on defence against gas warfare began at the research station at Porton in 1932, it was not until September 1936 that the Air Ministry's Chemical Warfare Defence Branch was set up. One of its responsibilities was to advise on gas protecton and filtration for essential airfield buildings such as operations rooms. It also designed the layout of the decontamination centre, a massive building still to be found at many former wartime aerodromes.

Not specifically connected with airfield defence, but a useful adjunct in the early stages of an attack, was the broadcasting system, colloquially known as the tannoy, which was introduced at RAF stations early in 1940. Its purpose was to enable operational instructions to be passed clearly, rapidly and simultaneously to personnel at dispersal points and other distant parts of the airfield. Microphones were placed in the main operational centres (such as the operations block, the watch office and the Battle Headquarters) and connected to the speech broadcasting building which housed the amplifying equipment. From this small blast-proofed building, usually found close to the watch office, cable ran to an average of 150 loudspeakers around the airfield.

To ensure that an airfield was operational again as soon as possible after air attack, a repair organization had been formed but, since it was composed mainly of civilians, it was feared that their capacity to continue work whilst under fire would be limited. It was fortuitous, therefore, that the evacuation of British forces from France in June 1940 made available a body of men who could be relied upon to maintain vital airfields under the worst conditions.

They were Royal Engineer units formed originally for the construction of airfields in Northern France. Detachments of 60 to 100 men each were immediately located on 66 aerodromes, and shortly afterwards a further 44 sites were covered. A total of 7,000 REs were available throughout the most critical stages of the Battle of Britain and performed work of the utmost importance. History shows that no airfield was ever out of use for more than a few hours. Though frequently without hangars or barracks, the pilots of Fighter Command were never short of airfields from which to operate.

Among the most serious raids on airfields during the Battle of Britain was the one on Manston on 12 August when 180 craters pitted the landing ground. With the help of station personnel and civilian contractors who repaired the drains, water and electrical services, the REs enabled flying to be resumed that same evening. Driffield in Yorkshire was heavily bombed on the afternoon of 15 August but was back in service by the following morning.

West Malling was attacked three times during August, the numerous craters being filled by the engineers each evening. In view of these

Top left *Rusty Turnbull machine gun mounting in a pillbox at Rednal, Shropshire.*
Top right *Economy design of pre-cast concrete pill-box at Southrop, Glos.*

Above left *Sunken pill-box at Carew Cheriton, Dyfed. This one probably had an AA post on the roof.*

Above right *An innocent-looking observation post built on top of a pill-box at Hinton-in-the-Hedges, Northants, no doubt to camouflage it.*

facts, it is surprising that the planners of the Falklands campaign believed that a single Vulcan attack on Port Stanley Airport would put it out of action permanently. The Argentinians even followed the old RAF ruse of making it appear that the craters had not been filled!

In the middle of 1943 with the war situation seeming more favourable, a policy decision was taken to restrict new construction of all forms of defence works to a coastal belt on the east and south of Britain. At all new aerodromes defence works were to be planned but not actually built. At the same time it was ruled that no more airfields would be prepared for demolition. Early in 1944 the maintenance of existing works was reduced to the minimum able to be performed by the station's own staff. The reason was the acute shortage of civilian labour which restricted the Works Directorate to essential tasks only.

On 18 April 1944 Churchill wrote:

'I do not think that we can afford to continue to maintain a special body of troops purely for the defence of aerodromes. The RAF Regiment was established at a time when the invasion of this country was likely, and when our life depended on the security of our fighter aerodromes.

Since then it has been reduced, but the time has now come to consider whether the greater part of it should not be taken to reinforce the field formations of the Army. I consider that at least 25,000 men should be transferred. They will be much better employed there than loafing around overcrowded airfields warding off dangers which have ceased to threaten.'

The suggestion was taken up, in part at least, and 2,000 men were transferred to the Guards in June 1944. In August of that year it was further decided to remove all explosive charges from the Canadian Pipe Mine System. However, the scarcity of skilled Army personnel greatly restricted progress, a fact that was apparent at Shoreham a few years ago when the new runway was being built! Certain devices had been lying quietly under the turf for 30 odd years.

The final nail in the coffin of airfield defence came in October 1944 when it was decided to abandon all defence works with the exception of limited light anti-aircraft facilities at about half-a-dozen airfields in south-east England and Shetland. It is estimated that over £3,000,000 was expended on these structures between 1940 and 1945, the average cost being about £5,000 for each airfield.

Top left *Purpose-built pill-box cunningly designed to look like a farm cottage. It is near the entrance to the former Maintenance Unit at High Ercall.* **Top right** *A rare local modification — a pill-box built into the end of a 'K' Type hangar at High Ercall, Shropshire.* **Above left** *In an emergency these sections of sewer pipe could be used as defensive positions. John Evans, author of* Flying Boat Haven, *looks into one at the old waterworks site near RAF Talbenny, Dyfed.* **Above right** *Massive pill-box built into a railway bridge on the edge of RAF Montrose, north-east Scotland. It had an AA position on the roof and served originally as the Battle HQ.* **Below left** *Another local improvisation: this time a ruined windmill near Angle, Dyfed, was turned into a pill-box by the addition of gun slits and an internal parapet.* **Below right** *A substantial strongpoint near the watch office at Windrush, Glos.* **Bottom left** *Cunningly concealed pill-box on the approach road to RNAS Burscough, Lancs (Keith Marsh).* **Bottom right** *Emergency field kitchen on a farm close to the perimeter of RAF Talbenny, Dyfed. Malcolm Cullen of the Pembrokeshire Aviation Group (seen here) discovered this relic.*

Of course all this work turned out to be unnecessary, but no one knew that at the time. The pillboxes did more damage to our own aircraft than they ever did to the enemy's, forming immovable obstacles if an aircraft was unfortunate enough to overrun the aerodrome at the wrong point on the perimeter. Perhaps their most useful function was providing illicit rendezvous for airmen and WAAFS! Their reinforced concrete will ensure that they outlive all other buildings on derelict airfields in years to come.

Since many defence works are not shown on airfield plans, it is worth looking out for them. They are usually gutted but some retain the Turnbull mounting for a machine-gun and I have found rusty ammunition boxes in at least one. In their original state they often had a light steel door, but few other fittings, one being a concrete bath with an air vent for the cooling of gun barrels. Gauze on a light frame was usually fitted externally to the loopholes to prevent grenades being thrown inside.

Airfield camouflage

It was not until 1937 that the Air Staff gave some consideration to the camouflage of aerodromes. Spurred on by the Munich Crisis, the Directorate of Works formed a Camouflage Section whose first job was to study the problems involved and devise solutions. Its conclusions became the basis on which all camouflage was carried out until it was finally discontinued in August 1944. The Section's chief was Colonel Sir John Turner and it was given the cover name 'Colonel Turner's Department'.

It was obviously impossible to hide completely such a large installation as an aerodrome but if an enemy pilot was unable to recognize it for what it was before he was almost over it, his attack was likely to be unsuccessful. The aim was to ensure that the target blended with its surroundings when observed from certain prescribed heights and distances. These were 10,000 ft at a range of six miles in fine weather, 5,000 ft at three and a half miles in cloudy weather and 300 ft at two and a half miles in bad weather.

Experimental work was conducted at Cranfield and other stations in 1938/39 with the main object of reducing the conspicuousness of buildings and roads and to break up the airfield into a pattern more closely resembling the surrounding countryside. Buildings were painted in a manner similar to the brown and green shadow shading seen on contemporary aircraft, while bold division lines were painted on the roofs and sides of hangars to break up the outline. Near built-up areas, Northolt and Squires Gate being good examples, they were

made to resemble rows of houses. Landing grounds were disrupted by the marking of hedge lines in black bitumen emulsion paint over the grass to simulate the continuation of the adjacent field patterns. This could be compromised by carelessness, however, an aerial photograph of RAF Penrhos showing Anson aircraft parked apparently on top of hedges!

On pre-war stations the buildings were more conspicuous than the airfield but as soon as runways, peri-tracks and dispersal points were introduced on a large scale, the balance was reversed. During the winter of 1939 the problem of 'shine' from concrete and tarmac surfaces was investigated at Stradishall and Gosport. At the former, paved areas were treated with fine pre-coloured slag chippings, and at Gosport with coarse pre-coloured stone chippings. These methods were suggested by the contractors and were based on customary practice with hard tennis courts. It was apparent from the trials that paved areas could be toned down and it was decided to treat all existing runways, particularly on fighter stations, in a similar manner.

At Hullavington tests were carried out with an open-textured bituminous surfacing which was so successful that it was adopted later for all Aircraft Storage Unit dispersal tracks and standings. By the spring of 1940 the Stradishall system came into use by agreement with all Commands except Fighter, which was unable to accept the excessive tyre wear on fighter aircraft caused by the abrasive chippings. The Hullavington specification was, however, acceptable and, although expensive, gave an effective non-shine surface.

Meanwhile, certain bomber stations were supplied with over-large or sharp chippings and the resulting tyre damage, although isolated, gave the whole method a bad name. Efforts were made to find some material in plentiful supply to produce a textured effect without the hardness of stone chippings and yet capable of firm adhesion. Sawdust, shavings and grass all proved unsuccessful, as did seaweed, heather and rounded pebbles. One material which showed promise was tan bark, a waste product of tanneries which, when sprayed with an iron salt, produced an intense black. The RAE staged a full-scale trial at the bomber OTU at Stanton Harcourt but soon found that the excellent camouflage effect was outweighed by the surface becoming soft and slushy in prolonged wet weather.

The work progressed to the use of granulated rubber and so successful was this that it became the standard texturing material for all fighter runways. The fall of Malaya brought this to an end, however, and all unused stocks on the airfields had to be returned for recy-

Above Watton, Norfolk on 18 April 1939. **Below** Watton on 4 October of the same year
showing the effectiveness of the camouflage (P.H.T. Green Collection).

cling. The search for a suitable substance eventually came back to wood as the one material that was strong, soft and in adequate supply. Experiments with wood chips were carried out at Pershore with the result that the method was standardized for all runways, 55,000 tons of wood chips being produced during 1942 alone. At the same time it had become obvious that the camouflage of landing grounds by painting hedge lines and spraying chemicals to colour the grass in irregular patches was extremely wasteful of manpower owing to the short life of these methods. The answer was a longer term scheme of agricultural treatment which simulated field effects by differential mowing of the grass and the fertilization of selected areas.

When dispersed sites were planned for a particular airfield, a specialist section advised on the siting of buildings to secure the best possible screening by woods and hedges and to avoid serried rows of huts in straight lines.

Above *Millom, Cumbria, from 3,000 ft in August 1942. The runways are camouflaged but the newly-painted 'hedges' are still very obtrusive. Note the 'bat handle' ends to the runways (RAF Museum).*

Below *Access road to the bomb dump at Templeton, Dyfed, follows the natural curve of a stream and hedge.*

Hedges, ditches, trees and other natural features were retained as far as practicable. Paths were provided in the most economical manner using local materials when available. They were to be inconspicous in colour and closely follow line features such as hedges. If there were no hedges long straight paths were to be avoided, although this recommendation was often ignored, the road to the operations block at Steeple Morden being just one example.

Nothing could be done about prominent local features such as lakes, as the newly-arrived Americans discovered to their cost at Gosfield, Essex on the evening of 10 December 1943. The bombing which cost eight lives was thought to have been attracted by the moonlight shining on nearby Gosfield Lake and revealing it as a landmark. When the USAAF Colonel received the British report on the incident, he commented 'What the hell do they want me to do, fill in the Goddam lake?'

The ultimate deception was to persuade the *Luftwaffe* to drop its bombs on a decoy site. During the war's early years, most RAF stations had such a decoy, usually located on common land as far from habitation as possible. The more elaborate day decoy, known as a 'K' site, had dummy aircraft and buildings, its night counterpart, the 'Q' site being equipped with a dummy Drem lighting system and means of simulating aircraft movement on the ground. Sometimes the 'K' and 'Q' sites were combined. A small hut and air raid shelter were usually supplied, as can be seen at Leamington Hastings, Warwickshire which was once a decoy for the Armstrong Whitworth works at Baginton.

By 1942 building camouflage consisted merely of painting irregularly in greens, browns and blacks and, in the spring of 1943, it was decided that the standard of camouflage could be relaxed in certain inland parts of the country. The requirements were reduced further in April 1944 and almost totally abandoned in the following August. As with all methods of passive defence, it is impossible to assess quantitively the effectiveness of camouflage but it was undoubtedly successful in misleading the *Luftwaffe* on a number of occasions.

Chapter 10

The development of approach and runway lighting

Drems, funnels, totem poles and goosenecks were all part of the peculiar jargon relating to lighting at RAF airfields during the Second World War. From rudimentary beginnings which had altered little since 1914-18 elaborate systems were devised, which, when used in conjunction with newly-invented radio aids, enabled the RAF to mount a round-the-clock, all-weather offensive.

The first steps in developing a night-flying technique were taken in 1913 when Captain G.S. Shepherd and Lieutenant K.P. Atkinson of 4 Squadron experimented with an electric searchlight on a BE 2a. In November trials were started with parachute flares to assist pilots in selecting suitable ground so that they could land with the aid of this searchlight. However, it was found better to release two flares, one at 1,500 ft and the other at 800 ft, falling at a rate of about 550 ft per minute, and using the light shed by these to land.

A rather less scientific approach was taken by Lieutenant Cholmondely of 3 Squadron in April 1913. He demonstrated that given a little luck, some moonlight and a lot of nerve, night flights could be made, and he proved it by flying at night from Larkhill to Upavon and back. The landing turned out to be exciting because although the moon had provided sufficient horizon while he was airborne, below 100 ft on the approach the horizon was poor and the moon too weak to illuminate the aerodrome. In later trials he tried landing by light streaming from open hangar doors.

In June 1913 Lieutenant G.I. Carmichael obtained permission to use petrol flares to light the landing area. Carmichael also asked his mechanic to install a 'night flying control', a simple switch which enabled him to illuminate his compass and tachometer together or separately. During the approach the flares proved their worth by giving the pilot depth perception so that he could judge accurately

the last few vital feet of the approach. Following this success, the petrol or paraffin flarepath was employed until well into 1917. It was laid out in a standard L-shaped pattern on the ground, the vertical line of the 'L' representing the direction of the runway into wind. It was incorporated into the 1914 RFC Training Manual and so far-seeing were the instructions that they remained unaltered in the 1916 edition.

I assume that the First World War flarepaths were similar to what were known as Money Flares, a term which crept in during the 'thirties in various memoirs and airfield information publications, and one which is mentioned sometimes in Second World War documents. They were merely round drums of paraffin with large wicks which consisted of swabs continuously soaked in the liquid and burning with a flame 3 to 4 ft high. A ground party had to keep running up and down the flarepath to replenish them and keep them alight.

Since the flares would obviously reveal an aerodrome's position to enemy aircraft, a different method was used in France. Each aircraft had a small signal lamp fixed beneath the fuselage. On returning to base, each pilot flashed his particular call-sign in morse code and, if it was safe to land, he was acknowledged by an electric torch on the ground. The aerodrome remained in darkness but at the edge of it was a small moveable trolley pointing into wind. On it were mounted four powerful Aldis lamps. As the aircraft descended, these were switched on, throwing a beam across the surface. The aircraft then landed in the beam and the lamps were switched off as soon as it was down.

It was very easy to get lost even with beacons behind the lines flashing different code letters. One pilot was unsure of his position and saw the beam of an Aldis trolley below. If it was not his own, at least it was some aerodrome. He flashed his call-sign but nobody answered. Reasoning that the beam was there so it must be safe, he landed but hit a telegraph pole and wrote off the aircraft. He had landed in the beam of a moving motor-cycle on a road 150 miles from base!

The growth of civil aviation in the 'twenties was accompanied by considerable improvements in ground lighting. Not surprisingly, Britain's premier airport at Croydon was the first to adopt many of them. Its night operating aids included a system of boundary lights to define the limits of the airport, a neon beacon to identify it at night and illuminated wind speed and direction indicators. Local obstructions were provided with red warning lights and experiments were also made with neon strip markers to delineate the main landing path at night and in daylight during foggy conditions. The grass landing area at Croydon was eventually floodlit in its entirety by multi-lamp units sited round the boundary.

The only standard provision of built-in runway lighting in the UK pre-war was designated 'contact lighting' and was installed at a very small number of RAF stations. It was unshielded and therefore could be seen all round the compass from the air. Primarily intended for use in poor visibility in conjunction with radio beam approach equipment, this became its only safe use in the wartime blackout.

After the outbreak of war it became increasingly apparent that if night operations were to be maintained, a remotely controlled form of built-in hooded runway lighting would have to be provided. This could only be seen by pilots when they were established in the correct position to approach and land, or when they were lined up on the runway for take-off. In addition, many new airfields were so close to one another that an outer circle of lights would have to be provided to define the circuit on

which aircraft should be flown to avoid collision whilst awaiting their turn to land.

Many attempts were made locally at aerodromes to design amateur equipment and installations which would meet the new requirements, using for example, ordinary lamp fittings inside discarded oil drums. A home-made scheme at Drem, the fighter station to the east of Edinburgh, was so successful that it was to give its name unofficially to the standard lighting at RAF airfields. 602 Squadron was flying Spitfires from Drem in 1940 on day and night patrols. The glare from their exhausts reduced the already poor view on final approach but matters were improved by arranging a circle of glim lamps so that they would follow the normal Spitfire curving approach. The idea was to become the basis for all RAF wartime lighting.

By the beginning of 1941 the Mechanical and Electrical Engineering Division of the Air Ministry Works Directorate evolved, in conjunction with the RAF, a system of lighting ultimately designated as Airfield Lighting Mark I but known colloquially as the Drem System. The initial requirement was for it to be installed at 80 bomber and 20 fighter stations by the end of 1941, a target that was almost attained.

The system comprised three main parts; the actual runway lighting itself, the approach lighting and the outer circle lighting. The runway section can be summarized as four main items, namely the runway flarepath, the 'totem pole' lights, the Angle of Glide Indicators (subsequently referred to as Angle of Approach Indicators or AAIs) and the runway floodlights. At fighter aerodromes, a fifth feature was added, this being the Taxiing Post Lights. The whole array was grouped under one control switch for any given direction of approach on any one runway. Thus on a three-runway

A Spitfire taxies in after a sweep shortly before sunset. It was the night-flying requirements of this type of aircraft which gave birth to the original Drem System.

Lined up on the flarepath at Leuchars in the beam of the Chance Light, BOAC Mosquito G-AGGF about to roll for Stockholm. Right rudder is already set to hold the swing (British Airways).

airfield six switches controlled the complete runway lighting system.

The runway marker light fittings were unidirectional with a 15 watt bulb housed beneath a cast iron dome showing through two apertures. Initially only one row was installed along each runway edge so that the left hand side could be delineated for a pilot landing in either direction. When the USAAF arrived in Britain, a need arose for both sides of the runway to be marked and fittings had to be doubled up at certain airfields.

Totem poles consisted of six light fittings mounted vertically on a post, screened so that they were visible only to a pilot on approach. On the reverse side, a similar assembly shone down the runway. Besides indicating to pilots the safe overrun from the runway ends, totem poles provided a visual guide at which to aim before touching down and an aligning point to enable the aircraft to stay on a straight course down the centre of the runway once it was on the ground.

The Angle of Glide Indicators were situated on the left-hand side at each end of each runway. By means of coloured slides in an optical projection lantern, a pilot approaching at too low an altitude and too flat an angle would see a red beam, at the correct height and angle a green one, whilst at too great a height and too steep an angle a yellow beam would be visible.

The floodlights were improvized from floodlighting units surplus to other services, mounted on a three-wheel trolley for ease of movement about the aerodrome. One was placed to the left of each end of each runway edge and 25 yd in from the GPIs so as to shine down the runway in the same direction as a landing aircraft.

The taxiing post lights, provided only at fighter stations, were the forerunners of Mk II Airfield Lighting taxi-track fittings. They consisted of a cast-iron dome with eight light apertures around the circumference. Only two such fittings were installed at each end of each runway, connected to the flarepath lights so that a pilot could readily tell at night the correct runway end to which to taxi for take-off. This was a considerable help in those days, when fighters were required to scramble at very short notice and when taxi-track lighting, as provided later, was unknown.

The approach lights, or funnels as they were later known, were six groups of six lights each, one to serve each direction of approach to each runway. They were mounted on poles and shone vertically upward, being arranged in a 90 degree vee shape with the axis pointing towards the runway. Feeding into the funnels were the outer circle lights, 23 units on poles equally spaced around the airfield on a circle of radius 2,000 yd from the geometrical centre of the aerodrome.

At fighter stations only, additional groups of lights designated 'outer lights' were placed beyond the outer circle, three miles from the centre of the aerodrome. Four such groups of lights were provided at opposite ends of two diameters of the outer circle at right angles to one another. The light fittings were installed in groups of three in the form of a triangle with the apex pointing towards the middle of the airfield. They were considered necessary for fighter aircraft in view of their speed being much greater than that of other operational types.

The Mk I system was crude compared to later developments but was adequate for the types of aircraft operating in the very early stages of the war. Since the limited time available for installation did not permit the deep

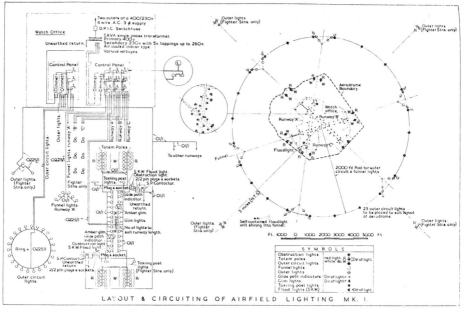

LAYOUT & CIRCUITING OF AIRFIELD LIGHTING MK. I

Layout and Circuiting of Airfield Lighting Mk 1.

burying of cables, a great deal of trouble was experienced with underground cabling outside the aerodrome being inadvertently ploughed up by farmers. Thus when the Mk II system was introduced, it was considered preferable to carry all circuits external to the airfield on overhead lines, except where these would cause obstruction on runway approaches.

While all this was being designed, some RAF units were forced to cope with conditions unthinkable in more normal times. Flight Lieutenant Brian Kingcombe quoted in Norman Gleb's book *Scramble*, flew Spitfires from Bibury in the Cotswolds where the squadron was told that it was responsible for the night defence of South Wales!

> 'We flew from this tiny strip — the sort of thing you'd never dream of doing in peacetime — *ever* — with no aids at all to get back, except four half-blacked out glim lamps and one Chance Light which was switched on for a second or two. We took off and groped our way around the night sky. It was black as sin. We were landing all over England because we couldn't find our way back. We were lucky no one was killed.'

Most of the grass aerodromes used by Training Command never aspired to electric lighting; they used paraffin flarepaths throughout the war. The flares were known as goosenecks

from the long-necked spout on a device which resembled a large watering can. A wick was placed in the spout and the neck was pointed downwind to prevent flaring. Although producing a bright light, their main drawback was the time taken to extinguish a line of them when an enemy intruder was approaching. The flares were set out to a pattern known as the 'Upavon Flarepath' which had been devised at that RAF station by a Warrant Officer Turnbull. His system was originally a portable electric flarepath deriving its power from a mobile floodlight and fully controlled from a central point.

To warn pilots on the ground of enemy intruder activity, the procedure was to switch on a hooded red light on the control building or other position plainly visible from all parts of the aerodrome. Aircraft already airborne were alerted by a triangle of red lights illuminated at the aerodrome identity beacon. Radio-equipped aircraft were then to circle the beacon, which was deliberately sited a mile or so from the airfield, and await further instructions. Those without radio would have to wait until the triangle was extinguished before rejoining the circuit.

Enemy bombers were encouraged to waste their loads on decoy 'Q' Sites. Some Q-Sites were fitted with a dummy Drem System which had a bar of red warning lights across the funnels, visible only when an aircraft was on final approach. Despite this precaution, several RAF aircraft crash-landed in error on Q-Sites. By the end of 1943 the decoys had all been withdrawn from use.

After some experimentation, Airfield Lighting Mk II was finally standardized late in 1941. The same general features as in the Mk I system were to be found, with much improved approach lighting. As before, the outer circle was laid out roughly in the form of a circle but enlarged to an approximate diameter of 6,500 yd, the total perimeter for an average bomber field being nearly 12 miles. A total of 52 light fittings were spaced 400 yd apart with a radial siting tolerance of 100 ft to allow for obstacles. The exact shape of the 'circle' was determined by the layout of the approach lighting and, as will be seen later, was therefore dependent on the alignment and lengths of the runways, normally up to three in number.

The Mk II approach light system was divided into four sections, the Lead-In String, Outer Funnel, Intermediate Funnel and Inner Funnel, the last two commonly being referred to under the combined title of Fog Funnel. The purpose of the lead-in string was to give visual indication of the point at which the aircraft should turn in from the outer circle towards the correct runway for landing and the curvature of turn required to ensure a smooth turn-on to the centre of the approach path.

The three funnel sections were arranged to give continuous visual indication to a pilot to enable him to keep his aircraft on the longitudinal centre-line of the runway on the approach. The inner and intermediate funnels also assisted night take-offs as 'horizon lights'. The funnels were vee-shaped as described above and the lead-in string of lights was spaced 200 yd apart to extend the left hand. At stations operating Spitfires, a special curved approach light path on an 800 yd radius was an extra fitment.

The runway marker lights were the same as before, but so circuited that all runway lights could only be switched on in one direction at a time in order to prevent inadvertent landings on the correct runway but in the wrong direction. If installed concurrently with the construction of the runway, they were embedded in the edge of the concrete. Otherwise, they were mounted on separate pre-cast concrete blocks alongside and as close as possible to the edge. They were usually spaced 100 yd apart longitudinally and exactly opposite to one another.

At 800 yd in from the end of each runway, a blue-screened cross-bar of lights was installed to warn pilots of the 'distance to go' and to mark the last safe point of touchdown. The totem poles were as described above, but weakened with saw cuts ('frangible' in today's jargon) to reduce damage to an aircraft striking them. Two AAIs were now provided, one on each side of the threshold, combinations of red, green and amber lights enabling a pilot

Layout of Airfield Lighting Mk II.

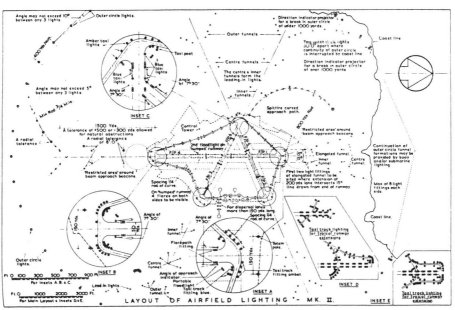

LAYOUT OF AIRFIELD LIGHTING - MK. II.

Above left *Airfield Identification Beacon on a trailer at Halfpenny Green with original watch office bungalow and replacement tower in background.*

Above *Mk II runway marker light fitting with scale provided by 35 mm camera.*

Left *This unique memorial at Cheddington, Bucks, incorporates the distinctive star-shape of a Mk I Contact Light fitting.*

to assume a safe approach angle. So that the light from the AAIs should not be confused with other lights in the vicinity, the indicators were fitted with a motor-driven shutter to produce intermittent beams.

Runway floodlights, known universally as Chance Lights after the manufacturers Chance Brothers, an old-established firm making light-house equipment, were positioned one at each end of each runway on the left-hand side when viewed from the approach. A second could be brought into use where a hump in the runway interfered with the floodlight beam. Being a hefty piece of machinery, they incorporated an obstruction light so aircraft could be alerted to the position of the ones not in use.

Taxi-track lighting was similar to the taxi post fitting of the Mk I system but with six light apertures around the cast iron dome instead of eight. They marked both sides of the taxi-way 150 yd apart with minor siting tolerances on the straight sections. On curved portions, the spacing intervals were reduced to a quarter of the radius of the curve. As with the runway cross-bar lights, coloured filters were employed to differentiate between the outside edge of the taxi-track (blue) and the inside edge (amber). This was found to assist

taxiing in low visibility and thus reduced the possibility of pilots straying off the paved area and getting bogged down or otherwise causing damage to their aircraft.

This did not prevent further local improvizations. For example, an experiment took place with amber lights along one side of the perimeter track at Langar in December 1942. Around the same time, amber and blue lighting was tried out at Elsham Wolds. At Lichfield, 27 OTU painted 1 ft wide white lines on all taxi-track bends, a simple idea which greatly reduced taxiing accidents. In 1945 1332 HCU, Nutts Corner's contribution to safety was to place thousands of four-gallon kerosene tins painted white along the taxiway edges.

In order to expedite the clearance of aircraft off the perimeter track on to the dispersals, where the length of any dispersal lane connecting the hard-standing to the taxi-track exceeded 150 yd, blue lights were provided for the dispersal lane for the first 150 yd of its length. The first pair of fittings was sited on either side of the lane where it joined the taxiway, a further six lights being installed, three on each side of the lane, spaced 500 yd apart.

Mounted in the watch tower was the panel controlling the entire airfield lighting system.

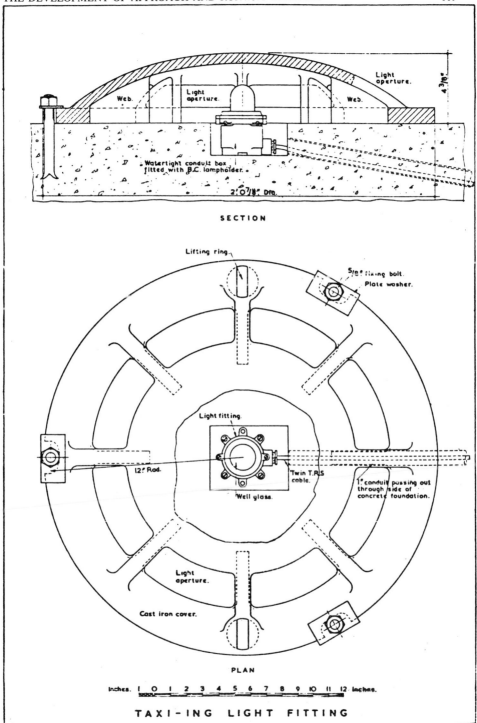

Taxiing Light Fitting.

The brilliance of the lights was adjustable in four stages from 25 per cent up to 100 per cent and a lamp failure indicator registered the percentage of lamps which had failed in a particular section. A mimic diagram on a panel approximately 2 ft square showed the layout of the aerodrome with a miniature representation of all lights on and around it. As each circuit was energized, the corresponding lamps on the mimic lit up, confirming that the switching was correct and enabling the Flying Control Officer to see at a glance the set-up of the lighting as a whole.

In the event of a national grid power failure, either accidental or from enemy action, standby power to essential services on an airfield was supplied by diesel engines. The changeover was automatic, the cables supplying the emergency current from the standby set house being routed separately at least 50 yd from the cable runs of the permanent circuit.

The Mk II system demanded cable lengths of approximately 30 miles for overhead lines and 22 miles of underground cabling for each station. The magnitude of the work was increased by having to carry out installations whilst airfields were in use and, outside their boundaries, with the minimum interference to farming activities, not to mention coping with rail, river and road crossings, forests, lakes, quarries and built-up areas.

Altogether, Mk II lighting necessitated the installation of over 12,000 miles of overhead lines in the UK, involving the erection of about 500,000 poles and over 9,000 miles of trenching or ducting. At airfields on the coast, the outer funnel lights were sometimes mounted on buoys. To indicate breaks in the continuity of the outer circle caused by coast lines, two lights were placed 50 ft apart and two projectors shone intersecting beams from each break point to indicate the correct direction in which to fly to remain on the circle.

So densely packed were the airfields of eastern England with their girdles of lights that on a clear night they made a breathtaking sight. Colonel Jean Calmel, DFC, in his book *Night Pilot* (William Kimber, 1955) wrote, 'These airfields were like close-set necklaces of pearls on raid nights, at the moment we left and again when we returned. England gleamed with all its fires like a woman wearing her diamonds.'

The ultimate development, Airfield Lighting MK III consisted basically of the MK II system, plus the following additional features which were common to all MK III systems: (a) closer spacing of taxi-track lighting on all curved tracks; (b) lighting on curved dispersal lanes; (c) illuminated dispersal indicators; (d) illuminated marshalling posts.

As well as the above, the following extra items, designated as part of the MK III system, were only installed at selected stations in accordance with operational requirements. They are described individually below:

a) sectionalization of taxi-track lighting where alternative taxiing routes existed;
b) dispersal lane lighting beyond the first 150 yards;
c) portable sodium lamp flarepath;
d) sodium lamp approach lighting;
e) remote control of runway cross-bar lighting;
f) illuminated station identification panels;
g) illuminated control tower sign;
h) traffic lights where interlocked with flarepath lighting;
i) treatment of overlapping or neighbouring outer circles of adjacent airfields.

Expanding these features in order, at operational stations where aircraft movements had to be maintained down to low visual conditions, it was found that the quarter radius rule for the spacing of lights on curved taxi-ways was inadequate. Pilots tended to follow the lights on the inside of the curve rather closely in poor visibility, taxiing in a straight line from one light to the next with the risk of bogging one wheel in the grass and causing chaos when aircraft were marshalling for an operation.

The answer to the problem was to reduce the spacing of the lights on curves so that the fittings would be closer together on the inside of the bends, the fittings on the outside of curves being spaced so as to pair with alternate fittings on the inside bends. For similar reasons, modifications were made to lights on dispersal lane bends. The entrances to these lanes were now to be marked with a metal box having holes punched in it in the pattern of a number, designating the dispersal and lit internally. In practice, the fittings were usually made from discarded four-gallon petrol cans.

Marshalling posts indicated the point on the taxi-track just short of the runway (known today as the holding point) at which pilots must halt for final checks and await a green light from the runway caravan. They consisted of an illuminated yellow-painted sign 2 ft square, with a blue 'M' or the runway QDM numerals superimposed according to whether the runway was grass or concrete. At night, they also acted as a guide for taxiing to the correct end of the runway-in-use.

As runways were lengthened at many airfields during the war, the original sections of the perimeter track were left in place to act as short-cuts for taxiing aircraft. There was, however, a danger that in bad visibility a pilot might turn on to the runway off the old taxi-way and thus find himself with a very much shorter take-off run than that actually available. Also, other taxiing aircraft and airfield vehicles might try inadvertently to cross an active runway. These dangers were obviated by arranging the lighting circuit so that the short-cut position was lit only when the lights on the appropriate runway were dead and *vice versa*.

The portable sodium flarepath was essential to increase the range of visibility over which it was possible to operate aircraft. It consisted simply of ordinary 140 watt sodium street lighting units placed on the ground so as to shine vertically upwards. Six were provided on each airfield, one on either side of the runway-in-use at the touchdown end, the remaining four being spaced down the left-hand side 200 yd apart longitudinally. The sodium lights were found as useful by day as by night and this led to the use of sodium approach lighting to complement the existing funnel lights. They were, however, fitted only on the main runway corresponding to the prevailing wind direction and one other subsidiary approach.

On certain airfields where it was found that no agreement could be obtained between the operating pilots as to what constituted an acceptable degree of brilliancy on the runway cross bar lights, provision was made for them to be adjusted by remote control from the watch office.

At some very large airfields like St Mawgan with complicated networks of runways and taxi-tracks, it was essential in the interests of safety to provide a light system to prevent perimeter traffic crossing active runways by day or night. Red and green traffic lights were used, normally showing green but changing to red when the master runway selector indicated that the associated runway was in use.

With airfields grouped so closely together, particularly in East Anglia, their outer circles often touched or even crossed one another. To ensure, by visual observation, that the correct airfield was being circled, a night identity panel was placed at the junction of the outer circle with the lead-in strings at opposite ends of the main runway. The panels were, in effect, an illuminated sign showing the two identification code letters (both 20 ft high) for the aerodrome, composed of light bulbs on a framework. A similar device, smaller and with hooded blue lights, also marked the location of the control tower at certain airfields.

Apart from the possibility of mistaking adjacent aerodromes, there was a very real danger of collision when large numbers of aircraft were waiting their turn to land. To overcome this where there were adjacent outer circles, a 'thousand yard light bar' was lit between the two outer circles to mark the extent of the safe flying distance outside the circle. This light bar was made up of six flashing yellow lights 200 yd apart.

Where outer circles touched or overlapped, additional lights at a tangent to both outer circles could be switched on to furnish one combined outer circle surrounding both the adjacent airfields. Control was arranged so that the composite circle could be lit from the tower at either station, with an overriding master control at one of them, usually the more important of the two from the operational aspect.

The ultimate in Mk III Airfield Lighting was probably that at St Mawgan. As described earlier, a comprehensive system of traffic lights was necessary owing to the volume of ground and air traffic on its complicated taxiways. Predating London Heathrow by many years, the taxi lighting was segregated into a number of separately-controlled sections so that, at night, the Flying Control Officer was able to route aircraft and vehicles along the most convenient routes.

One other important lighting application requires explanation, namely High Intensity-Low Visibility (HILV) Lighting. This was American in origin and was employed on USAAF and RAF-occupied airfields in the UK. Inevitably, it had considerable influence on British practice, particularly in respect of colour coding where widely differing standards could lead to confusion and hazardous situations. The runway and approach lighting closely followed British design, but there was no outer circle and the system was more akin to today's installations. It was confined to the main runway and in the last year of the war 70 complete sets of this type were installed in the UK.

HILV lighting was almost identical to the RAF system known as Contact Lighting, which had been developed separately from the Mk I, II and III systems. Contact lighting installations were intended primarily for use in association with radio landing aids in bad visibility. Their function was to indicate to pilots the limits of the runway once the aircraft had been guided by radio to a point where a visual landing could be made. Only the main runway was so equipped as mist and fog are usually prevalent in conditions of little or no wind.

Mk I Contact Lighting, already mentioned, was a pre-war development which, by 1944, was to be found at a total of 175 airfields. The introduction of American HILV then drew attention to the relatively low brilliance of the British system and the RAE was given the task

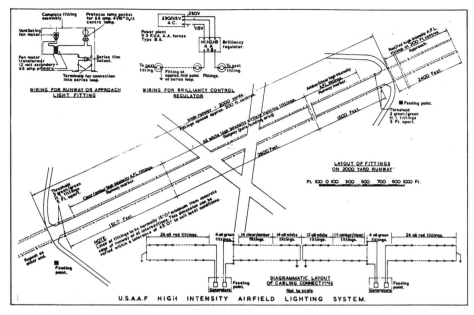

U.S.A.A.F HIGH INTENSITY AIRFIELD LIGHTING SYSTEM.

of developing a new flush-type screened contact lighting with a greater light intensity than that given by any previous type of British marker light fitting. Working in conjunction with the Directorate General of Works, RAE designed the Contact Lighting Mk II fitting, along with a more efficient type of approach lighting.

As the work and expense involved in putting in completely new bad weather runway lighting on 175 airfields would have been prohibitive, research was carried out with a view to improving the old type fitting. Simple modifications which could be done on the spot with minimal interference with aircraft movements, resulted in a six-fold increase in candle power. This adaptation was designated Contact Lighting Mk IA.

In 1945, with the likelihood that large transports and very heavy bomber types such as the B-29 would soon be operating from UK bases, it was decided to scrap the Mk II outer circle approach funnel at certain locations and replace it with long, straight, lighted approach paths. The approach lighting finally agreed upon at places like Heathrow was essentially a compromise between the Mk II funnel and the HILV system previously described.

It consisted of a 3,000 yd long double run of lights leading in to the ends of the runways, the two lines being at an angle of 40 degrees to each other, forming in effect an elongated funnel which narrowed as the runway was approached. The lights were coloured in accordance with practice in the USA, pend-

USAAF High Intensity Airfield Lighting System.

ing any post-war international agreement to the contrary.

A coded system of distance marking along the approach path was also provided at intervals of 500, 1,000, 1,500 and 2,000 yd from the runway end. At these points, the markings consisted of four, three, two and one additional light fittings on either side of the centre-line. Each group of distance markers was laid out in a straight line at about 45° to the line of flight as delineated by the approach lights. This gave the appearance of barbs on an arrow pointing towards the runway.

A further aspect which had to be considered throughout the war was obstruction lighting. Prior to the general provision of hard runways, flying obstructions were confined to three categories only; airfield obstructions within the boundary, such as hangars; obstacles in the area surrounding the aerodrome for a distance of 3,500 yd from its perimeter and, beyond this, air navigation obstructions like radio masts. When runways came on the scene, a fourth classification was brought in, namely approach and circuit obstructions.

The criteria for the latter are too complicated to detail but suffice it to say that over 1,000 obstruction light installations were fitted in Britain during the Second World War. One small grass aerodrome in Shropshire which never achieved such sophistication was Bridleway Gate, used as a relief landing ground by Shawbury's Oxfords. When night flying was arranged, the occupants of a cottage on the aerodrome boundary were asked to keep a light burning upstairs to warn pilots of its location!

Coverage of the fairly basic lighting aids at flying boat bases can be found in Chapter 16. Another specialist application was to be found at the three Bomber Command Emergency Landing Grounds at Manston, Carnaby and Woodbridge. Each had a single runway 3,000 yd long and 250 yd wide, on which a disabled aircraft could crash-land if necessary. The runway lighting was sectionalized in three colour-coded parallel lanes to indicate the clear portion if part of the strip was blocked by a crashed or immobile aircraft.

The remainder of the lighting was the stand-ard Mk II system plus an extra ring of sodium lights on the outer circle for use in low visibility. On the main direction of approach from the east, sodium lamps at quarter-mile intervals out to about 4½ miles led the pilot to the normal funnel lights. At about 2½ miles from touch-down, a distance marker was provided in the form of a cross-bar of sodiums 100 yd apart. This unique straight-in approach system was intended to assist aircraft which were in no condition to be flown around the normal circuit on reaching the airfield. In fog, FIDO petrol burners dissipated the fog and outlined the runway.

Without all the time and effort devoted to improving ground lighting aids, the scale of night bombing and other operations which was achieved would have been quite impossible. Well over £10 million was expended on lighting installations in the UK alone, a total of 421

Contact Lighting Mk II.

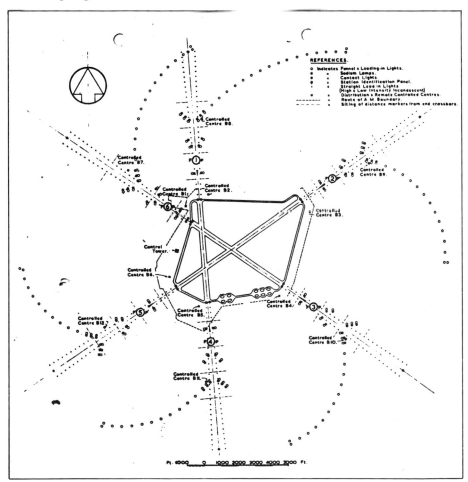

airfields being equipped with Airfield Lighting Mks I, II or III.

Lifting the total blackout on 14 December 1944 seriously compromised outer circle lighting which had depended for its effectiveness on the absence of other lights. The solution was to reimpose a blackout at certain airfields out to a radius of 3,000 yd from the perimeter. This was not quite so drastic as it sounds because it applied only to lights visible through angles above the horizon such as street lamps. As an alternative it was suggested that the whole of the outer circle and funnels could be made flashing in character and thus readily distinguishable from other civilian lighting. However, this would have entailed considerable work and reduced bulb life drastically so it was not adopted.

Chapter 11

Flying Control and Radio Aids

Between the wars, radio, or wireless as it was then known, was not in general use in the RAF but a certain amount of development work took place. The introduction of VHF radio immediately before the war meant that direct speech was far more viable, but it was a long time before it replaced W/T in Morse Code or the static-laden H/F frequency band. It was employed initially for communications between fighters and their ground controller, bombers still relying on W/T or ordinary speech on H/F.

The RAF had never before found it necessary to control its traffic, but suddenly realized that this deficiency was causing many accidents. A total of 1,451 aircraft were written off or badly damaged as a result of airfield accidents during the second half of 1941. Concern was expressed that standardization of Flying Control was essential before the Americans arrived with thousands more aircraft. At that time it had not even been standardized within the Commands, each Group having its own system.

Training aircraft of smaller types were not normally fitted with radio equipment and a solution to the large number of runway collisions was to place a caravan alongside the touchdown area. On runway airfields it had its own hard-standing and access track. An Aerodrome Control Pilot (ACP) manned it, armed with an Aldis signalling lamp and a Very pistol to warn pilots to go round again if they were approaching with another machine in a blind spot or with the undercarriage retracted. RAF Woodvale claimed the credit for the caravan idea in the summer of 1942, but it seems to have evolved simultaneously at several other locations.

RAF Lichfield, home of a Maintenance Unit and a Wellington Operational Training Unit, was the proving ground for many procedures which were adopted throughout the service.

Early developments here were the regulation of vehicle movements, the clearance of airfield obstructions where possible and the control of taxiing. Standard taxi routes were devised and, to assist aircraft movement at night, white lines were painted on all perimeter track bends, a simple but effective measure.

The runway-in-use at an aerodrome obviously depended upon wind direction and was differentiated by a number from one to six (assuming there were three strips) beginning with the one nearest north and continuing in a clockwise direction. The appropriate runway would be passed to an aircraft by radio but if it was not so equipped, a landing 'Tee' displayed in the signals square near the tower would indicate the direction. This was confirmed by another 'Tee' placed at the downwind end of the runway. The cross-bar was always nearest to the approaching wind. In addition, large boards bearing the runway number would be hung on the side of the tower. From March 1944 runways were referred to by their magnetic heading, for example, '23' for 230°, 235° and above would be rounded up to '24' and so on. The idea was American.

For an aircraft in an emergency there was a variety of aids which could lead to a safe landing. The basic life-saver was *Darky*, a system by which an aircraft could call for a homing using the call-sign *Darky*. Most RAF stations operated a permanent *Darky* watch on a common frequency with a transmitter receiver of limited range to avoid too much overlap with other stations. By taking bearings and comparing them by telephone, they were rapidly able to fix a lost aircraft's position. In areas where RAF coverage was poor, Royal Observer Corps posts were also equipped with *Darky* sets.

Apart from this, all ROC posts plotted aircraft movements both visually and by sound,

Left *Horsa on characteristic steep approach at Tilstock with chequered control caravan in foreground* (R.R. Glass).

Above *Original watch office at RNAS Dale displaying '03' as runway-in-use* (FAA Museum).

and passed the information to their Group operations room where a complete picture was built up on an operations table. On a clear night searchlight beams could be arranged to point towards the nearest suitable aerodrome. Three searchlights on an airfield, known as *Sandra* Lights, were directed upwards to form a cone overhead and, if there was a low cloud-base, the glow could often be seen from above. As a last resort, a night fighter could be vectored to a lost aircraft by radar and lead it down to a landing. Other visual aids included rockets, Very lights and a signal mortar which fired a brilliant flare high in the sky.

The *Occult* Scheme delineated the coastline of the British Isles by means of 'aerial light-houses' operating from fixed sites. They flashed code letters which were changed periodically and were intended to be visible to aircraft approaching the coast. Where practicable the locations were to be no more than 15 miles inland and had to meet the following criteria: 40 mile intervals from Cape Wrath to West Hartlepool and from the Bristol Channel to the Solway Firth, 30 miles between Hartlepool and the Bristol Channel via the South Coast. Each site was easily accessible from a main road, not closer than 800 yds from the nearest village and there was to be a telephone within a reasonable distance. Ideally, slight screening of the light to seawards by the terrain was desirable to prevent the signals confusing coastal shipping. When this was not possible,

fixed screens were used to block the light at low angles.

Moving on to approach aids, one of the first to be adopted by the RAF in wartime was the civil 'ZZ' procedure. The pilot was given the local barometric pressure to set on his altimeter, then D/F guidance to overhead the aerodrome. When audible at the appropriate moment, 'Motors overhead' was signalled and the aircraft would then head in the direction from which the landing would be made. After a set time, the pilot would reverse course and with continuing D/F assistance descend and land. The 'ZZ' signal from which the system took its name indicated that altitude and course were correct.

'ZZ' was replaced eventually by QGH, the code for Controlled Descent Through Cloud. This used D/F to place the aircraft within a safety lane down to the runway. Experienced controllers could handle as many as five returning bombers at a time, all in different stages of the procedure, with separations which by today's standards were minimal but that were considered acceptable in wartime.

The most important approach aid during the mid-war years was, however, Standard Beam Approach (SBA) which was ironically a German invention dating back to the early 'thirties and produced by C. Lorenz AG and Telefunken. By 1935 it was in regular use by *Lufthansa*, having been installed at Berlin-Tempelhof and Hanover, amongst others. Mar-

Sandra *Lights 'somewhere in England'* (Via Dr A.A. Duncan).

coni supplied their own beam approach equipment to Croydon and Liverpool's Speke Airport and the RAF was not slow to recognize the possibilities of blind landing systems for all-weather operations. The RAE tried out six different systems of British, Dutch, American and German origin at Abingdon between 1935 and 1939. The system by Lorenz was judged the most effective, British rights having been obtained by Standard Telephones and Cables as early as 1936.

The first RAF SBA system for training was installed at Watchfield, Berkshire in October 1940, the Lorenz equipment having been shipped from Holland immediately before the invasion of that country. The Beam Approach School was formed at Watchfield on 17 October 1940 and began training in radio letdown procedures. The Blind Approach Training and Development Unit, which had been established at Boscombe Down in September 1939, had given limited instruction to experienced pilots, but its main effort was now diverted to investigation into the *Luftwaffe*'s use of wireless beams for target finding. To reflect this new role it was renamed the Wireless Intelligence Development Unit.

In March 1941 Bomber Command was pressing for the replacement of the cumbersome 'ZZ' Procedure by Lorenz but noted that they considered the latter a blind *approach* system rather than one for blind *landings*. In practice, however, it was good for landings with a cloud base down to 50 ft and virtually blind landings were made on a regular basis, returning bomber crews low on fuel having little choice. By 1945, more than 40 Blind Approach Training Flights had been formed, most of them affiliated to Advanced Flying Units. The name was later amended to *Beam Approach Training Flight* and by 1945 some became Radio Aids Training Flights, such were the variety of electronic aids then available.

Briefly, SBA consisted of a radio beam transmitted along the runway approach track from a ground station. A receiver in the aircraft indicated deviations from the centre line to the pilot both visually and aurally. The visual method was a directional indicator synchronized with the magnetic compass which was confirmed by differing tones in the pilot's earphones. A zone of dashes showed he was right of final approach, dots if to the left and a continuous note when on the centre line. Two low-powered marker beacons, one on the aerodrome boundary and the other about two miles out, gave the pilot both visual and aural indication of his distance from the runway threshold.

The drawback with SBA was that the minimum safe landing rate was five minutes between aircraft and it demanded the utmost concentration when a pilot was obviously at

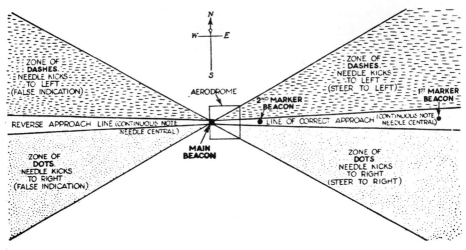

Above *Visual and Aural Indications of Lorenz System.*

Left *Oxford PG943 'T' of No 1 Beam Approach School at Watchfield in 1945. Bellman hangar in background* (Via Roy Bonser).

Below *Hinton-in-the-Hedges, Northants, scene of some of the early ILS trials. Partly farmed but still in use today for gliding and private flying* (Tony Hooper).

his most tired. The aid which was destined to replace it came on the scene in 1944; the American Signals Corps System 51 (SCS 51). Conceived as long ago as 1939, SCS 51 was brought rapidly to the production stage in response to a plea from the 8th Air Force for a better landing aid than SBA. The Americans were apparently so appalled at the British climate that some thought it safer flying over Germany than trying to land back at their bases! Subsequently abbreviated to ILS (Instrument Landing System), it is still the standard approach aid in military and civil aviation.

Two ground transmitters provided an approach path for the aircraft's exact alignment and final descent to the runway. One, known as the *localizer*, gave the pilot course guidance which enabled him to line up with the runway. The other was the so-called glide-slope transmitter. This unit sent a narrow radio beam directly at the incoming aircraft at an angle of about 3° from the ground. On the pilot's instrument panel a pair of intersecting needles interpreted these guiding signals visually. When the vertical needle for course and the horizontal needle for descent crossed at right angles, the line-up was accurate and if the needles were kept that way the landing approach would be successful.

The USAAF's initial programme announced in June 1944 envisaged installations at 16 airfields, with all bomber stations being equipped with them in the near future. However, this was not achieved even by VE-Day. In the meantime the RAF continued to rely upon SBA but the Signals Development Unit carried out trials with the SCS 51 at Hinton-in-the-Hedges, Northamptonshire. Not until late 1945 were some Transport Command aircraft equipped with ILS receivers.

BABS, the Beam Approach Beacon System, was introduced in 1944 and consisted of an airborne interrogator which worked with a ground responder beacon. It was suitable only for large aircraft as the information was presented on a cathode-ray tube to the navigator who passed it to the pilot on the intercom. Another type of approach aid was installed at a number of American Atlantic Ferry terminals in Britain. Known as the Radio Range, it became the main airways navigation aid throughout North America and later spread worldwide until progressively replaced by more modern systems in the 'fifties.

Bombers departing for a night raid were dispatched by light signals to avoid intense radio traffic alerting the German monitoring service. The American daylight bombing missions brought their own problems as formations attempted to join up from 20 or more differ-

ent airfields. To facilitate the climb through cloud which had caused so many mid-air collisions, a network of radio beacons known as *Bunchers* and *Splashers* was used, over which the aircraft could climb in a race track pattern at predetermined intervals. Once above cloud they were able to formate visually. These beacons were also used for instrument letdowns on the return from a raid.

Ground Controlled Approach by radar (GCA) was perfected too late to have much impact on wartime flying. Using American equipment, some of the first experimental landings in Britain were made at St Eval in Cornwall by Signals Development Unit. The apparatus was bulky and was installed in covered trucks for ease of transport as it had to be positioned carefully near the end of the active runway. For a good account of GCA in its infancy Arthur C. Clarke's book *Glide Path* can be recommended, a novel with authentic background details.

Control of circuit traffic differed in detail between RAF Groups but generally the traffic zone was considered to extend to 3,000 yd from the airfield perimeter and up to 2,000 ft overhead. In visual conditions at training stations radio was rarely used, although a listening watch was kept on a common frequency of 6,440 khz, all instructions being given by Aldis lamp from the ACP. Many wartime airfields were far too close to each other and their traffic had to be co-ordinated. Prestwick and Ayr, for example, had a common circuit. At Ford and Tangmere, aircraft orbiting the former were required to fly at odd thousands of feet, those at Tangmere at even thousands.

At night when downwind in the circuit, a pilot would flash his code letter in morse on the downward identification lamp. A green light from the ACP meant 'You may land', a flashing red indicated 'Wait and try again' and a steady white 'You may not land here, go away.' On receipt of a green, the pilot would switch the identification light to 'steady' and keep it on until after landing. An aircraft in emergency and requesting a priority landing had three alternatives, namely to call the watch tower on R/T, make a series of short flashes on navigation lights or Aldis lamp, or fire a white Very light.

The *ad hoc* method of detailing a spare pilot as ACP gave way to a new RAF trade in July 1942, that of Airfield Controller. The principal object of its introduction was to cut down the number of accidents, particularly at airfields with runways. The School of Flying Control was established at Watchfield and the syllabus gradually widened as experience was gained. Many of the Flying Control Officers who supervized the Airfield Controllers were

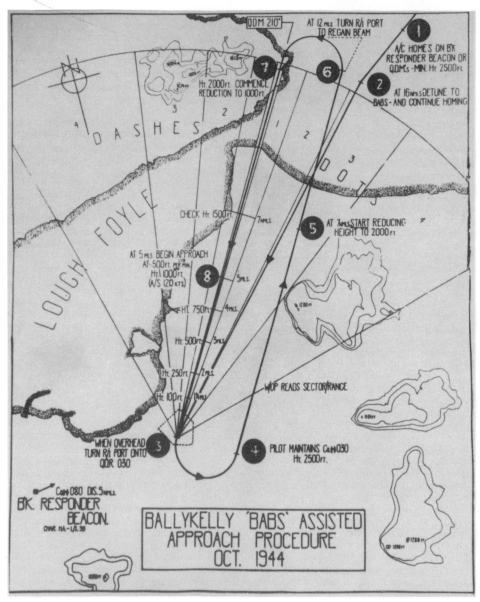

BABS chart for Ballykelly, Northern Ireland, 1944.

ex-aircrew, perhaps tour-expired or medically unfit, so the pilot's traditional resistance to any form of interference from the ground was soon overcome when it was realized that Flying Control could render valuable assistance.

There was still only a system in the immediate vicinity of airfields, however. The only form of area control in the British Isles was set up at Ramsey on the Isle of Man in March 1943 to reduce the number of accidents to training aircraft in the Irish Sea area. Train-

ing Area Flying Control, as it was known, had moved to Nutts Corner in Northern Ireland by 1945 and was now also responsible for aircraft flying over the north of Scotland and the northwest Atlantic. HF/DF fixer stations at Nutts Corner, Stornoway, Prestwick and Doncaster could give a lost aircrew its position with relative ease.

Airfield identification codes

Between the wars there was a simple and fool-proof method of identifying civil airfields from the air. It consisted of a circle of chalk in the approximate centre of the landing area in which the location was written in large letters that were easily visible from an altitude of 2,000 ft or so. The RAF does not seem to have adopted this system, although a plain white circle was often employed as a target for practice bombing. However, as more and more aerodromes were constructed in wartime, often close together as in East Anglia, it became obvious that visual confirmation of identity was essential.

A system of two-letter codes was adopted, chosen from the letters making up the airfield's name. These were displayed in the signals square in characters which were about 10 ft high. If it was a double-barrelled name, like Church Lawford or Castle Donington, the initial letters of each part would be used, viz 'CL' and 'CD'.

This worked very well for a while until it became difficult to allocate codes to new airfields which did not duplicate previous combinations. There were few aerodrome names beginning with 'I', 'J', 'U', 'V' or 'Z' and, of course, none with 'X', so these letters became a ready source of new codes. Often there was no clue to the derivation — for example 'JO' was used by Bungay and 'AC' by Breighton, but, if at all possible, a letter was taken from the name, such as 'XF' for Blakehill Farm.

Some apparently unconnected codes stemmed from airfield name changes, such as 'IA' for Merryfield (formerly Isle Abbotts) and 'CE' for Peplow (formerly Childs Ercall). Similarly, Andrews Field in Essex inherited 'GZ' from its former title of Great Saling.

These ground signals were obviously of no value at night so a mobile beacon known as a Pundit was employed to flash in red the identity letters in Morse Code. Since they would obviously attract enemy raiders, they were not actually sited on the aerodrome, normally being positioned several miles away and moved periodically. Crews were briefed on their relative position to the airfield before night flying commenced. Inevitably, many drew machine gun fire and even bombs from enemy aircraft, so they were not too popular with local residents! Despite these arrangements aircraft still contrived to land at the wrong airfield having perhaps in the heat of the moment on returning from operations misread the code.

Where a number of airfields were located so close to one another that their outer circle lighting nearly touched, it was essential to ensure by visual observation from the air that the correct airfield was being circled prior to a landing approach. The confusion which might possibly arise with three squadrons returning on each other's tails to land at three adjacent fields can be readily imagined.

A further requirement was the provision of a means of identification at night in a blacked-out area by a pilot whose radio had failed. Consequently, after a certain amount of research into the problem, a type of night identification panel was evolved and installed at most of the airfields provided with airfield lighting.

At those airfields equipped with an illuminated outer circle, the panels were connected to the outer circle circuit and installed at the junction of the outer circle with the lead-in lights at opposite ends of the main runway. The panels consisted of an illuminated sign showing the identification letters of the airfield. The overall length of each letter was 20 ft, this being found to be the minimum size compatible with conspicuousness.

The light fittings consisted of 15 watt bulbs spaced 12 in apart and supported on a timber or steel framework mounted on the ground at an angle of 60° so as to face towards a pilot making a normal left-hand circuit. It was found that making up letters of the size finally decided upon with lamps of greater brightness than 15 watt, or spaced closer than 12 in apart, merely resulted in a confused blur of light.

At those stations where an illuminated identification panel was required but where the 3 mile radius outer circle was not installed, a single panel similar to that described was employed. This was mounted on the ground in a horizontal position in the signals area.

Few examples of the concrete letters have survived and those which do exist on disused airfields are usually very overgrown. Sometimes, the broken-up concrete still lies in the long grass in front of the derelict control tower. The signals square itself was normally outlined in white-painted concrete and many of these can still be discerned. The 'TW' code of Turweston, near Brackley in Northamptonshire, lasted until quite recently and was easily visible from the air. Unfortunately, the farmer destroyed it last year. Conversely, at Little Staughton, the original 'LX' code is still well-maintained.

The tower at Wigtown in Southern Scotland may have been demolished by now to make way for development. The letters 'JO' were still visible a few years ago, this being rather interesting because Wigtown's code was actually 'GO', 'JO' being allocated as a fin code when the Royal Navy was considering taking over this facility in 1945-46.

Above *Tower at Ridgewell, Essex, with prominent 'RD' code.*

Below *Locally-designed glasshouse on the roof of Polebrook tower. Note B-17 nose glazing, signals square and 'PK' code.*

I have only been able to trace one code for a naval airfield, this being 'QM' which was used by Eglinton. Since there are so few other 'Q' prefixes, it seems reasonable to suspect that many of them fell within this block. Similarly, I have not been able to find all the letters for flying boat stations, which were displayed on the adjacent shoreline.

To confuse things somewhat, the list for mid-1944 contains some duplications. These are 'AM' for Acaster Malbis and Aldermaston,

'BN' for Brunton and Balderton, 'KT' for Calshot and Stansted, 'PM' for Pembroke Dock and Podington, 'SP' for Spilsby and Sculthorpe, 'TG' for Tealing and Toome, 'UM' for Sumburgh and Wombleton, 'WD' for Watchfield and Wymeswold, 'XB' for Deanland and Hartford Bridge (Blackbushe) and 'XM' for Syerston and Manston. Since many of these locations are separated by 100 miles or more and since there are often distinguishing features such as one being a flying boat base and the other a land base, it was perhaps presumed that only a gross navigation error could lead to confusion.

After the war it was possible to allocate the surviving RAF stations a rational system of code letters easily linked to their actual names such as 'SY' for Shawbury and 'CD' for Cosford. Few civil aerodromes continued to use this practice, although Halfpenny Green does retain the concrete 'HG' code in front of the tower, this being laid when the airfield was refurbished for the RAF way back in 1952.

It was intended that the three or four beacon sites allocated to an aerodrome would have an air raid shelter and gunpost although it seems extremely doubtful that these were provided in every case. There was certainly a brick building at one of Bramcote's beacon sites close to the village of Arnesby, Leicestershire, as the rubble was still there in 1987.

When a Lancaster of 1654 HCU was wrecked in an over-shoot at the small Condover aerodrome near Shrewsbury in September 1942, the accident was attributed directly to a beacon flashing the wrong characteristic. The crew observed code letters which indicated they were in the vicinity of Dover and, already uncertain of their position and now thoroughly confused, they landed at the first available aerodrome.

Airfield code letters

Abingdon	AB
Acaster Malbis	AM
Acklington	AI
Alconbury	AY
Aldergrove	JV
Aldermaston	AM
Alness	YS
Andreas	VS
Angle	AE
Annan	AG
Ashbourne	AS
Aston Down	AD
Atcham	AP
Attlebridge	AT
Ayr	AR
Babdown Farm	BF
Baginton	NG
Balderton	BN
Ballyhalbert	YB
Ballykelly	IY
Banff	AF
Bardney	BA
Barford St John	BJ
Barkston Heath	BH
Bassingbourn	BS
Beccles	BE
Benbecula	BB
Benson	EB
Bentwaters	BY
Bibury	BI
Bicester	BC
Binbrook	BK
Bircotes	BR
Birch	JB
Bishops Court	IC
Bitteswell	BT
Blakehill Farm	XF
Blyton	AL
Bodney	BO
Bolt Head	OH
Boreham	JM
Boscombe Down	BD
Bottesford	AQ
Bottisham	IM
Boulmer	BM
Bourn	AU
Bovingdon	BV
Boxted	BX
Brawdy	BW
Breighton	AC
Brize Norton	BZ
Broadwell	JR
Bruntingthorpe	BP
Brunton	BN
Bungay	JO
Burn	AZ
Bury St Edmunds	BU
Calshot	KT
Calveley	KY
Castle Archdale	QA
Cark	KA
Castle Camps	CC
Castle Donington	CD
Castle Kennedy	QK
Castletown	AX
Catfoss	CA
Catterick	AK
Charmy Down	CH
Charterhall	KH
Chedburgh	CU
Cheddington	CZ
Chedworth	YW
Chelveston	CV
Chilbolton	CI
Chipping Ongar	JC
Chipping Warden	CW
Chivenor	IV
Church Broughton	CB
Church Fenton	CF
Church Lawford	CL
Cluntoe	UK
Coleby Grange	CG
Colerne	CQ
Coltishall	CS
Condover	DV
Coningsby	CY
Connel	KO
Cottam	CM
Cottesmore	CT
Cranage	RG

Cranfield	CX	Full Sutton	FS
Cranwell	CP	Gamston	GB
Croft	CR	Gaydon	GP
Crosby-on-Eden	KX	Glatton	GT
Croughton	AW	Gosfield	GF
Culmhead	UC	Goxhill	GX
Dalcross	DZ	Grafton Underwood	GU
Dallachy	DI	Grangemouth	GW
Dalton	DA	Gransden Lodge	GL
Darley Moor	DM	Graveley	GR
Davidstow Moor	DD	Great Dunmow	GD
Debach	DC	Great Massingham	GM
Debden	DB	Great Orton	GE
Deenethorpe	DP	Great Saling (Andrews Field)	GZ
Defford	DF	Great Sampford	GS
Deopham Green	DG	Greencastle	GQ
Desborough	DS	Greenham Common	GC
Digby	DJ	Grimsby	GY
Dishforth	DH	Grove	GV
Docking	DK	Halesworth	HA
Donna Nook	ZN	Halfpenny Green	HG
Dounreay	DN	Hampstead Norris	HN
Down Ampney	XA	Hardwick	HC
Downham Market	DO	Harlaxton	HH
Drem	DE	Harrington	HR
Driffield	DR	Harrowbeer	QB
Dumfries	DU	Harwell	HW
Dunholme Lodge	DL	Haverfordwest	AV
Dunkeswell	DW	Hawarden	HK
Duxford	DX	Hells Mouth	HU
Dyce	DY	Hemswell	HL
Earls Colne	EC	Hethel	HJ
East Fortune	EF	Hibaldstow	HE
East Kirkby	EK	High Ercall	HC
East Moor	EM	Hinton-in-the-Hedges	HI
East Wretham	UT	Hixon	HX
Edgehill	EH	Holme-on-Spalding-Moor	HM
Edzell	EZ	Honeybourne	HQ
Eglinton	QM	Honiley	HY
Elsham Wolds	ES	Honington	HT
Elvington	EV	Horham	JH
Enstone	EN	Horsham St Faith	HF
Errol	ER	Hullavington	HV
Evanton	ET	Hunsdon	HD
Exeter	EX	Husbands Bosworth	HZ
Eye	EY	Hutton Cranswick	CK
Fairwood Common	FC	Jurby	JY
Faldingworth	FH	Keevil	KV
Feltwell	FL	Kelstern	KS
Fersfield	WF	Kemble	KM
Findo Gask	FG	Kidlington	KD
Finmere	FI	Kimbolton	KI
Finningley	FB	Kingscliffe	KC
Fiskerton	FN	Kingston Bagpuize	KB
Folkingham	FO	Kinloss	KW
Fordoun	FR	Kinnel	KL
Foulsham	FU	Kirkistown	IK
Fowlmere	FW	Kirknewton	KK
Framlingham	FM	Kirmington	KG
Fraserburgh	FB	Knettishall	KN
Fulbeck	FK	Lakenheath	LK

Langar	LA	Mullaghmore	UL
Langham	LJ	Newmarket	NM
Lavenham	LV	Newton	NA
Leconfield	LC	New Zealand Farm	NZ
Leeming	LG	North Coates	NC
Leicester East	LE	North Creake	NO
Leiston	LI	Northolt	NH
Leuchars	LY	North Killingholme	NK
Lichfield	LF	North Luffenham	NL
Limavady	VA	North Pickenham	NP
Lindholme	LB	North Witham	NW
Linton-on-Ouse	LO	Nuneaton	NU
Lissett	LT	Nuthampstead	NT
Little Horwood	LH	Nutts Corner	XU
Little Rissington	LR	Oakington	OA
Little Snoring	LS	Oakley	OY
Little Staughton	LX	Oban	OQ
Little Walden	LL	Old Buckenham	OE
Llandwrog	LW	Old Sarum	OM
Long Kesh	JK	Ossington	ON
Long Marston	JS	Oulton	OU
Long Newnton	LN	Ouston	OS
Longtown	IO	Overton Heath	OV
Lossiemouth	OR	Pembroke Dock	PM
Ludford Magna	LM	Peplow (Childs Ercall)	CE
Ludham	LU	Perranporth	PP
Lulsgate Bottom	LP	Pershore	PR
Lyneham	YM	Perton	PT
Maghaberry	VM	Peterborough	PB
Macmerry	VC	Peterhead	PH
Manby	MY	Pocklington	PC
Marham	MR	Podington	PM
Market Harborough	MB	Polebrook	PK
Marston Moor	MA	Port Ellen	PE
Martlesham Heath	MH	Portreath	PA
Matching	MC	Poulton	PU
Matlask	MK	Predannack	PD
Melbourne	ME	Prestwick	PW
Melton Mowbray	MM	Rackheath	RK
Membury	XY	Ramsbury	RY
Mendlesham	MZ	Rattlesden	RS
Mepal	MP	Raydon	RA
Merryfield	IA	Rhoose	RH
Metfield	MT	Riccall	RC
Metheringham	MN	Ridgewell	RD
Methwold	ML	Rivenhall	RL
Middleton St George	MG	Rufforth	RU
Middle Wallop	MW	St Angelo	JA
Mildenhall	MI	St Athan	ZA
Milfield	IL	St Davids	SD
Millom	MJ	St Eval	ZE
Milltown	IT	St Mawgan	ZM
Molesworth	MX	Saltby	SY
Mona	MU	Sandtoft	SF
Montrose	MS	Scampton	SA
Moreton-in-Marsh	MO	Scorton	SO
Moreton Valence	MV	Sculthorpe	SP
Morpeth	EP	Seething	SE
Mount Batten	ZB	Seighford	YD
Mount Farm	MF	Shawbury	ZY
Montford Bridge	MD	Sherburn-in-Elmet	SH

Shepherds Grove	HP	Upottery	UO
Shipdham	SJ	Upper Heyford	UH
Shobdon	SR	Upwood	UD
Sibson	SI	Valley	VY
Silloth	IS	Waddington	WA
Silverstone	SV	Warboys	WB
Skeabrae	KJ	Warton	OT
Skellingthorpe	SG	Watchfield	WE
Skipton-on-Swale	SK	Waterbeach	WJ
Skitten	NS	Wattisham	WT
Sleap	YP	Watton	WN
Snailwell	SW	Welford	WZ
Snaith	SX	Wellesbourne Mountford	WM
Snetterton Heath	SN	Wellingore	JW
Snitterfield	KF	Wendling	WU
South Cerney	SC	Westcott	WX
Southrop	KP	West Freugh	EW
Spanhoe	UY	Westley	UL
Speke	PZ	Weston-on-the-Green	WG
Spilsby	SL	Weston Zoyland	ZW
Spitalgate	GH	West Raynham	WR
Squires Gate	ZG	Wethersfield	UW
Stansted	KT	Wheaton Aston	WH
Stanton Harcourt	ST	Wick	WC
Stapleford Tawney	KZ	Wickenby	UI
Steeple Morden	KR	Wigsley	UG
Stornoway	ZX	Wigtown	GO
Stracathro	ZO	Winfield	IW
Stradishall	NX	Wing	UX
Stratford	NF	Winkleigh	WK
Strubby	NY	Winthorpe	WE
Sturgate	US	Witchford	EL
Sudbury	SU	Wittering	WI
Sullom Voe	QV	Wombleton	UM
Sumburgh	UM	Woodhall Spa	WS
Sutton Bridge	SB	Woodhaven	OW
Swannington	NG	Woodvale	OD
Swanton Morley	SM	Woolfox Lodge	WL
Swinderby	NR	Worksop	WP
Syerston	YM	Wormingford	WO
Tain	TN	Wratting Common	WW
Talbenny	TZ	Wrexham	RW
Tatenhill	VL	Wymeswold	WD
Templeton	TV	Wyton	WY
Tempsford	TE	Zeals	ZL
Ternhill	TR	*For Day Use Only:*	
Tholthorpe	TH	Aberporth	AH
Thornaby	TB	Appledram	AO
Thorpe Abbots	TA	Ashford	ZF
Thurleigh	TL	Beaulieu	BQ
Tibenham	TM	Biggin Hill	GI
Tilstock	OK	Bisterne	IZ
Tiree	TI	Bognor	OG
Tollerton	TO	Bradwell Bay	RB
Toome	TG	Brenzett	ZT
Topcliffe	TP	Castle Combe	CJ
Tuddenham	TD	Chailey	AJ
Turnberry	TU	Chipping Norton	CN
Turnhouse	TS	Christchurch	XC
Turweston	TW	Coolham	XQ
Twinwoods Farm	TF	Croydon	CO

Deanland	XB	Needs Oar Point	NI
Detling	DQ	Netheravon	NE
Dunsfold	DT	Newchurch	XK
Eastchurch	EA	New Romney	XR
Fairlop	FP	North Weald	NQ
Fairford	FA	Odiham	OI
Ford	FD	Penshurst	PS
Friston	FX	Redhill	RI
Funtington	FJ	Rochford	RO
Gatwick	GK	Rollestone	RZ
Gosport	GJ	Sawbridgeworth	ZH
Gravesend	GM	Selsey	ZS
Hartford Bridge	XB	Shoreham	SQ
Hawkinge	VK	Shrewton	RE
Headcorn	ED	Staplehurst	XS
Hendon	ND	Stoke Orchard	SZ
Heston	HS	Stoney Cross	SS
High Halden	IH	Swingfield	IF
Hornchurch	HO	Tangmere	RN
Horne	OR	Tarrant Rushton	TK
Hurn	KU	Tealing	TG
Ibsley	IB	Thorney Island	TC
Kenley	KE	Thruxton	TX
Kingsnorth	IN	Towyn	TY
Lasham	LQ	Upavon	UA
Lashenden	XL	Warmwell	XW
Lydd	YL	Wasthampnett	WQ
Lymington	LZ	West Malling	VG
Lympne	PY	Windrush	UR
Manston	MQ	Winkton	XT
Merston	XM	Woodchurch	XO

Chapter 12

Fido

Many unlikely ideas proved their worth during the Second World War. One of the most weird was Fido, which used heat to disperse fog from an airfield runway. In round figures, Fido saved 2,500 aircraft and 10,000 aircrew at a cost of 30 million gallons of petrol.

There is still controversy as to the precise meaning of the term *Fido*, but both versions are, in fact, correct. Originally it stood for 'Fog Investigation Dispersal Operation' but in June 1945 the RAF announced officially that it preferred 'Fog, Intensive, Dispersal Of'. The system owed its origin to pre-war experiments held at the Royal Aircraft Establishments at Martlesham Heath and Farnborough. Alcohol fuels were burned in these trials but the results were disappointing and research was abandoned in the summer of 1939. Even before this, in 1921 the possibility of dispersing fog over airfields had been discussed in the publications of the Aeronautical Research Committee but, apart from the meteorological study of fogs, no practical experiments were made until 1937.

RAF Bomber Command's strength increased enormously in 1941 and 1942 but operations were still very much at the mercy of the weather with early morning fog often playing havoc with returning bombers. Many aircraft were destroyed because the crews had to bale out as a safe landing was impossible. On a typical night, seven Wellingtons were lost with four airmen killed. The problem seemed insoluble and could be alleviated only very slightly by better training in approaches on radio beams. Winston Churchill was aware of the pre-war trials and issued a directive on 26 September 1942 to Geoffrey Lloyd, the Minister responsible for the Petroleum Warfare Department. In this, he stated, 'It is of great importance to find means to dissipate fog at aerodromes so that aircraft can land safely. Let full experiments to this end be put in hand with all expedition by the Petroleum Warfare

Department. They should be given every support.'

A full-scale experimental station was set up in an uncompleted reservoir near Staines, loaned by the Metropolitan Water Board. An illustration of the urgency of the situation is that the development work was performed simultaneously with the first trial installation at an operational airfield, namely Graveley, near St Neots. The scientists had been greeted with apathy when they approached Bomber Command Main Force Groups in order to secure the use of an airfield for trials. Despite Churchill's backing for the scheme, various excuses were given as to why no operational base was available. Accordingly, the last hope was No 8 (Pathfinder Force) Group and here they found an unexpected ally in the shape of the then Air Commodore D.C.T. Bennett, DSO. Bennett was highly enthusiastic about the idea and immediately nominated Graveley as the most suitable aerodrome for their use.

Model experiments began at the Earls Court ice-skating rink using a wind tunnel and heat from small-scale butane burners. Almost 500,000 readings were analysed to ascertain heat flow paths under variations of wind speed and direction, and rates of heat evolution. Problems investigated included the intrusion of fog through gaps, the effects of greater runway width and the special requirements of a coastal station. Field tests were carried out at Staines with lines of experimental burners, using 100 ft fire ladders and a balloon for observation. Both full and small-scale tests showed that fog would always be cleared if the air temperature could be increased by 4-7° Fahrenheit.

The first aerodrome installation required 6,900 burners and 30 in stand-pipes, 2 ft apart in a double row, which caused serious obstruction. Another snag was the dense smoke emitted when petrol was used, clear combustion

Lancaster of 35 Squadron, part of the Pathfinder Force at Graveley during a Fido test. The picture illustrates the intense heat generated by the system and the distance from the runway at which the pipes were sided (IWM CH15271).

only being obtainable when a mixture containing 80 per cent alcohol was employed. The latter was not available on the scale envisaged but, fortunately, the answer soon revealed itself. It was discovered that petrol in the feed pipes was heated by conduction and, by the time it reached the farthest point from its entry into the system, it was vaporized sufficiently to burn with a smaller and cleaner flame. The petrol flow was rearranged so that it travelled three times up and down the length of the burners in order to absorb enough radiant heat. The principle was exactly the same as a Primus stove but on an enormous scale.

The resultant burner became known as the Haigas (Hartley Anglo-Iranian Gas, after its designer, Hartley) and 50 yds was the maximum practical length, enabling one man to control from one point a pair of burners covering 100 yd of runway. With the increase in heat output, only one line was now required on each side of the Graveley runway and construction was hurriedly adapted. The system was almost perfected with the addition of a modification known as the Haigill Burner (Hartley Anglo-Iranian Gill), which became standard equipment for all 15 wartime installations.

Difficulties were dealt with as they occurred. For example, bomber airfields usually had three intersecting runways which effectively cut the Fido-equipped runway into two or three parts. It was essential to prevent the intrusion of fog through the 150 yd gap in the burner lines without obstructing the intersecting runways. A temporary solution was obtained at Graveley by mounting Haigas Burners on steel 'gates' hinged at one end and mounted on rollers, which were manhandled or tractored into position across intersections. A second problem was fog drifting into the open ends of the Fido installation, such as at the opposite end of the runway from touchdown. Various methods of overcoming this were tried but lengthening the burner lines to beyond the runway's end proved to be the most effective remedy. Similarly, the intersecting runway difficulty was also solved by trenching the burner lines to prevent obstruction.

The Graveley Fido was ready for use in January 1943, the first test burn causing so much smoke and flame that fire engines rushed to the airfield from a 20 mile radius resulting in the mess's beer supplies being consumed in record time as consolation! The first flying test was made by Air Commodore Bennett on 18 February 1943. He borrowed Lancaster W4854 of 156 Sqn and flew it over from Oakington to Graveley in clear weather and reported that, although the glare was considerable, the turbulence was not excessive. The first test landing in fog was made by an Oxford on 17 July 1943, the pilot being Wing Commander John Wooldridge, Aeronautical Adviser to the Petroleum Warfare Department. After early trials it was decided that seven more airfields were to be equipped with Fido,

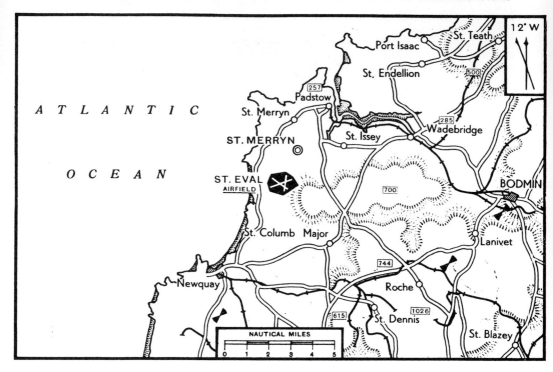

ALL HEIGHTS IN FEET ABOVE MEAN SEA LEVEL

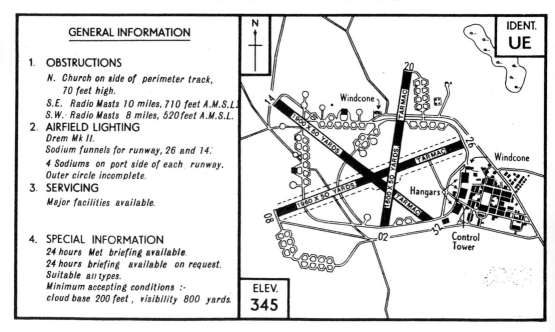

GENERAL INFORMATION

1. **OBSTRUCTIONS**
   N. Church on side of perimeter track,
   70 feet high.
   S.E. Radio Masts 10 miles, 710 feet A.M.S.L.
   S.W. Radio Masts 8 miles, 520 feet A.M.S.L.

2. **AIRFIELD LIGHTING**
   Drem Mk II.
   Sodium funnels for runway, 26 and 14.
   4 Sodiums on port side of each runway.
   Outer circle incomplete.

3. **SERVICING**
   Major facilities available.

4. **SPECIAL INFORMATION**
   24 hours Met briefing available.
   24 hours briefing available on request.
   Suitable all types.
   Minimum accepting conditions :-
   cloud base 200 feet, visibility 800 yards.

IDENT.
UE

ELEV.
345

St Eval, Cornwall, was selected as one of the Fido stations.

the first of these being Downham Market in Norfolk.

Wing Commander Wooldridge made most of the Fido tests in an Oxford, one being flown under the worst possible conditions for fog clearance — heavy moist mist with rain clouds drifting above. His report read:

'At 1600 hours on November 21 1943 the test aircraft took off from RAF Feltwell and set course for RAF Downham Market, where a specimen landing was to be attempted. The ground was obscured immediately after take-off and the fog bank eventually cleared between 300-400 feet. A cloud layer was then seen to be lying 300 feet above the aircraft and there were additional indications of cloud extending in further layers up to 15,000 feet. The windscreen of the aircraft was misted over with moisture throughout.

'The aircraft set course for Downham, flying solely on instruments, and the Downham beam was picked up successfully shortly after take-off. So bad were general conditions, however, that the lighted burners were not sighted until the aircraft was flying at 1,500 feet across the aerodrome and they first appeared as a considerable diffused red glow. By the time we were directly overhead, the plan of the burners could be seen quite clearly through the intervening mist and low cloud.

'Normal beam approach procedure was carried out, with the aircraft again flying in completely blind conditions until it reached a point almost 1,000 yards from the beginning of the runway. From that point on, the burners became progressively more visible and the pilot was able to 'line up' his aircraft by *looking out ahead* and a satisfactory landing was made. The local meteorology office informed us that the cloud base was below 100 feet with moderately heavy rain.

'Conclusions: Only a moderately accurate blind approach was necessary to get the aircraft to within 1000 yards of the runway. It should be borne in mind that the weather conditions were so bad that they could hardly be expected to have materialized in a few hours, as would be the case in a return from operations. The fog over Downham Market had lain for three days and large amounts of cloud had drifted in above. This cloud was giving a percentage of precipitation which implied that Fido had to deal with moisture 60 per cent beyond its capacity. Nevertheless, it is the considered opinion of the two pilots in the aircraft that a medium experienced four-engined pilot (400 hours) could have landed his machine safely.'

Experiments revealed that if the apparatus was moved downwind, the pilot would find 500 yds of his approach cleared and 500 yds of the runway after that, which was obviously better than breaking out of the fog suddenly and trying to land at the same time. Another discovery was that even in the filthiest weather the fierce crimson light given off was visible for some distance from the aerodrome and penetrating as much as 1,500 ft of cloud. Parallel trials at Lakenheath with coke burners were abandoned because it took three hours before the initial smoke drifted away and sufficient heat was generated to clear the fog. An even worse problem was how to extinguish the fires quickly, coupled with the fact that the heavy iron braziers were an unacceptable obstruction.

Squadron Leader K.F. Jolly, the Commanding Officer of 1519 Beam Approach Training Flight at Feltwell, made a test landing on 11 November 1943 in Oxford HN748, probably because a less biased opinion was needed. He too was converted and commented, 'Fido is a practical emergency aid, provided the pilot is sufficiently competent in instrument flying and beam approach on the aircraft type.'

History was made on the night of 19 November 1943 when four Halifaxes of 35 Sqn which were returning from the Ruhr found their base at Graveley covered by radiation fog with a visibility of 100 yds. Within 10 minutes of lighting up, Fido cleared a lane along the runway in which the equivalent visibility was 2 to 4 miles and the bombers landed without incident.

Other installations followed at Ludford Magna, Fiskerton, Metheringham and Sturgate in Lincolnshire, Melbourne and Carnaby in Yorkshire, Foulsham in Norfolk, Tuddenham and Woodbridge in Suffolk, Bradwell Bay in Essex, Manston in Kent, Blackbushe in Hampshire and St Eval in Cornwall. The intention was to provide at least one Fido-equipped airfield in each area where there was a concentration of bomber bases, together with installations at the three emergency landing grounds. St Eval was the exception since it was a Coastal Command station which required additional lines of burners 75 yd outside the normal lines to cope with wet sea fogs. Basic Haigill Burners were also installed in the USA during 1944 at Wright Field, Dayton, Ohio and in the Aleutian Islands where the constant fogs played havoc with the 11th Air Force's bombing campaign against the Japanese.

Experience soon showed that fog was not only dispersed from the runway, but that low stratus cloud was also lifted to a base of about 400 ft. Official guidance to pilots on the use of Fido was brief:

'Cockpit lighting should be turned up fully during the approach. A member of the crew should monitor and repeat height and airspeed. Slight turbulence may be encountered when entering the cleared approach but no worse than that expected on a hot summer's afternoon. Pilots should keep their eyes on the centre of the runway between the burner lines. They should also anticipate and correct any tendency to flatten out too high.'

The late Maurice A. Smith, DFC, a former editor of *Flight* magazine described a Fido landing thus:

'For a pilot it was a most encouraging — and warming — beacon to guide him home and down. there was, perhaps, some doubt about the turn in to the funnel if the fog layer was very deep and thick, but, once settled on the approach, all was normal and the first slight turbulence was met near the runway end. After that, it was a case of flying — slightly dazzled — into a great glowing cathedral with fire-framed nave and landing much as though high-powered goosenecks marked the runway.'

Wartime Fido was provided with manual control of lighting-up. Single Haigill Burners took three minutes to light up and disperse initial smoke, but multiple installations required 20 minutes since the lack of manpower necessitated lighting up in sequence. Paraffin flares placed near burners were later used to give semi-automatic ignition and quicker starting. Burners could be idled at low rates in between aircraft landing in order to economize on fuel. If an aircraft swung on to the pipes, the petrol flow through the appropriate section could be cut off immediately by means of a valve. At the three Emergency Landing Grounds, gaps were left in the burner lines so that ground crews could tow damaged or immobile aircraft clear of the runway without delay.

Fido-assisted landings soon became routine, 65 being made at Carnaby ELG alone in December 1944. At the same strip in 31 January 1945, 65 USAAF Liberators and 6 Halifaxes landed safely in thick fog. Things did not always go so well, however, such as in the early hours of 2 August 1944 when a Halifax struck a house chimney with its port outer engine. It staggered on and made a good landing with the propeller missing and the engine

on fire. Carnaby also witnessed several intentional wheels-up landings between the flames.

Fido's other great contribution to the war effort was stated officially to be the defeat of Field-Marshal von Runstedt's Ardennes offensive in December 1944. Bomber Command was asked by the Army for help in stopping the attack as the 2nd TAF was grounded by poor weather. Great accuracy was essential in marking the target as it was so near to our own troops. The Main Force stations were clear but the Pathfinder fields were in fog. Fido was lit at Graveley and 11 Lancasters took off and were able to mark the target with their usual accuracy.

Fido also enabled Bomber Command to maintain its continuity of operations despite doubtful weather forecasts, as there was always somewhere the force could land safely provided that the number of aircraft was kept within certain limits. Without it, the bombing of Berlin by Mosquitoes on 30 consecutive nights could never have been risked.

To supply the enormous amounts of fuel needed, special sidings for petrol trains were constructed on the nearest railway to each aerodrome and large pipelines were laid to pump the fuel to tankage adjacent to the airstrip. Apart from the permanent installations, development work was done on a portable system to meet an anticipated demand for Fido on the Continent after the coming invasion. The result was the Haifox (Portable) Burner (Hartley Anglo-Iranian Fox) and a further improvement, the Light Portable Marker Burner, evolved in November 1944 in response to requests for runway or approach funnel marker flames for use at airfields lacking full Fido equipment. These markers were issued to TAF Wings with semi-rotary hand pumps, whilst a USAAF station used them with road tankers.

The burner types described above were designed for ease of installation on an existing airfield with minimal disruption to traffic and were therefore above ground except where crossing intersecting runways. Early in 1944 it was decided, as a long-term policy for possible peace-time use, to design permanent underground installations which eliminated all obstruction to aircraft. The first development along these lines was the Rapex Burner (*Rap*idly *Ex*tinguished) which was placed in troughs beneath a cast iron grid capable of supporting a heavy bomber. The Rapex was installed across two emergency runways at Carnaby and Woodbridge in 1944, so as to 'seal off' the ends of the extra-wide strips.

A similar burner, the Hades, was introduced for normal side-line fitting and the Manston Fido was totally converted to this type. Further improvements led to the Hairpin Burner

Mosquito landing at Graveley during a Fido test (IWM CH15273).

which was installed at Blackbushe at the far end of the earlier Haigill system. It was so promising that it eventually replaced the latter but it was found, however, that Hairpin Burners in long lines became starved of air in certain wind conditions, resulting in slow starting and reduced heat output. A modification cured this fault completely and, known as Haiflot, this became the ultimate Fido design, providing quicker starting than that of any previous type.

As soon as the war ended, Fido was progressively withdrawn until the only operational station remaining was Manston, although the RAF would have liked to have retained Graveley as well. A Notam issued in 1947 laid down these conditions for the provision of Fido: (a) when, owing to a sudden widespread deterioration in weather, an aircraft having passed its point-of-no-return is unable to reach an aerodrome outside the fog-affected area; and (b) when an aircraft is in a state of emergency and must effect a landing quickly within the area affected by fog. It was stressed that Fido was strictly an emergency facility which must in no way influence operators to undertake flights which were unlikely to terminate at an aerodrome fit for visual approach or for normal instrument landings.

The Ministry of Civil Aviation reserved the right to investigate each cause of its use. Apart from the normal landing fee, no extra charge was made in cases of genuine emergency, but if the enquiry showed that it could have been avoided by better planning or airmanship, the operator could be compelled to pay the full cost of the burn. The Manston charges at that time were £500 for the warming-up period of 15 minutes and £250 for each subsequent minute. If the aircraft was positioned correctly, it was possible to land within the last three or four minutes of the warming-up period.

Early in May 1948, Blackbushe became the second peace-time Fido airfield, although it used a Haigill Mk 5 surface-type system, not its original sub-surface installation. A test burn was laid on for interested aircraft operators but it appears that the system was only once used in anger, and this for a take-off. On 30 November 1948 Airwork Viking G-AJFS took off from Blackbushe with a priority cargo of banknotes. The aircraft had been chartered by the Crown Agents and the destination was Accra on the Gold Coast, via Gibraltar. The 30 yd visibility increased with Fido to between 600 and 800 yd even though the whole system was not lit.

In November 1952, the Blackbushe Fido was given a thorough overhaul prior to being placed on a care and maintenance basis, and this was adjudged to be a good opportunity for a test burn. The chance was seized by the Ministry of Civil Aviation and the airline corporations to arrange some trial Fido landings by civil aircraft, a BEA Ambassador and Viking, a BOAC York and an MCA Dove taking part. One reason for the exercise was to ascertain passenger reaction which turned out to be favourable but perhaps not truly representative as the people concerned were mainly from the aircraft industry. It was proposed to install Fido at Heathrow, the cost to be shared by user airlines, but the plan was dropped owing to a general unwillingness, apart from BEA, to furnish the necessary finance. The only work carried out at Heathrow was confined to No 1 Runway, being limited to a few foundations for tanks and pipeline channels in the concrete.

Blackbushe Fido was retained as a standby in the event of the Manston Fido becoming unserviceable, but as nobody seemed to need the equipment in peace-time Manston's was finally withdrawn in about 1959. The Category III Instrument Landing System and the oil crisis ensured that it would never be revived. Difficult to control and with a voracious appetite, Fido was nobody's pet, except to a few thousand aircrew who saw him as a St Bernard.

Chapter 13

Advanced Landing Grounds in south-east England

During the RAF's pre-war expansion, almost all new airfields were sited in East Anglia to meet a possible threat from Germany which lay to the east. France, the traditional enemy, had long been an ally so there was little point in augmenting the few RAF stations located in the south and south-east. However, when France fell in 1940, the *Luftwaffe* took over its northern bases and the handful of airfields in the Home Counties were barely able to cope with the onslaught.

When the time came to prepare for an invasion of the Continent, temporary airfields known as Advanced Landing Grounds (ALGs) were laid to accommodate dozens of RAF and USAAF squadrons. Redundant when the war moved on, the ALGs were soon torn up and restored to their former owners, and those few months of hectic activity, vital to establish a foothold in Europe, have left almost no trace on the landscape today.

It is a measure of British optimism that we would eventually win the war despite Germany's apparent invincibility that, as early as 4 May 1942, an Air Ministry staff officer wrote:

> 'One of the limiting factors of the intensive operations envisaged in the Pas-de-Calais area is the number of landing grounds available in Kent and Sussex. Therefore, then, at least six more airfields should if possible be provided in this area. The construction of permanent aerodromes would prove too long a process. They would not require full facilities normally provided at permanent stations but it would, however, be necessary to provide runways. Sommerfeld Track would suffice with perimeter track, refuelling and re-arming facilities, and a limited number of hard-standings and blister hangars for day-to-day maintenance. All major repair work on aircraft would be carried out on permanent stations.'

The Air Ministry planning staff were indeed working on a proposed landing in the Pas-de-Calais, known as Operation *Hadrian* and the rudimentary aerodromes were termed ALGs to give a measure of security. The plan was postponed indefinitely, however, presumably because of the débâcle at Dieppe in August 1942, but ALG construction was allowed to proceed. It was now on a more ambitious scale, the search for sites being extended to cover the entire area south of a line Frinton-Reading-Weston-Super-Mare and the suggestion of six ALGs soon being increased to more than 20, with 70 possible sites from which to choose. It should be noted that the term 'ALG' had been used before by the RAF but merely to indicate a forward airfield near the coast where a refuelling or re-arming stop could be made, rather than a specially-built base.

Space does not permit the listing of all the projected locations but examples were No 51 at Linstead, three miles south-east of Sittingbourne, No 53 at Ryde, Isle of Wight, No 56 at Somerton, Isle of Wight (presumably on the site of Saunders-Roe's airfield), No 58 at Frost Hill, one mile south of Overton, Hants, No 64 at Stowry, eight miles south of Bristol and No 68 at Chitterne, Wilts. None of these was developed to the relief of the landowners (if they ever knew what was going on). A few sites were chosen for full-size airfields, an example being Dunsfold.

Work started on the ALGs in the autumn of 1942. The specification was now standardized at two metal track runways, one 1,600 yd and the other 1,400 yd in length, 50 yd wide and with a further width of 50 yd at each side to be levelled and cleared of obstructions. The longer runway was to be aligned with the prevailing wind and, as it was essential to take up as little agricultural land as possible, the perimeter track was placed as close to the runways as was permissible. This led to taxi-tracks running parallel to and crossing runways, with numerous ground collisions as a result when the ALGs became operational.

Four blister hangars were planned at each with two being erected initially and the remainder as and when supplies and labour permitted. Accommodation was provided on a standard scale of 100 officers and 2,000 other ranks. In practice, this meant tents and locally requisitioned property, but some of the fields acquired hutted camps in 1944. The total number of aircraft to be based was 50 and no night flying or beam approach facilities were considered necessary. Bomb stores were built only at Lashenden and Woodchurch to begin with, both being earmarked for light bombers. For the others it was said that a number of woodland areas adjacent to roads and central to clutches of ALGs could be used as Air Ammunition Parks.

Since civilian labour was already being hard-pressed to finish permanent airfields, the ALGs were built in the main by RAF Airfield Construction units with some help from the US Army, and some were laid by Airfield Construction Groups of the Royal Engineers. No 16 ACG, for example, built Swingfield in Sussex between 10 May and 16 June 1943. The same ACG started work on Deanland on 2 July, a Spitfire with a wounded pilot making a forced landing on the new runway two days later. Amongst those prepared solely by RAF personnel were Needs Oar Point, Appledram, Bisterne, Selsey and Lymington.

Wherever possible, poor quality farmland was chosen when the original list of sites was narrowed down. There was, however, friction with the Ministry of Agriculture who demanded that the development of certain

Surviving Blister hangar at ex-Thunderbolt ALG, Lymington, Hants (Brian Martin).

sites, including Appledram, Bisterne and Selsey, be abandoned. Air Ministry planners refused to give them up but, as a compromise, some ALGs not required immediately were utilized for grazing land, others such as Winkton being kept clear as emergency landing grounds.

The development of the metal tracking which formed the runways and taxi-ways at ALGs is an interesting study in its own right. The function of the tracking was to distribute wheel loads over a larger area of ground than the contact area of the tyres, thus enabling aircraft to operate under surface conditions which might otherwise prove difficult or impossible. It also delayed deterioration of the soil's natural bearing capacity owing to abrasion.

Possibly the first occasion when metal track was used as an aid to wheeled traffic occurred in the Middle East during the First World War when it was discovered in the course of Allenby's campaign that ordinary wire netting laid on the desert sand helped the passage of vehicles. Its first recorded use by aircraft was at Kilia near Constantinople in 1922 when the British Army was in occupation. The mud was so bad that a rough runway was made with wire netting stretched over canvas and pegged. By this means it was hoped to get the Bristol Fighters of 4 Squadron to flying speed before they became bogged down. Even on this 'runway' they sank 5 or 6 in and conditions worsened until aircraft had to stand on planks even when in their hangars.

Between the wars, the British Army used a material known as Army Track to make temporary roads. It consisted of diamond-shaped wire mesh supplied in rolls 35 ft long and 12 ft wide. Its use as an airfield track was considered early in the Second World War and several sites were provided with it. It had many defects, however, the main one being the difficulty experienced in making it lie flat on the ground. Another experimental surface tested in 1939 was Chevron Grid which was

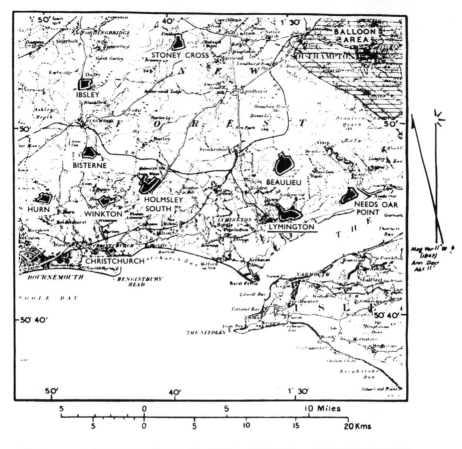

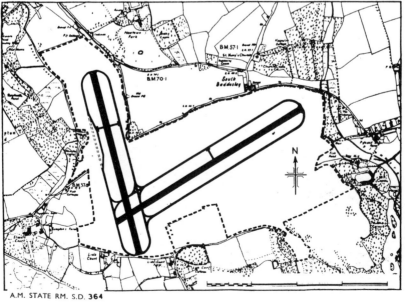

A.M. STATE RM. S.D. **364**

designed on the principle of certain Swiss and French types. It took its name from its construction of flat, steel bars laced in a chevron pattern into tee-bar stringers. Despite considerable load-bearing capacity, it suffered from the disadvantage of slow and cumbersome panel connection and was never produced in quantity.

To remedy this lack of a satisfactory surfacing medium, Kurt Sommerfeld, an expatriate Austrian engineer, adapted the First World War wire-netting idea. The result was known as Sommerfeld Track and a full-scale trial carried out by the Royal Engineers early in 1941 proved sufficiently encouraging to justify its production. It was first used operationally in the North African campaign and soon earned the nickname *Tin Lino*. Mild steel bars and rods were employed to hold the netting rigid and angle iron pickets kept it on the ground. All the ALGs started life with Sommerfeld runways, but wear and tear and heavier aircraft were to change this.

Experience with Sommerfeld Track led to the formulation of service requirements for airfield tracking. Summarized, they stated that the track should lend itself to production on a large scale using simple manufacturing processes which utilized readily available raw materials. The units which made up the track should be easily transportable by ship, rail or

cargo aircraft, robust enough to withstand rough handling and heavy traffic, and easily laid under active service conditions by unskilled labour. Track sections damaged by enemy action or aircraft accident were to be capable of quick replacement and it should be possible to dismantle tracks for transport and use elsewhere. Finally, the track should possess a reasonably non-skid surface, be inconspicuous from the air or readily lend itself to camouflage treatment.

The second major advance in British track design was Square Mesh Track (SMT), a development of the welded mesh used as a reinforcement in concrete roads and other structures. Devised and patented by the British Reinforced Engineering Co Ltd and sometimes known as BRC Track, it consisted of 3 in square mesh and was usually supplied in rolls 7 ft 3 in wide and 77 ft 3 in long. It was easy to make, and at one time production in the UK was running at a rate of over 1,000,000 sq yd per month. The unrolled sections were connected by overlapping one or two meshes and clipping them together.

SMT runways were tested with aircraft by British and American engineers independently during 1943. It was found that there was a pronounced tendency for a billow or wave to form, sometimes reaching a magnitude which damaged aircraft undercarriages. This alarm-

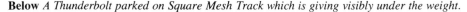

Left *A typical South Coast ALG: Lymington, Hampshire.*

Below *A Thunderbolt parked on Square Mesh Track which is giving visibly under the weight.*

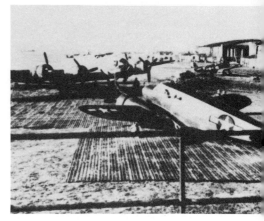

Above left *PSP and Channel Track on a farm on the edge of the former Bisterne ALG in Hampshire.*

Above right *Bobcat and B-17 parked on extensive areas of PSP adjacent to the tower at Duxford in 1944.*

ing characteristic was eventually cured by tensioning the track and picketing it down. SMT was probably the most widely used temporary runway material in the UK and Northern Europe, and had the distinction of forming the first tracked runway laid in the Normandy beach-head.

As 2nd Tactical Air Force squadrons began to operate from ALGs in the summer of 1943, the shortcomings of the Sommerfeld surfaces were revealed. Many Spitfires had their tailwheels torn off on loose tracking and a modification had to be introduced early in 1944 to give greater clearance to the tailwheel fork on 2nd TAF Spitfires. The best answer, however, was to replace the Sommerfeld Track with SMT and this was done at most, if not all, the ALGs in the spring of 1944. The other reason was the seven ton weight of the 9th USAAF's Thunderbolts which were now being stationed on them.

Moving on a little in time, we come to the final type to be devised in the UK during the war, namely Channel Track. This was an attempt to obtain a large measure of load distribution with a relatively small amount of material. The track comprised rectangular panels 11 ft by 16 ft connected to each other across the runway by an interlocking joint and longitudinally by shaped joint cover plates. When tested on soft ground early in 1945, the track behaved very well, with no undue tyre wear being caused. However, the war finished before this type was used in any quantity but odd panels can still be seen at a few airfield locations in England.

The Americans, meanwhile, had been designing their own tracks, unhindered by the limitations on the supply of steel which had forced the British to concentrate on wire mesh types. Pierced Steel Plank (PSP), the best known of all, was developed in the USA prior to that country's entry into the war, and was subsequently used far more widely than any other kind, British or American. Initially called Marstron Strip after the first trial installation during manoeuvres near the town of this name in North Carolina, it was employed extensively in every theatre of war and was produced in enormous quantities.

PSP was made in panels 1 ft 3 in wide by 10 ft long with longitudinal ribs for stiffness and punched holes to reduce weight and assist drainage. Lugs and slots on both edges enabled connections to be made and spring clips locked them together. Simple to manufacture and requiring less shipping space per ton than any other type it was, however, comparatively heavy and uneconomical in material. It shared the advantage common to all metal runways of providing natural camouflage, since the holes permitted grass and weeds to grow and merge with the surrounding area. It could also be painted if necessary.

In use, it had a few limitations, namely a tendency to retain moisture and pump up mud through the holes when subjected to repeated loads in wet weather. To counter this and also to reduce dust in hot weather, PSP was frequently laid on a bed of straw. Several permanent grass airfields in Britain were given PSP runways when supplies allowed. Cranage in Cheshire had two excellent runways of the material to replace the worn out Army Track which its Navigation School Ansons and Oxfords had suffered for years. Photographs exist showing how the plates were neatly cut and welded at the runway intersection and they even had cut-outs for light fittings.

The other unfortunate characteristic was revealed when PSP was laid on ground of bearing capacity inadequate for the traffic loads which it was to carry, namely that the panels would curl at the edges making a dangerous hazard for aircraft. This was avoided by laying a base of hard core first when the soil was considered unstable. A similar problem was encountered with SMT and, shortly before D-Day to give the strength necessary for Thunderbolt operations, one runway on each of their ALGs had to be relaid. Fortunately, Hampshire is well served with sources of gravel and sand as nearly 10,000 tons were needed to complete the work in time.

The other major American design was Bar and Rod Track, but though comparable in performance and lighter than PSP, it was far more difficult to manufacture. Produced in two versions, heavy and light, it was made up of panels 12 ft long by 3 ft wide, consisting of a framework of flat, round-edged bars welded to transverse rods. Each section was fastened to the next by clips. Its use was confined mainly to reinforcing areas of heavy wear on ALGs, such as taxi-way bends and marshalling points. Elsewhere, it was laid at many permanent airfields to augment the existing dispersals. When these stations were abandoned after the war, the local farmers removed sections *en masse*, with the result that Bar and Rod — and SMT as well — can be seen for a radius of many miles doing service as fencing or plugging gaps in hedges.

A US variety which was produced on a limited scale only was Irving Grid, based on the grid flooring used in ships' engine rooms. Made up of sections 12 ft 6 in long by 22 in

wide, it suffered from a structural weakness caused by the rivet holes in the longitudinal bars. Production was complicated and the weight was relatively high for the performance given. The only piece I have ever seen is at Condover aerodrome in Shropshire, in use as a fence.

One of the most significant innovations in temporary runways was Prefabricated Bitumen Surfacing (PBS), a carpet of hessian cloth impregnated with bitumen to render it waterproof. Used mainly on the Continent and hardly at all in England, except for parts of the Thunderbolt ALGs in Hampshire, I shall cover its development in the next chapter.

Non-metallic surfacing had been tried out before at Redhill where coir matting runways were laid by the Royal Engineers in the winter of 1940-41 when that airfield was almost a swamp. Used continuously by fighters, the matting required constant maintenance, 20 men being employed on it daily. Sawbridgeworth in Hertfordshire also had coir runways and at Montrose in Scotland, the training aerodrome had this material covering the worn out grass runway intersections. Montrose was later given Army Track strips and stretches of them can still be seen today. During the war, few ostensibly grass airfields were operated without some form of artificial surface, as intensive flying activity was just not possible in all weathers, except perhaps by light aircraft such as the Tiger Moth.

When spring arrived in 1944 and the ALGs became dry enough for use by aircraft and motor transport, 2nd TAF and 9th Air Force units began to occupy them. About 12 had been active for varying periods during the summer and autumn of 1943 but as soon as rainfall began to affect them, aircraft moved to permanent airfields and left the ALGs under care and maintenance.

In April 1944, Horne in Sussex was a typical ALG, having two SMT runways with marshalling areas and perimeter tracks in a

A typical scene on an ALG: Tempest being serviced at Newchurch, Kent (IWM CH14088).

Butler Combat hangar under construction with parked Mustang.

mixture of Sommerfeld and Army Track. SMT was later to replace the last-named types. Four blister hangars were sited off the northern taxi-way and four refuelling hard-standings were provided, together with a 24,000 gallon fuel installation. Tented sleeping sites, eight in number, were positioned just to the north of the landing ground and part of a nearby dairy was used as an officers' dining room. About 50 mesh hard-standings led off the peri-track to park the three squadrons of Spitfires flying from here as part of the air cover for the Invasion.

Most of the RAF squadrons had been flying operations for some time, often from ALGs, but many of those joining the 9th Air Force came straight from the USA and were not impressed with the new bases from which they were expected to work up as effective combat units. The historian of the 371st Fighter Bomber Group at Bisterne wrote:

> 'Personnel adjusted quickly to living and working conditions although both were very primitive. The area was so swampy that tent floors had to be built up to prevent flooding. We learned to make use of the smallest items. Cut trees became clothes racks, bits of wire were twisted into clothes hangers and an old metal bed made an excellent grille upon which to boil water for washing. The operating factor, however, presented a more difficult problem. The airfield had been, and still was, a cow pasture overlaid with 'chicken wire' (steel wire mesh) and one week of heavy pounding under P-47 landings and take-offs reduced the runways to a series of ruts and bumps which were extremely hazardous. Administrative inspectors from 9th Air Force Service Command finally closed the field for reconstruction, and the airplanes and enough equipment to operate were moved to a concrete strip at Ibsley, three miles away.'

The aircraft returned to Bisterne on 1 May 1944 and flew from there until 23 June 1944. The farmer at Bisterne whose land became a busy air base almost overnight remembers how the trucks delivering bombs just before D-Day used to get bogged down. A half-mile long road was built in 24 hours to remedy the situation, typical of how quickly things were done in wartime, especially by the Americans.

The majority of the flying units at ALGs followed the ground forces to the Continent, leaving only a few squadrons for air defence, including the Tempests at Newchurch. Most of the sites were de-requisitioned early in 1945. The majority of the PSP had already been taken up and transported to Europe for re-use. Some traces of the ALGs can still be found, particularly at Bisterne where the main runway was bulldozed, leaving a bank about 4 ft high which now divides two fields. Rusty pickets and bits of SMT stick out all over it.

Looking at the stretches of peaceful farmland today, it is almost impossible to imagine the Thunderbolts and Typhoons laden with bombs and rockets, thundering off to wreak havoc across the Channel. Crops grow where Mustangs and Spitfires once took to the air but the plough still turns up twisted runway mesh, spent shell cases and corroded aircraft parts.

Chapter 14

Toehold in Europe: perfecting the techniques of Advanced Landing Grounds

Side by side with the ALG programme in England ran the development of techniques for rapid airfield construction essential to support a beach-head on the Continent, and thereafter to keep pace with the advancing Allied armies. William the Conqueror brought pre-fabricated wooden forts to England in 1066; the modern parallel was the shipping of thousands of rolls of wire mesh runway surfacing to permit the deployment of air power where it was needed.

Planning of Operation *Overlord*, the invasion of Europe, had begun as early as 1942. The original intention was to land on the Cotentin Peninsula near Cherbourg, with the object of capturing the port rapidly. Unfortunately, the countryside was unsuitable for the fast construction of airfields, being hilly with small fields, separated by high banks and hedges. In contrast, the area between Caen and Bayeux was not only gently undulating but also very well drained.

Geological advice was given to Major-General Drummond, the Chief Engineer of the 21st Army Group, the British Commonwealth element of the invading forces, by Professor King of Cambridge University. This, together with a careful study of reconnaissance photographs, influenced the locations of the ALG sites. Theoretically, by D-Day plus 10 (16 June) we would have at our disposal three Emergency Landing Strips (ELS) of reasonably level ground at least 1,800 by 90 ft with an ambulance and fire tender, four Refuelling and Rearming Strips of well-rolled ground 3,600 ft long with two dispersal areas of 100 by 50 yd, one at each end, and eight ALGs of minimum length 3,600 by 120 ft with sufficient dispersal space for 54 aircraft. An increase to 5,000 ft was required for fighters.

Specially-trained RAF Servicing Commandos were earmarked for the ALGs. Nos 3205, 3206 and 3208 served in Europe and followed the advance, each having personnel trained to work on the types of aircraft most likely to use their airstrips. They were soon reinforced by the ordinary RAF ground crew. It was decided that the responsibility for providing RAF bases in Europe should be shared between Airfield Construction Groups of the Royal Engineers and the RAF Airfield Construction Service, the latter to provide five complete Construction Wings. The first, 5357 Wing, came into being in February 1944 and consisted of a Wing Headquarters and two Airfield Construction Squadrons each of which, in addition to their construction and artisan flights, had a field plant flight equipped with the type of machinery necessary for the rapid construction of airstrips in forward areas.

Apart from training and preparation, the ACSs had an important pre-D-Day task, a mobile blitz repair scheme covering 74 airfields in the southern counties, including the 23 ALGs which the ACSs had themselves built. A concentrated assault by the *Luftwaffe* on these vital fields was regarded as the enemy's most likely counter-measure, although it did not in fact occur.

Practical preparation for the RAF's role in an invasion began in the summer of 1943 when the ground staff and base organization of certain tactical units were radically altered. A series of numbered Airfields were set up, pairs of them forming sectors. All such Airfields — the title was independent of geographical situation — were fully mobile and were capable of operating efficiently for indefinite periods from forward strips. It was thus essential that all personnel be familiar with life under canvas and if necessary be able to defend their base from attack.

Ground crews were removed from their squadrons and formed into independent servicing echelons which were to be attached to particular Airfields to look after any squadrons which landed there. The loss of *esprit de corps*

Typhoons of 198 Squadron throwing up dust at either B-5 (Camilly) or B-10 (Plumetot) (IWM CL472).

and resulting drop in morale was slowly regained as, after the initial upheaval, particular squadrons tended to become identified with specific Airfields and Wings and to move around with them. Thus, the servicing unit looking after a particular squadron soon had the essential personal involvement in its fortunes. The first Airfields to be organized were numbered from 121 to 127 inclusive, some being at satellite airfields and others at main sector stations, more being added as 1943 progressed.

A major exercise, code-named *Toby*, took place in October 1943. Its dual purpose was to give practice in the construction of an ALG under operational conditions, including the provision of AA defences, and its immediate occupation by RAF fighter units. An undeveloped and abandoned site for a heavy bomber airfield at Huggate Wold in Yorkshire was the location.

The first Sommerfeld Track 'flightway', as these strips were originally known, was to be ready on 12 October but bad weather and deep mud delayed completion of the two runways until the 23 October. Fog then prevented its use by 168 and 170 Squadrons of No 123 Airfield, then at Hutton Cranswick, until 26 October. Their Mustangs eventually did some extensive flying from the strips, the pilots finding them adequate but bumpy.

In May 1943 No 16 ACG, Royal Engineers laid a strip on Fairmile Common near Eastbourne as an exercise. Prior to this, during Exercise *Spartan* in March 1943, Sommerfeld Track runways were laid by No 13 ACG at Red Barn and Eastmanton Down near Lambourne in Berkshire. RAF squadrons flew from them

until they were withdrawn from use and cleared a few months later. American engineers built an ALG at Slapton on the Devon coast in support of the ill-fated amphibious landing exercise, P-47s of the 365th Fighter Group using it for several days.

Developed concurrently with ALG trials were two British ideas to give continuous fighter support to troops on a beach-head. *Scheme Habbakuk*, named after an obscure book of the Old Testament, was the brain-child of a Mr Pyke who served on Mountbatten's staff. His idea was to form a ship-like construction of ice large enough to serve as a runway. It would displace one *million* tons, be self-propelled at slow speed, have its own AA defence and repair facilities and would be equipped with a small refrigeration plant to preserve its existence. It had been found that by adding a proportion of wood pulp to ordinary sea water the mixture lost the brittle qualities normally associated with ice, and became extremely tough.

This substance, known as 'Pykrete' after its inventor, seemed to offer great possibilities, not only for our needs in North-West Europe but also elsewhere. It was found that as the ice melted, the fibrous content quickly formed a furry outer surface which acted as an insulator and greatly retarded the melting process. Much development work was done up to about 1946, particularly in Canada, but for a number of reasons the scheme was eventually abandoned.

The name *Habbakuk*, by the way, had been chosen by Churchill from the Biblical text, 'Behold ye among the heathen, and regard, and wonder marvellously: for I will work a work in your days which ye will not believe, though it be told you.' The idea of a floating iceberg met with widespread scepticism, so much so that one scientist proposed using the term 'milli-Habbakuk' as a new unit for measuring impracticability.

Tentacle was marginally less fanciful, being a floating landing strip 1,800 ft long by 75 ft, supported on steel pontoons. A full-sized replica was marked out on a runway at Ford in Sussex and a rehearsal held on 8 October 1943. Three Spitfire squadrons, including Nos 412 and 416, were present, along with examples of the Beaufighters, Mosquito, Fulmar, Hurricane, Mustang and Typhoon. No less than 23 of the aircraft over-ran the limits of the strip and became 'casualties' so it was decided that a length of at least 2,500 ft would be required.

Little hope was expressed for successful development, towing and moving *Tentacle* being a major problem and their very size would render them vulnerable to air attack. Equally, there was already a heavy enough training programme without adding deck landing to it. Drop tanks and the new ALGs being built in southern England killed the project, although it was not totally abandoned until January 1945. As a footnote, one should mention that Piper Cubs were flown off special platforms on ships for artillery spotting in Normandy. Aircraft carriers were not employed in the invasion because of their obvious vulnerability. To test the feasibility of their

use in amphibious operations in the Pacific, *Lily* and *Clover* were built on a small scale at Rosyth and tried out successfully by an Auster and a Swordfish. The trials took place off the Isle of Arran during March and April 1945. *Lily* had been designed in the first instance as a floating pierhead formed of horizontal steel buoyancy units hinged together to make a flexible mat on the surface of the sea. *Clover* consisted of a wooden decking laid at right angles over steel buoyancy tubes. The war moved faster than the projects, however, and they were never used in anger.

As Allied supremacy in the air became daily more apparent over France and the Low Countries, the planners began to feel that complete control of the air on D-Day was by no means an idle dream. They urged the destruction of aircraft maintenance facilities on all 40 main aerodromes within a radius of 150 miles from Caen. When this had been accomplished attacks were to be switched to runways, hangars, parked aircraft and control centres. The raids, mainly by the USAAF, began on 11 May and were continued intermittently until D-Day when the programme was almost complete. This was a two-edged sword, however, as the Allies were effectively denying themselves any usable airfields once they had got a foothold in Europe. They would have to build their own from scratch, but no one doubted the abilities of the construction units to carry out this task.

The Americans had their own organization for the laying of temporary airstrips in a battle

Thunderbolts in France parked on SMT with Hadrian gliders in the background (IWM).

zone and, although there was some co-opera-tion with the British, training was largely done separately. US Army engineering personnel had arrived in England as early as August 1942 and had since built such airfields as Gosfield, Stansted and Andrews Field, all in Essex. They had also carried out runway extensions at RAF bases, including Kinloss and Lossie-mouth. The 9th Air Force which was to bear the brunt of American tactical support for the invasion, proposed the establishment of an Engineer Command within its structure. The US War Department, however, was reluctant to authorize such a move, perhaps because a precedent might be set for Ordnance, Signal, Chemical Warfare and other services to ele-vate their status.

A decision was postponed for months but, in the meantime, the 9th activated a provisional Engineer Command. A total of 17,000 officers and men made up 16 Engineer Aviation Bat-talions which were grouped under four Regi-ments, three Airborne Battalions and a Camouflage Battalion. The men wore a shoul-der flash similar to that of the Royal Engineers' ACGs, a triangle representing three runways. The EABs later adopted their own unit insig-nia, one of which was a winged caricature of a bulldozer clutching a piece of PSP and a tommy-gun! Brigadier General James B. Newman Jr became the first commander of the 9th Engineer Command.

Since the officers were specialists and the men already seasoned, not more than two months' new training was deemed necessary. At Great Barrington Park in Gloucestershire and other centres during the first part of 1944, the EABs practised the techniques they would soon use as mobile units under enemy fire, and if some found it rough in cold, paraffin-lit tents, it meant they were acquiring precious experience. A large grass airfield at Kingston Bagpuize in Berkshire was made available for experiments in laying a new type of temporary runway, Prefabricated Bitumenized Surfacing (PBS), in other words tarred canvas.

The varieties of metal tracking have already been described but PBS was only referred to in passing. The material was the idea of a Canadian Army engineer who considered that, since paved runway construction was obviously impossible in the early stages of an invasion battle, a short term answer was to select air-field sites on hard, dry ground and ensure their serviceability for a limited time in wet weather by laying a waterproof membrane to form a runway. Trials held in the summer of 1943 were sufficiently promising to authorize the subsequent manufacture of large quantities, some 20 million sq yds being produced in the UK alone by the end of the European war.

It required extremely careful laying and constant maintenance when in use, but its main advantages were speed of application (150 men could surface a runway 3,600 ft by 120 ft in about 14 hours), and low weight. To construct an average ALG required about 800 tons of PBS, as against 4,800 tons of PSP for an equivalent site.

At Kingston Bagpuize in March 1944, 'C' Company of the 816th EAB put down the first PBS runway to be completed by American troops. It was tested in April by up to 50 Thun-derbolts of the 368th FG from Chilbolton, who refuelled and rearmed for several missions to targets in France. C-47s and Havocs also tried it out without any significant wear. Between D-Day and 28 October 1944 it was used to sur-face 30 airfields, the first being a terminal strip for C-47s at A-22, overlooking Omaha Beach.

Royal Engineer and ACS units went ashore on D-Day and by 10 June had completed three Emergency Landing Strips and four R & R strips, B-1 at Asnelles being ready on D + 1 for emergency landings. At noon on the 10 June the first British landings in the beach-head were made by Spitfires of 222 Squadron at B-3 (St Croix-sur-Mer). Dust was a terri-ble problem and Pierre Closterman in his book *The Big Show* describes landing at the half-finished B-2 at Bazenville on 11 June:

'It was white and as fine as flour. Stirred up by the slipstream of the propellors, it infiltrated everywhere, darkened the sky, suffocated us and found its way into our eyes and ears. For 500 yards around the landing strip all traces of green had dis-appeared — every growing thing was covered by a thick layer stirred up by the slightest breeze.'

Water spraying was tried to lay the dust but it dried too soon to be effective. Fuel oil sal-vaged from a beached destroyer proved to be much more successful. Square Mesh Track was employed for the first runway laid in Nor-mandy, but PBS was found to be the ideal sur-facing medium for dust-free runways.

An RAF Beach Group provided the organi-zation for the distribution of the materials required for ALG construction. It also defended the beach with barrage balloons. The Allied engineers often had to act as infantry, fighting off enemy counter-attacks and deal-ing with snipers while they removed anti-glider posts, wrecked vehicles and high hedges. They also had to flatten fully-grown crops and fill in ditches and craters, all with the ever-present danger of mines.

A sergeant of the 816th EAB was awarded a Bronze Star after his survey team staked out the centre line of a proposed runway under

Rolls of SMT for ALGs being unloaded on a French beach just after D-Day.

shellfire. The engineers were also in peril from their own aircraft as the ALGs were often in use before full completion. There were a number of fatal accidents, such as the two men killed at A-3 by a P-47 as they were laying wire mesh. The mesh had been laid only half-way across the strip and aircraft were operating during the process.

Ground facilities at the ALGs were rudimentary, Flying Control, for example, usually operating from a tent with a handy slit trench in case things got hot. At one strip a Horsa glider fuselage was occupied to good effect. Ground signals were limited to a 'Tee' to indicate the direction of landing, and the site's code number.

The first US engineers ashore on D-Day were detachments of the 819th EAB on Utah Beach, just after H + 4 (4 hours after the initial landing), somewhat seasick after two days on their LSTs. Wading ashore, they found their heavy equipment bogged down on the beach and it took seven hours to move it to the planned site of an ELS. Devastating fire on Omaha prevented the 834th EAB from landing all that day and the 820th's ferry was crippled by a shell. Next day they were towed ashore but found their ALG site had still to be captured!

On their own initiative, the 820th went ahead and prepared an earth strip at St Marsur-Mer which was ready on D + 3 (9 June). C-47s immediately began to fly in supplies and evacuate wounded. This unplanned strip on Omaha Beach turned out to be the first operational American aerodrome in France. An average of 100 transport aircraft landed there daily for the first six weeks.

The scheduled ALG at St Pierre du Mont was speedily completed and occupied by the 366th FG's Thunderbolts on 20 June. It was known as A-1 under a scheme whereby all Continental airfields, temporary or permanent, were allocated a code number. The prefix 'A' denoted American usage, 'B' British, 'Y' airfields taken over by the American and French armies advancing from Southern France, and 'R' for airfields in Germany occupied by American troops. Since the British and, even more so, the Americans are adept at mangling foreign languages, it reduced confusion considerably!

Throughout the swift advance, 2nd Tactical Air Force and the 9th Air Force kept pace with the armies only through the prodigious efforts of the engineers. The beach-head strips were soon far out of range in the rear so a field reconnaissance party in armoured cars followed the leading armoured units and looked for suitable sites. The general policy was to repair damaged airfields rather than to build new ones. The standard was low but adequate, with one runway 1,200 yds long, sufficiently smooth to enable a light car to run along it without undue bumping.

Metz (Y-34) in Alsace-Lorraine, to take but one example, had been devastated, but US engineers filled hundreds of craters and laid

Mustangs on an unidentified French ALG (Via Dr A.A. Duncan).

a 5,000 ft PSP runway and SMT hardstandings for up to 150 fighters. All runways on these fields were given a parallel crash strip so that belly-landings would not hinder operations. Engineers laid out many 'Cub Strips', as they were known, to a standard 2,000 by 100 ft. Supply and Evacuation Strips for use by C-47s were generally 3,000 by 120 ft of turf or rolled earth, Y-85 at Ettinghausen being a typical example.

Two days was the average time for their completion and they were essential for the airborne supply of fuel for the tanks and the evacuation of the wounded. Pierced Aluminium Plank (PAP) came into use during the closing stages of the campaign, identical in design but half the weight of the earlier PSP. It has since been employed extensively in Korea and Vietnam.

The British Airfield Construction Squadrons, meanwhile, continued to make their presence felt. The airfield at Eindhoven (B-78) stands out as one of their greatest accomplishments in north-west Europe. Always within range of the enemy and frequently threatened by counter-attack, the men overcame innumerable obstacles to keep the aircraft of the 2nd TAF in the air under appalling weather conditions. The Germans had more than doubled the size of the airfield, building three runways and redraining the entire surface, but more than 500 bombs had wrecked it. On top of this, they had blown up all buildings before departing. The worst problem was drainage, Dutch forced labour employed in construction having deliberately laid many incorrect falls! There was no time to lay a completely new system so a temporary scheme of open ditches was substituted.

The ALGs in Normandy were soon abandoned but, as in England, traces can still be found. SMT is often employed for fencing and a thorough investigation would probably uncover aircraft parts and other contemporary relics. It was to be many years before the devastated permanent airfields were fully reinstated but PSP is still around in vast quantities in Europe doing service as parking areas on small aerodromes. Static display parking at the Paris Air Show relied heavily upon it until well into the 1960s and a photograph in *Flight* magazine *circa* 1947 shows the interior of the passenger lounge at Orly Airport, its walls faced with painted PSP. The effect is remarkably decorative!

The Harrier makes the whole ALG concept a thing of the past, but what do they use for many of its pads in the field but dear old PSP again! This ubiquitous material was one of the unsung successes of the Second World War and lengths of it turn up in all sorts of places. The RAF Museum even has some but not for display, for it is doing useful service between the car park and the Battle of Britain Museum building. Perhaps one day it will join the exhibits.

Chapter 15

Royal Naval Air Stations

Before the Second World War, the requirements for Naval Air Stations were nominal. A few locations near to naval ports and anchorages sufficed to service aircraft flown off from carriers between cruises and to prepare and store replacements. The enormous wartime expansion of the Fleet Air Arm produced a need for new training bases and by 1945 a total of 27 had been constructed, most of them in an Admiralty building programme which was entirely separate from that of the Air Ministry.

On 3 July 1937, Prime Minister Neville Chamberlain announced in Parliament that the FAA, then a branch of the RAF, should come completely under Admiralty control. This did not happen, however, until 24 May 1939 when the Navy inherited Lee-on-Solent, Donibristle, Ford, Worthy Down and Eastleigh. The Air Ministry's Aerodromes Board had, in the meantime, collaborated with the Admiralty and made suggestions for sites which seemed to fit in with the latter's requirements.

One of the first was selected in August 1938 when the Aerodromes Board was informed that a full-sized airfield was needed to act as a relief landing ground for Donibristle. A former First World War site at Crail and two undeveloped ones at nearby Kilrenny were the alternatives and Crail duly became HMS *Jackdaw*, being commissioned on 1 October 1940.

During 1938 Skeabrae in Orkney was accepted by the Navy but, while still under construction in May 1940, it was handed over to the RAF in order to meet Orkney fighter defence requirements. Shortly before the war, the following sites were offered: Fifehead Magdalen, Syles Farm, Maiston Magna, Ibsley North, Holmsley South, Yeovilton, Hillingham, South Ripley, Kingston, Frimston Down, Hartfordbridge Flats and Eversleigh Common.

I have been unable to identify all of these locations but some, notably Ibsley, Holmsley South and Hartfordbridge (Blackbushe), ultimately became RAF stations. Yeovilton will be familiar to all and Syles Farm became its satellite, Henstridge, the farm itself serving as the Station headquarters. Towards the end of December 1938 the Admiralty's Engineer had taken up options on Yeovilton, Crail and South Ripley, others being accepted soon afterwards.

After the initial planning, liaison between the Admiralty and the Aerodromes Board appears to have been sporadic, chiefly owing to the fact that the former did not have any definite programme of further requirements and so had no need to apply for further sites. Unfortunately, during the summer of 1942 when naval forward planning necessitated a number of new airfields, it was found that the RAF had already developed most of the suitable locations.

The first purpose-built RNAS at Hatston in Orkney opened on 2 October 1939, followed by Yeovilton on 1 June 1940, Arbroath on 19 June 1940, St Merryn on 10 August 1949 and Crail on 1 October 1940. With certain exceptions, such as HMS *Daedalus* (Lee-on-Solent), RNASs were named after birds. Unfortunately, as airfields proliferated, those responsible for such matters began to delve more deeply into the ornithology text books and came up with some rather obscure names. Examples are Belfast (HMS *Gadwall*), Macrihanish (*Landrail*) and Ronaldsway (*Urley*) while the training camp for WRNS air mechanics at Milmeece in Staffordshire was appropriately known as HMS *Fledgling*. Satellites — 'tenders' in naval parlance — were identified by a 'II' after the name, Dunino, controlled by Crail, being HMS *Jackdaw II*.

The Admiralty's share of construction labour allocated by the Government was already heavily committed to building shore installations for the Fleet and new airfields

Barracudas and Seafires at Henstridge, Somerset, one of only two airfields in Britain to have five runways (FAA Museum).

were an extra burden. There was much argument when the Admiralty proposed a labour force of 2,000 men to construct a large air station. This was challenged by the Ministry of Works, which pointed out that the Air Ministry were having airfields built for the RAF with a little over 1,000 men each.

This apparent fact was used to suggest a reduction in the naval construction programme but, on investigation, the Admiralty was able to show that the charge of under-production by its work force was unfounded. The reason was that the high output figures for the Air Ministry were achieved on concrete runways laid during the summer months of 1942 at bomber stations, a type of construction which lent itself to extensive mechanization. The method used by the Admiralty for its relatively light aircraft was Tarmac on a hardcore foundation, a method which, it was noted, was easier to repair after air raid damage.

FAA stations also included a considerable number of buildings for training duties, the construction of which could not reach as high output figures in terms of manhours as the mechanized runway job. Moreover, the site and climate conditions at FAA stations situated mainly in Scotland and north-west England were not as favourable as those for the bomber bases in East Anglia.

The bleak and inhospitable nature of most of the sites seems to have been *de rigueur* with wartime RNASs. Only a handful, including Yeovilton and Lee-on-Solent, were in any way pleasingly located; the rest were miserable affairs, relying heavily on the ubiquitous Nissen hut for creature comforts.

Purpose-built RNASs are readily identified by their runway pattern and building types. The standard was four runways, three of 1,000 yd in length and the fourth, which was generally aligned with the prevailing wind, of

1,100 yd. Length was not a problem with the small types of aircraft in naval service and the strips were much narrower than the norm for RAF stations, being 30 yd wide compared with 50 yd.

It has been suggested that the naval standard of four runways was necessary because its pilots had little experience in cross-wind landings and take-offs, always operating from carriers streaming into wind! However, the real reason was that so many air stations were situated in windy coastal areas and many of the aircraft in service were extremely susceptible to ground-looping in cross-winds, the narrow-tracked Martlet being notorious for this.

Henstridge in Somerset had the distinction of being one of only two airfields in Britain with five runways, two of them being parallel so that one could be used for dummy deck landing training. The other contender was Arbroath which also had a dummy deck on a much shorter fifth runway measuring 530 yd by 33 yd.

The Navy developed its own style of control tower with three storeys to the equivalent RAF building's two. With a glasshouse superimposed, it offered an excellent view of the airfield and it is perhaps no coincidence that the later design of RAF watch tower also incorporated three floors, the building at Farnborough being a surviving example. Former RAF aerodromes taken over by the FAA usually retained their original towers, thus betraying their ancestry. At Fearn, a naval three-storey type was erected close to the rudimentary RAF satellite watch office.

The Admiralty also designed its own hangars, including the Pentad which was similar to the T2 but with sloping sides, perhaps to present less wind resistance in gale-prone areas. Another common sight was a small 72 by 60 ft building with doors at one end only.

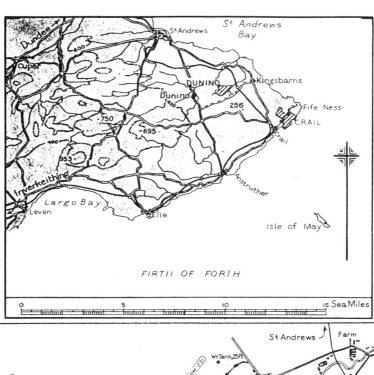

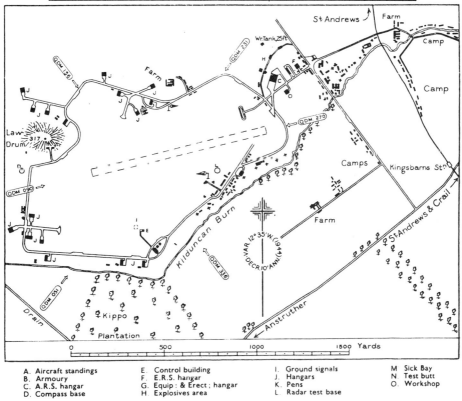

A. Aircraft standings	E. Control building	I. Ground signals	M. Sick Bay
B. Armoury	F. E.R.S. hangar	J. Hangars	N. Test butt
C. A.R.S. hangar	G. Equip.: & Erect ; hangar	K. Pens	O. Workshop
D. Compass base	H. Explosives area	L. Radar test base	

RNAS Dunino, Fife, of which it was said that the personnel would suffer more from pneumonia than enemy action!

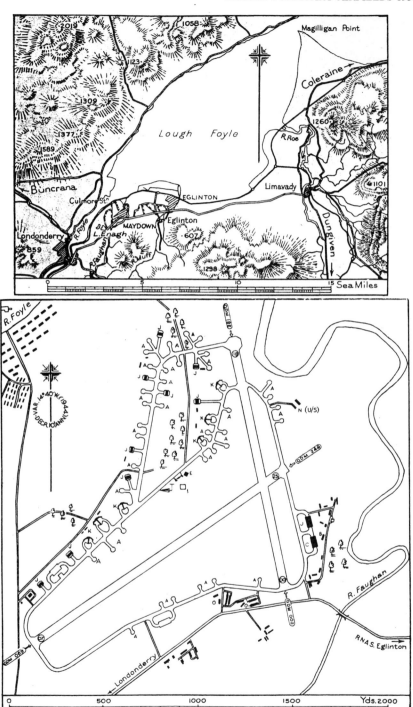

A. Aircraft standings   E. Control building   I. Ground signals   M. Sick Bay
B. Armoury   F. E.R.S. hangar   J. Hangars   N. Test butt
C. A.R.S. hangar   G. Equip: & Erect: hangar K. Pens   O. Workshop
D. Compass base   H. Explosives area   L. Radar test base

Above *Seafire NN609 'P3-N' of 790 Squadron in front of a Mains or Mainhill hangar at Dale in 1946* (Via M.J. Burrow).

Left *RNAS Maydown, Northern Ireland, an ex-RAF fighter satellite with two runways and dispersal pens.*

It was intended for aircraft with folded wings and some RNASs had as many as 30 dispersed around the perimeter. Its correct nomenclature is something of a mystery, Mains or Mainhill apparently being alternative names for it.

Naval aerodromes established before the war usually had Bellmans and by 1945 some had acquired a curious mixture of naval and RAF hangars. Blister hangars were common and the Navy also had its own similar pattern known as the Fromson. At Worthy Down, 48 Dutch barns were erected for the dispersed storage of aircraft with wings folded. Late in the war, the FAA built rectangular servicing aprons at many of its stations, these being a distinctive feature in aerial photographs.

Nissen huts were used for most of the personnel accommodation, rather than the brick and cement-rendered hutting so beloved of the RAF. Again, non-availability of bricks in the remote regions favoured by the FAA for its aerodromes encouraged the employment of corrugated iron.

By the summer of 1942, the Admiralty was forced to accept that its programme of new air stations would not allow anything like the complete training of all FAA personnel at its own airfields and establishments. It would still have to rely largely upon training facilities at RAF stations and at bases overseas.

One of the reasons why the Navy willingly

continued its dependence for much of the training on the RAF was that, even when the airfields they had asked for were ready, they had to face the consequences of having cut out of the 1942 works programme three stations so that other essential work could be completed by the limited labour allocation then available. The results of this cut were now appearing and it seemed probable that they would be still more evident in 1943, so that a further reduction would have been disastrous to naval interests. Requirements had been kept to an absolute minimum and had been based upon the expected first-line strength in aircraft, rather than on the theoretical first-line strength needed to equip all the new carriers soon to come into service.

In June 1942 the FAA forecast that it was due to expand from a strength of all types of aircraft of 2,665 at the end of the previous year to 6,350 by the end of December 1943. Shore accommodation in the UK would be needed for some 1,200 naval aircraft, so to alleviate the situation somewhat, the Air Ministry was persuaded to give up a certain number of RAF stations to the FAA and grant lodger facilities at others.

Not surprisingly, the RAF handed over various unwanted or surplus sites, some of which were of little use to the FAA either. Maydown in Northern Ireland, for example, had two runways, there being insufficient room

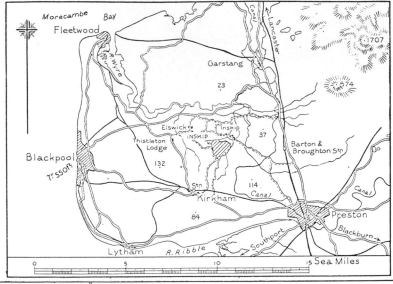

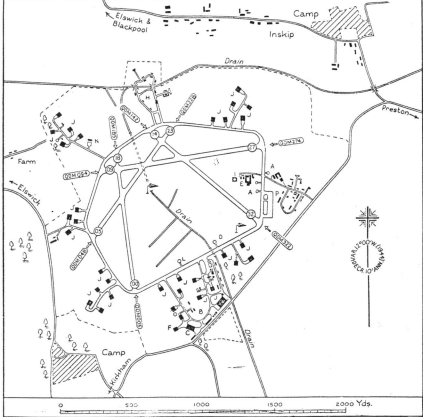

A. Aircraft standings	E. Control building	I. Ground signals
B. Armoury	F. E.R.S. hangar	J. Hangars
C. A.R.S. hangar	G. Equip: & Erect: hangar	K. Pens
D. Compass base	H. Explosives area	L. Radar test base

M. Sick Bay
N. Test butt
O. Workshop
P. Fuel: apron

Left *RNAS Inskip, Lancs, with standard four runway layout.*

Above *New Fireflies and Seafires await collection from the Aircraft Receipt and Dispatch Unit at Culham, Oxfordshire, in 1945* (FAA Museum).

Right *Firefly at Culham in 1945. Note Dutch barn hangar in use as a fire tender shed* (FAA Museum).

for a third. Its weather was 'not very suitable for night flying' and Eglinton, the original parent station, was too close. It did, however, serve a useful purpose as the shore headquarters of 836 Squadron, the 'private air force' of over 100 Swordfish which operated from the Merchant Aircraft Carriers.

Nearby Eglinton was a little better, but there was still the hazard of overlapping circuits. Both stations were on loan and due to be returned by October 1944 as they were required after this date 'by the Americans', an event which never came to pass. Stretton in Cheshire had been built as a night fighter field, but with the *Luftwaffe* turning its attentions elsewhere was now redundant. Unfortunately, it suffered badly from fog and industrial haze. A site at Burscough, north-west of Liverpool and earmarked for the RAF, was given up without demur and this later became a fine airfield, HMS *Ringtail*.

The RAF extracted a price for its 'generosity', however, demanding lodger rights at a number of the airfields and also at existing RNASs. For example, accommodation was reserved at Machrihanish for one RAF fighter squadron in exchange for the FAA's use of Stretton. In June 1943, the RAF was urging the exchange of St Merryn for Talbenny in south-west Wales so that the former might be used for the maintenance of Liberators based at adjacent St Eval. The plan was not taken up, however, perhaps because the runways were too short.

The Navy had its eye on several other airfields, but for various reasons they were not made available. Among them were Lossiemouth, Kinloss, Jurby, Banff, Andreas and Barrow, but it was not until 1946 that the FAA acquired the first named. Turnberry was another site which the RAF refused to give up, the reason being that it was 'the only first-

class torpedo training centre in the RAF'.
There was no room there either for the FAA
as a lodger.

Kidsdale, a grass aerodrome in the south of
Scotland, was proffered for development, as
were Dunino in Fife and Findo Gask, north
of Perth. The FAA by now had learned to be
very suspicious of the RAF's unconditional
offers! Kidsdale was found to be surrounded
by army firing ranges while Dunino was grass-
surfaced and, looking at it today, it is hard to
believe that it was once an aerodrome. Findo
Gask was also grass but was later used as the
Southern Terminal of the FAA's ferry service
to and from the Orkneys. Kidsdale was refused
but Dunino was accepted, despite its shortcomings.

Hinstock in Shropshire, on the site of a
former Ministry of Aircraft production SLG
known as Ollerton, was one of the furthest
RNASs from the sea, but since it was used
by an instrument training unit, this was of little
importance. More serious was the proximity
of the bomber OTU at RAF Peplow for the
aerodrome boundaries at their closest point
were less than a mile apart.

At the end of 1942, the FAA was becoming
increasingly concerned about its continued

relegation to a minor role. An official minute
summarized contemporary feeling:

> 'It is imperative to the national interest
> that naval requirements for air stations
> and facilities should be given equal con-
> sideration with RAF requirements, irre-
> spective of the fact that the RAF being
> first in the field have earmarked all suit-
> able facilities. The present system where-
> by the Royal Navy has to adapt itself to
> sites which the RAF, with its wider scope
> of interests, has found of no value, can
> but lead to naval and therefore national
> disaster.'

A case in point was the search for a site for

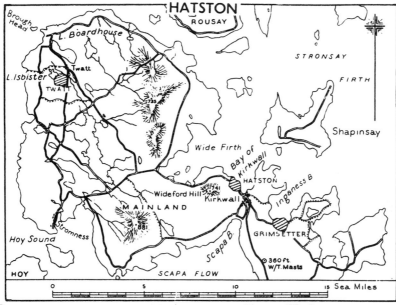

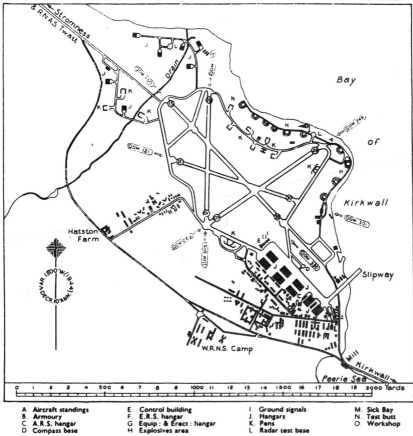

A.	Aircraft standings	E.	Control building	I.	Ground signals	M.	Sick Bay
B.	Armoury	F.	E.R.S. hangar	J.	Hangars	N.	Test butt
C.	A.R.S. hangar	G.	Equip: & Erect: hangar	K.	Pens	O.	Workshop
D.	Compass base	H.	Explosives area	L.	Radar test base		

A 763 Squadron Barracuda at St Merryn, Cornwall, March 1945. The hangar is an Admiralty 'S' Shed (FAA Museum).

an observer school which was desperately needed by the spring of 1943. Much naval observer training was already being performed piecemeal by the RAF, but specialized amenities like target vessels were not available. Nor were naval instructors exactly thick on the ground, and a lack of proper naval background was felt to be another major disadvantage.

One contender for the school was Arbroath, but it was already suffering from chronic overcrowding and its satellite at East Haven was not yet finished. The Navy looked at RAF Sealand and thought that it might just be suitable if the RAF could be induced to move its EFTS somewhere else. The Aircraft Packing Depot would have to stay, however, and this and other considerations led to the idea being dropped.

The Air Ministry rejected approaches for the use of several other stations, including Lossiemouth, Kinloss and Jurby, but offered Dallachy in north-east Scotland as a temporary solution. Naval tenure was to last three months after its scheduled completion date of 31 March 1943. The Admiralty would, in the meantime, have to build its own new base or, alternatively, construct a new station for the RAF out of its own funds and retain Dallachy permanently.

The FAA was not happy with Dallachy as it had only two runways and the inevitable cross-winds would make intensive flying training very difficult. It was also in the middle of what was described as 'one of the most air-congested areas of Britain' and close to a number of firing ranges. The Navy thus decided to find its own airfield site and for the moment expand the existing observer training programme at Arbroath. Dallachy eventually housed a Beaufighter Strike Wing and the only naval unit which ever flew from there was 828

Squadron with Swordfish under Coastal Command's control for most of October 1944.

Stemming directly from this débâcle was the discovery of an aerodrome site at Crimond by the Admiralty, an event almost unique because, as previously described, this was normally the responsibility of the Air Ministry's Aerodromes Board. It was hoped to open this by September 1943 but delays meant that it was not ready until the summer of 1944.

By that time, events had overtaken the need for a new observer school, so it became a TBR training unit equipped with Barracudas. The station was renamed Rattray or Rattray Head on 1 July 1945 after a nearby coastal feature. It has been suggested that the accident rate on the evil Barracuda and the gloomy associations of Crimond and the 23rd Psalm were responsible for the change of title, but the real reason was misdirected mail and equipment. There was no RNAS with a similar name but perhaps there was a naval facility at Cramond on the Firth of Forth.

During 1944 the Admiralty found a number of potential aerodromes in Cheshire, Lancashire and Flintshire, but the Ministry of Agriculture raised so many objections to the loss of valuable farmland at that late stage of the war that none was developed. Yet again, the FAA was forced to fall back on its existing stations, although it had managed to secure Ronaldsway on the Isle of Man for operational training, noting with foresight that the Isle of Man Government would probably wish to purchase the site at some future date for use as the island's main airport.

The FAA equivalent of an RAF Maintenance Unit was the Aircraft Maintenance Yard and, as the service expanded, more of them were established. Abbotsinch was one of the first, being commissioned on 20 September 1943 as HMS *Sanderling*. Other Yards were operated at Belfast (Sydenham), Stretton, Donibristle, Evanton and Fleetlands, the latter being a non-airfield camp in Hampshire. A subsidiary function was the storage of reserve aircraft. As with the RAF, the Air Transport Auxiliary performed most of the ferrying, but some was done by the Aircraft Receipt and Despatch Units, No 1 being located at Anthorn in Cumberland and No 2 at Culham in Oxfordshire.

The Aircraft Yards, however, never achieved the capacity to prepare and maintain all the FAA's aircraft, the task being handled chiefly by RAF MUs, including No 15 at Wroughton, No 29 at High Ercall and No 51 at Lichfield. Early in 1944, High Ercall's commitment was

almost entirely FAA aircraft with 69 naval ratings assisting almost 700 civilian employees. In April 1944 over 150 Corsairs, Avengers and Wildcats were on the unit, as well as 120 Swordfish, the latter awaiting the installation of American radar.

In May 1945 storage for up to 300 aircraft was urgently required as was a satellite for Hinstock's beam approach training school. It was hoped that these needs could be met by one aerodrome. RAF Condover near Shrewsbury was tentatively offered but as usual negotiations were so protracted that the needs were met elsewhere.

In contrast to the rapid shrinkage of the RAF after VE-Day, the FAA was still expanding for the part it was going to take in what was seen

Right *Some FAA aircraft were based at RAF airfields. This is Mosquito TW241 of the Royal Navy Section, TRE Defford, Worcs, just after the war* (Via Glyn Warren).

Below *RNAS Twatt, Orkney, in the snow of 1945* (FAA Museum).

Above left *RNAS Dale on 19 October 1944 with a newly-built control tower and standard naval parking apron* (FAA Museum).

Above right *Worthy Down, Hants, a former RAF station inherited by the Royal Navy* (FAA Museum).

as the final amphibious assault on Japan. One of the important requirements was a new repair yard in the north of England to replace the accommodation soon to be lost at Donibristle when certain property was de-requisitioned. The Air Ministry was asked to release Warton, recently vacated by a USAAF Air Depot, for this purpose and was also prepared to lend Macmerry, east of Edinburgh, for an indefinite period to house a Fleet Requirements Unit.

Accommodation for a fighter school with 78 aircraft was needed in Central Scotland. The Admiralty suggested East Fortune, Charterhall or Milfield while the RAF countered with Dyce (Aberdeen Airport) which was refused as 'unsuitable'. Drem, near the Firth of Forth, was offered as an alternative and was accepted although considered 'unsuitable for the safe operation of modern aircraft'.

The summer of 1945 also saw the loan of some airfields in Northern Ireland — Ballyhalbert, Kirkistown and Nutt's Corner — to the FAA. A request for an aerodrome for torpedo training to be available by August 1945 centred around Tain or Leuchars. The former was the more desirable, being located close to the existing RNAS at Fearn, but in the event neither was acquired.

The Navy was still building one of its airfields long after the war ended. This was Culdrose in Cornwall and a question was asked in Parliament in June 1945 why an entirely new site was under construction when RAF Predannack already existed virtually next door.

Since Culdrose had been requisitioned as early as 1943 and was in an advanced state of completion, it was retained and commissioned on 17 April 1947, Predannack having become redundant and been on a care and maintenance basis for almost a year by then!

A clutch of former USAAF bases in East Anglia — Beccles, Bungay and Halesworth — were taken over for a short period in 1945-46. However, the sudden end of the war in the Pacific meant the rapid run down of the FAA and most of the airfields on loan were duly returned to the RAF.

Of the longer established RNASs, Ayr, Crail, Dale, Evanton, Fearn and Worthy Down were all closed to flying by mid-1948 and the FAA was left with just a mere handful of its wartime acquisitions. Some well-known names were included, Abbotsinch, Arbroath, Ford, Gosport and Lee-on-Solent being amongst them. As naval aviation declined, so did the number of active air stations. Arbroath became a ground training station in 1954, Gosport closed in 1956, Anthorn, Bramcote, Ford and Stretton succumbed in 1958, followed by Donibristle a year later.

In 1963 Eglinton and Abbotsinch closed and during 1971 and 1972 Brawdy and Lossiemouth respectively were transferred to the RAF. RNAS Belfast, better known as Sydenham, was given up in 1973 and today only Yeovilton and Culdrose remain operational, together with a helicopter base at Prestwick and a communications airfield at Lee-on-Solent.

Chapter 16

Flying boat bases

Marine aircraft are such a thing of the past in Britain that on the rare occasions that a large flying boat makes an appearance, there are few suitable places from which it can operate. During the Second World War, however, it was a very different picture for there were more than 40 marine bases around these shores and on inland waters. In addition to these, there were numerous alighting and mooring areas in sheltered waters which had no land facilities but provided a haven in bad weather, and enabled flying boats to be dispersed away from vulnerable sites like Sullom Voe in the Shetlands.

More than 30 stations for marine aircraft were created in the First World War, most of them in existing harbours. Between the wars, the numbers dwindled to a mere handful but they included some famous names such as Calshot and Felixstowe. The First World War seaplane station at Cattewater in Plymouth Harbour was retained as a reserve and storage base, but it was revived in September 1928 for operational use. On 1 October 1929 it was renamed Mount Batten.

In September 1939 there were still only about seven flying boat bases at strategic points around the British Isles. More were obviously required as quickly as possible and the Air Ministry Works Directorate, apart from its urgent commitment to find suitable sites for land aerodromes, was also expected to survey potential flying boat stations. This involved soundings over many square miles for seaplane docks and piers, slipways and moorings, and by the end of the war approximately 20 coastal areas had been exhaustively surveyed in this way.

Flying boat maintenance was another problem. Previously, most of it had been done at Calshot on the Solent, but with the possibility of invasion 50 per cent of the Flying Boat Servicing Unit was dispersed to Scotland. A requisitioned boat-building yard at Greenock on the Clyde was to be used and RAF Greenock duly opened on 10 October 1940.

On 12 March 1942 Wig Bay near Stranraer became the home of 1 Flying Boat Servicing Unit. The latter was absorbed by 57 MU which formed here on 8 October 1943. The site was located on the shores of Loch Ryan close to the existing RAF Stranraer, and was constructed on a scale sufficient to allow for the major servicing of eight flying boat squadrons.

Stranraer had been used by operational flying boats for a short period before assuming a training role in mid-1940. It was reduced to Care and Maintenance in July 1943 but Wig Bay remained active until 1957. Sunderlands were the only boats still in RAF service by that time and from October 1951, when 57 MU disbanded, all maintenance was taken over by Short Brothers under contract.

With U-boats ranging almost at will in the North Atlantic in late 1940, it was imperative that air cover for convoys should be extended. At that time flying boats were the only aircraft with anything like the necessary endurance but Pembroke Dock, the farthest base west, was still a long way from the North-West Approaches to the Clyde ports and Liverpool. The answer was found on Lough Erne, a beautiful scenic site in Northern Ireland.

It was opened as RAF Station Castle Archdale early in February 1941, but renamed RAF Lough Erne on Air Ministry orders on 18 February, this title reverting to Castle Archdale in January 1943. At first, there were few support services and no ground protection against air attack, but the risk was deemed acceptable. Nos 209 and 240 Squadrons with Lerwicks and Catalinas flew from here and within months one of the Cats sighted *Bismarck* and sent the position report which led directly to its sinking.

Top *Technical area at Castle Archdale crowded with Sunderlands and Catalinas in 1944. Note operations block at bottom right, now a tourist information centre* (P.H.T. Green Collection).

Above *Swordfish and Seafoxes beside the seaplane ramp at Lee-on-Solent in 1939* (Via M.J. Burrow).

Below *Beaching party waiting for Sunderland to be towed in at Pembroke Dock* (Via John Evans).

Even before Lough Erne was used for operations, an agreement had been reached with the Irish Government to allow certain RAF aircraft free passage across the narrow neck of neutral territory which separates the Ulster lake from the Atlantic. It saved a long detour which would have reduced the radius of action considerably. Obviously the arrangement compromised Eire's neutrality and one of the conditions was that it should be kept as secret as possible.

As is now well-known, long before the USA entered the war the US and British Governments were laying plans on the co-ordination of strategy should America be drawn into the conflict. One of the agreements was that two naval and two flying boat bases were to be placed at the disposal of the United States in Northern Ireland and Scotland. The air bases were to be on Lough Erne and Loch Ryan, the last-named being adjacent to Stranraer. Pairs of bases were selected in case the *Luftwaffe* bombed American forces out of one of them.

The plan was to establish a base large enough to support four squadrons of Catalinas. American civilians began work in August 1941 at Ely Lodge on Lough Erne and within five months it was completed. However, by that time the USA was at war and events in the Pacific were no doubt the reason why the Lough was never used by US flying boats. Although commissioned by the US Navy in early 1942, steps were taken in June to make the installations and accommodation available to the US Army, units of which were arriving in Northern Ireland. Soon afterwards, the seaplane repair and operating facilities were placed at the disposal of the British.

Since nearby Castle Archdale was already operational, it was decided that Killadeas, as the American-built station had come to be known, would be relegated to training. On 20 July 1942 131 OTU formed here and took over the Catalina training commitment of 4 OTU at Invergordon. Castle Archdale's flare-path was employed for night flying and a satellite known variously as Rock Bay or Boa Island was taken into use.

Sullom Voe in the north of the Shetlands was another wartime utility station, its possibilities having not escaped notice during the 'thirties, as it was first utilized by Sunderlands just before the war began. Initially a depot ship housed the personnel until a hutted camp was built. Such was the scarcity of bricks in the islands that all the station buildings were of timber or Nissen construction.

Marine aircraft bases were unique in that, unlike land airfields, the aircraft were often there before the facilities, hangars and slipways

being built later. Bowmore on Loch Indaal, Islay, was another place hastily pressed into service, chiefly as a satellite for RAF Oban. It never even aspired to a slipway, but three dispersed living sites, a communal site and bomb dump were supplied.

Difficulties with handling operational aircraft at Bowmore were exacerbated by an exposed mooring area and it was finally closed in January 1944. A small party of airmen was retained, however, to look after any diverted aircraft and 131 OTU continued to use the loch for water landing practice.

Storms were the greatest enemy of moored flying boats and it was at Bowmore that Sunderland DD831 belonging to 422 Squadron foundered on 25 January 1944. When a gale warning was received it was customary to position a skeleton crew on board aircraft at their moorings so that the engines could be used to keep station if necessary. On this occasion the gale crew took to their dinghy when the aircraft began to sink. The Second Pilot, however, was unable to reach it and was later rescued from the tailplane by a pinnace!

One of the worst catastrophes happened in a storm at Wig Bay when a number of Catalinas and Sunderlands were sunk and driven ashore, fortunately without loss of life. Ice was not a common problem in British waters but it did overtake Castle Archdale one night in January 1945, badly damaging several Sunderlands with its squeezing effect despite the efforts of many steel-bottomed marine craft acting as ice-breakers day and night. It was one of the few occasions that it was possible to walk out to a moored flying boat!

Night flying aids at marine stations were extremely basic right up to 1945 when steps were at last being taken to rectify this situation. Part of a report by Flight Lieutenant H.J. King attached to 201 Squadron in August/September 1943, described operations on Lough Erne as follows:

> 'The take-off path is denoted by three small lights on anchored floats which can be changed. After the elaborate lay-out of the Aerodrome Lighting Mk II, this appeared to be very scanty and during take-off, once the third light is passed, there is nothing to keep straight on in the form of totem poles on the shores of the Lough and, as boats fully laden require a very large run (sometimes up to three minutes), quite a long part of the take-off is in darkness. The Lough is buoyed for day and night flying, but pilots are required to "know" the areas which are safe, as they are not defined as are runways.'

Above *The unique flying boat dock at Castle Archdale, reputedly built for the Short Shetland which never entered service* (E.A. Cromie).

Left *Sign on a door inside one of Pembroke Dock's surviving hangars. FBTS stands for Flying Boat Training Squadron.*

By the end of 1945 four flying boat bases in the UK were being, or had already been, equipped with a system of landing lights to be used in conjunction with the buoyed flare-paths. The principles governing the layout of these flarepaths were quite complicated, but can be summarized as an ideal length of 3,000 yd with a minimum of 2,000 yd and an ideal interval between lights of 100 yd but up to 500 yd if there was difficulty in laying so many buoys. In addition, outer circle and approach lighting was provided in a modified form of the Airfield Lighting Mk II. Where aircraft were liable to conflict with shipping in a channel, red and green traffic lights were used as a means of signalling to ships entering and leaving these waters.

One of the host of scientific devices invented during the war was a system of switching marine flarepaths and associated lights on and off by the mere pressing of a button on shore, without either connections or the use of radio. The electrical engineer, Dr W. Stren, discovered that by passing an electric current through the water itself in the form of an impulse, every switch on the buoys could be operated simultaneously. The initial tests were made in a swimming pool at Millbank and were so successful that further full scale tests were carried out in Poole Harbour with satisfactory results.

Briefly, a 50-cycle AC current of between one and 3 kw (depending on depth of water, coastal configuration, etc) was fed into the water from leads about a quarter of a mile apart. This ionized the water for an area of some 25 square miles to an average depth of about 60 ft, giving an operational range from the shore control point of roughly five miles. Each buoy was fitted with three equidistant electrodes protected by a cylindrical apron and the minute electrical impulses picked up were passed through an amplifier to operate the switch. By using varying numbers of impulses, different combinations of light could be activated as required.

There were still some technical difficulties with the scheme, however, so that by the time the war ended its universal issue was withheld, pending further operational experience. Replacement buoys were made with sufficient space for the remote control equipment but for the moment continued to be operated by manual on-off switches. In peacetime this was more acceptable and it seems that remote control was not further developed, although I have been unable to obtain any data on this.

Essential for the smooth running of a flying boat base was a small fleet of marine craft. By the end of the war the RAF's Marine Branch operated nearly 700 of them throughout the world. They ranged from 18 ft planing dinghies, through fire floats, seaplane tenders, bomb scows and refuellers, to 60 ft

Above *Civilianized seaplane tender at Pembroke Dock in 1986.*

Right *Sunderland of 201 Squadron on the slipway at Pembroke Dock* (Roy Bonser Collection).

general purpose pinnaces. A few survive in civilian hands, including an ex-tender at Pembroke Dock, while at Castle Archdale, a beached tender in poor condition but still in RAF blue-grey, could be seen as recently as 1983.

Flying boat handling was originally taught to marine craft personnel at Calshot. The Marine Training School, as it was known, moved to Kirkcolm, just north of RAF Wig Bay in May 1942. Kirkcolm was renamed RAF Carsewall on 1 August 1942, several retired Sunderlands with M-serials being available for practice towing, mooring and beaching.

The servicing of flying boats was never easy, a dropped spanner being a lost spanner. A typical routine for the Sunderlands of 201 Squadron in 1943 was a minor inspection every 45 flying hours, that is to say after approximately three operational sorties. This was performed in one day and the aircraft was kept at its buoy throughout. After 90 hours it was brought ashore and inspected, a process which took about two-and-a-half days. The number of hours flown averaged about 1,650 per month, which gives some indication of the servicing crew's workload.

Hangarage for major maintenance was provided at the more permanent stations. At Sullom Voe, for example, there were two Bellmans but, since these were not big enough to house a Sunderland, a TFB was built later.

Another hangar type, unique to marine bases, was the Shetland. Wig Bay had some, long since dismantled and I have yet to find a good photograph of one of them. Castle Archdale and other places, including Wig Bay, had buildings called flying boat pens. They resembled boat sheds under which an aircraft could be pulled nose first for attention. They provided a measure of protection from the elements for aircraft and ground crew.

The great distances between the more northerly stations are put into perspective by an entry in the Operations Record Book for Sullom Voe:

'The question of diversion to alternate seaplane bases for aircraft airborne when Sullom Voe becomes unfit, has to be carefully watched as the reserve endurance of Sunderlands is very limited compared to Catalinas. The nearest base on the East Coast is Alness, 190 nautical miles away, whilst the next, Woodhaven, is 260 miles and can only be used in daylight. The nearest West Coast base is Oban, 325 miles via the Minches route.'

In December 1944 the same ORB had this to say about other everyday difficulties of running a marine base:

'The state of the sea in Garth's Voe also interfered with daily inspections, refuell-

ing and rearming, as it was dangerous to take pinnaces, refuelling and bomb scows alongside the aircraft without risk of damage. It was, however, sometimes possible to take off on operations during lulls with a heavily loaded aircraft on a long run and return with a lighter aircraft on a short run in the lee of the land.'

Flying Control at most sites was eventually located in a proper watch office overlooking the water. In the early days at Castle Archdale it was performed from the operations block but this was obviously unsatisfactory and a new building was provided giving a good view of the Lough. Most watch offices seem to have been simple huts, perhaps with a bay window, but Felixstowe had a pre-war 'fort' type which still exists. Pembroke Dock's call sign in October 1944 was 'Rhymster' and that of its control pinnace a rather apt 'Quackduck'.

Radio contact was maintained between watch office and pinnace, the local orders for Wig Bay in February 1945 stating:

'The control pinnace will be to the left of the downwind end of the alighting strip and will be distinguished by a black and white checked flag at the yardarm and another spread over the deck. After the aircraft has landed, a tender will lead it to the buoy or tow it if necessary.'

Apart from the operational stations of Coastal Command and its training bases, there were many other marine sites from which manufacturers tested new flying boats and seaplanes. Pre-war factories such as Saunders-Roe at Cowes, Shorts at Queens Island and Rochester and Supermarine at Woolston were joined by several duration-only establishments which included Blackburn at Dumbarton and Shorts on Lake Windermere. In addition, Saunders-Roe ran a modification centre at Beaumaris, Anglesey for American flying boats, chiefly Catalinas.

The use of Hamworthy in Poole Harbour

Above left *Royal New Zealand Air Force Sunderland in flying boat pen at Wig Bay* (D. Shepherd).

Above right *Sunderlands and Shetland hangar at Wig Bay, near Stranraer, in the 'fifties* (D. Shepherd).

as a BOAC terminal is well-known, unlike the US Navy operation through Sandy Bay on Lough Neagh in Ulster. Coronadoes of the US Naval Transport Service flew a regular service between May and October 1944 to and from New York, via either Botwood in Newfoundland or Port Lyautey in North Africa.

A mere handful of the marine installations survived the war for more than a few months, the principal RAF ones being Pembroke Dock, Calshot, Felixstowe and Wig Bay. Alness continued to be used spasmodically and Sullom Voe, although allowed to fall into disrepair, was revived for Exercise *Mainbrace* in the summer of 1952. No 201 Squadron's Sunderlands shared the Voe with Mariners of the US Navy, the latter supported by the seaplane tender USS *Timbalier*.

In the autumn of 1945, Wig Bay witnessed the largest assembly of flying boats ever seen in Britain. There were more than 170 Catalinas and Sunderlands but most were destined to be cut up for scrap. Today, the concrete hard-standings on Scar Point can still be discerned but there is little else left of this once busy station.

Sullom Voe was swallowed by the oil terminal, while Felixstowe now forms part of a container port. Pembroke Dock, as befits its former position as one of the RAF's premier flying boat stations, is one of the best preserved. Its main hangars still stand, although the 50-year-old slipway was demolished recently to improve deep water facilities. The magnificent Georgian-style Officers Mess is deteriorating rapidly but it may not be too late to save it. Calshot on the Solent alone retains most of the flavour of its past.

Chapter 17

Satellite Landing Grounds for aircraft storage

During the Second World War there were about 50 airfields throughout Britain which never appeared on aeronautical charts. Secrecy was their watchword and no wonder because this was where hundreds of replacement aircraft were stored and prepared, safe from the eyes of the *Luftwaffe*. Parks, race courses, golf links and humble farms were requisitioned overnight and Spitfires, Hurricanes and Wellingtons replaced pheasants in the woodland margins. These temporary sites are almost forgotten but there are still plenty of traces of their former use.

Aircraft, especially fighters, were the nation's life blood in the summer of 1940 and, as they poured from the factories, hiding places were needed until they were required by operational squadrons. In August 1940 the Secretary of State for Air, Sir Archibald Sinclair, wrote:

> 'There are many large private estates and huge parklands which, if the trees were taken down, would be suitable as landing grounds, if not aerodromes. We are out to win this war and should not be put off by a desire to maintain intact the stately homes of England or the future of horse racing and horse breeding.'

Strong words indeed and although Sinclair probably envisaged fighters operating from prepared strips, the idea was instead adapted for the dispersal of new aircraft.

Sir Alan Cobham, nationally famous for his pre-war air circuses, had great experience in improvizing airfields in unlikely places. He was therefore approached by Lord Beaverbrook, head of the Ministry of Aircraft Production, to select sites where aircraft could be landed, camouflaged and eventually flown off again when needed. A surveyor and a team of battle-weary pilots helped him with the field-work which was by no means easy for

there was little time and many of the recommended sites in fact proved to be useless. Some, however, were adopted but their shortcomings soon became obvious, as we shall see. They were known as Satellite Landing Grounds (SLGs), a term which should not be confused with the RAF's satellite stations which were proper aerodromes, usually equipped with paved runways.

Something in the region of 50 sites were prepared under the direction of consultant engineers Rendall, Palmer and Tritton, each being allotted a number from one to 49. The discrepancy arises from the fact that several were abandoned without being used whilst in the case of a few of the others there is some controversy as to whether or not they were technically SLGs. A few were short-lived, being developed as full airfields and transferred to RAF or FAA control and some were released for other purposes later in the war. There was a certain amount of re-numbering of sites before the final designations were agreed. For example, there were two adjacent SLGs in South Wales, No 5 at St Brides East and No 6, St Brides West but they were amalgamated to become No 6 SLG, No 5 being allocated to Berrow.

Buildings at SLGs were deliberately kept to a minimum with existing farmhouses and cottages generally being commandeered to house the small number of personnel. Miniature hangars, known as Robins, were designed to resemble private houses and each could hold two aircraft of Spitfire size. They had sliding doors at one end only and were fitted with a dummy chimney. The illusion was completed by the painting of doors and windows on the sides. Some were cleverly disguised to look like barns, wayside garages and other innocent structures. An average of four Robins or the slightly larger Super-Robin were sited around each SLG. Watch offices were of stan-

Robin Hangar on one of Shawbury's far-flung dispersal sites with dummy chimney and faded 'half-timbered' paint scheme to match houses in the village.

dard design very like a civilian bungalow and mess rooms and armouries were, as far as possible, made to resemble farm outbuildings. Access tracks followed existing farm roads where practicable.

One or more SLGs were allocated to each Maintenance Unit which acted as an Aircraft Storage Unit (ASU) and they were to be brought into service as soon as the landing strip was usable and when approximately ten aircraft were capable of being stored. Hides made from steel wool were erected and extensive use was made also of camouflage netting. Windsocks were too conspicuous so a smoke generator was installed to indicate the wind direction whenever a landing was anticipated.

The first SLG, No 1, opened at Slade Farm in Oxfordshire on 1 December 1940 under the control of 8 MU at Little Rissington. However, winter weather and labour shortages restricted implementation of the plan and only four more were ready for use by the end of March 1941. They were at Middle Farm in Oxfordshire (8 MU), Berrow in Worcestershire (5 MU), Hornby Hall in Cumberland (12 MU) and Aberffraw on Anglesey (48 MU). The latter, soon renamed Bodorgan, was unique in that it was already an established grass aerodrome with many buildings and could therefore never be camouflaged adequately.

Thereafter, expansion was rapid and by 1 July 1941 27 SLGs were active, each defended in theory by one army platoon with 12 Tommy guns between them and three improvized armoured cars, *Beaverettes*. To save valuable manpower, however, SLGs were often guarded

by a local Home Guard unit or one that was raised from civilian employees of the parent MU. At others, soldiers who were based or in training locally made periodic anti-sabotage patrols. SLGs were amongst the first RAF installations to be protected by guard dogs, No 7 SLG at Chepstow having a team of seven Airedales early in 1942. One at least died on active service when poor Rex (dog No 41) choked on his food at St Brides in February 1942!

By 1944 there seems to have been a relaxing of security, for some SLGs were totally unguarded. An example of this is provided by Hoar Cross in Staffordshire which, during a visit made at this time, revealed a few parked Whitleys along the roadside but no other signs of life!

A total of 34 sites were in operation by 1 September 1941 and instructions had been issued in June to the effect that replacement fighter aircraft were so essential to the country's security that they were to be dispersed amongst ASUs and SLGs to the maximum degree. The sites were still cunningly concealed and often had the aircraft parking areas fenced off in order to permit livestock grazing on the landing strips when these were not in use. Dummy hedges were painted across the grass in either tar or creosote. The dispersal of Coastal Command aircraft with their conspicuous white fuselage sides caused a headache until sufficient camouflage netting became available and such aircraft were initially banned from storage at SLGs.

The camouflage was often so effective that

it caused some embarrassment. For example, on 3 September 1941, an Air Transport Auxiliary pilot landed a Piper Cub on one of the dispersal fields at Hornby Hall because he was unable to distinguish the runway. Another incident occurred on 4 June 1942 when a Spitfire of 53 OTU caught fire in the air and crash-landed in a field. The pilot was annoyed to learn later that he was only two miles from a usable airfield, namely No 7 SLG at Chepstow! Despite there being 17 aircraft on the ground here he failed to notice any indication of its existence. Conversely at Knowsley Park, two Gloster Gauntlets on a ferry flight force-landed owing to bad weather. When interviewed both pilots said it looked like an aerodrome and could not be mistaken for anything else! The regular use of SLGs by RAF units was heavily discouraged to avoid compromising the camouflage, any local arrangements being swiftly quashed when higher authority learned of them.

Northern Ireland was provided with five SLGs, all being intended for use by 23 MU at Aldergrove, but such was the scarcity of suitable airfield sites in the province that three of them were developed into full airfields, leaving just two SLGs for the MU. The first to open was Murlough, also known as Dundrum, the initial trial landing being performed by a Blenheim on 11 March 1941 with the field being brought into full use just four days later. Maydown was visited by an Anson on 10 April 1941 and opened on 14 April when a Whitley V was flown in for storage. St Angelo was also available for use from April and was quickly followed by Langford Lodge on 9 May. Both of these sites were on very poorly drained land and it was found necessary to build two concrete runways at each.

On 12 September 1941, Maydown and Langford Lodge were handed over to the RAF on the understanding that they could be used by 41 Group, Maintenance Command when required for the storage of aircraft. Maydown subsequently became a satellite of RAF Eglinton and was later to acquire full Royal Naval Air Station status. Langford Lodge was expanded into a vast Base Air Depot for the USAAF, this being particularly ironic for it lay on the ancestral estate of General Sir Edward Packenham, the British Officer who was defeated by Andrew Jackson at the Battle of New Orleans in 1815.

St Angelo also was lost to the MU when it was enlarged to become a Combat Crew Replacement Centre for American fighter pilots, although it was destined never to be used in this role. Ballywalter opened on 1 June 1941 and remained in use until March 1945, while another field known as Blaris was considered as an emergency dispersal site. Unfortunately, after a test landing in April 1941, an Anson sank into an unsuspected soft spot and was damaged, resulting in Blaris being abandoned as unsuitable.

On the mainland more and more SLGs were being opened, although some were used only briefly owing to the wet winter weather. Remedial work was carried out so that they would be ready in the spring of 1942. The last to open were at Grove Park in Nottinghamshire in the summer of 1942 and Brayton Park, Cumberland on 29 May 1942. Five sites which

Robin at former No 1 SLG Slade Farm, Oxfordshire, adapted for farm use.

Left *Standard tractor shed at former No 33 SLG, Weston Park, Staffs.*

Right *No 40 SLG, Dornoch, seen from the cathedral tower in 1945. Lancasters and Beaufighters are among the aircraft visible* (Via D.A. Goskirk).

were planned but never brought into use are known to be Calmsden in Gloucestershire, Southgrove in Wiltshire, Picton in Pembrokeshire, Kayshill in Ayrshire and Macaroni Down. Kayshill was intended as an SLG for Prestwick, presumably to disperse aircraft after transatlantic ferry flights, and was under construction in November 1941, although it was soon abandoned and I can find no trace of it today. Macaroni Down's exact location is problematical but one theory is that the proximity of RAF Southrop, Gloucestershire caused its closure.

The cumulative cost of providing SLGs was estimated by the Ministry of Aircraft Production in 1943 as £1,355,000, a sum roughly equivalent to that required to build one three-runway airfield of the period. The hasty choice of some sites inevitably caused problems, Dornoch for example costing £5,000 more than the original estimate of £33,000. Expenditure on SLGs was kept to a minimum as it usually had no residual value and there would obviously be further expense on reinstatement for deterioration of land and loss of shadow due to the felling of trees, and replacement of fencing.

The spring of 1943 saw a revoking of the long-standing rule that aircraft at SLGs and MUs should never be parked in groups of more than two. They could now be positioned in threes or fours, provided that aircraft in these groups were so placed that a burst of fire from any one direction would not damage more than one aircraft. The distance between the groups was never to be less than 50 yd. This was an attempt to reduce the cost of building hard-standings at airfields and of laying wire mesh dispersals at SLGs. The holdings at the latter increased sharply by the end of May 1943 when there were 83 aircraft at Middle Farm, 71 at Brocton and the highest number, 93, at Down Farm.

Plans for the projected invasion of Europe included a scheme to provide accommodation by the winter of 1943 for 10,000 aircraft with 41 Group, Maintenance Command. It was expected that the ASUs would cater for 7,000 of them but the remaining 3,000, including anything up to 200 four-engined types, would have to go the SLGs. During the previous winter, SLGs had held only about 1,000 and a lot of work on drainage of runways and improved access tracks was necessary to render them fit for the greatly increased traffic that was expected. At the same time, the work had, as far as possible, to avoid prejudicing the existing camouflage.

In 1943 only 30 of the 42 SLGs then in being were in active use by 41 Group, the remaining 12 being held in reserve on a care and maintenance basis. It was decided to reduce the latter number to eight by giving up Rudbaxton, always unsatisfactory because of high ground and adjacent RAF stations; Winterseugh owing to poor drainage; Grove Park which had an inadequate landing strip for modern types and Hardwick Park which was used partly by Airborne Forces for training with live ammunition.

The other eight SLGs were retained because, on more than one occasion, the entire output of a certain type of aeroplane had to be directed to storage for a variety of reasons, thus stretching existing facilities to the limit. There was also the possibility of a renewed enemy attack on the British Isles which would necessitate even wider aircraft dispersal. Five of the reserve SLGs — at Stravithie, Townsend, Bush Barn and Leanach — were in daily use by Flying Training Command as RLGs and all were under grazing agreements so there was no loss of food production.

The forecast storage requirements for the winter of 1943-44 proved to be an over-

estimate, the average monthly SLG holding being just 1,136 aircraft. In February 1944 it was calculated that the 30 SLGs could accommodate up to 2,560 aircraft, but despite such tasks as removing the engines from 100 Hampdens and storing the airframes for a considerable time, this capacity was never reached. De-requisitioning began early in 1945 and by the beginning of June that year only 17 sites remained to help deal with the huge quantities of surplus aircraft that had to be scrapped.

Concealment was obviously unnecessary during the final months of their life so the SLGs were soon packed with aircraft. As an instance of this, Woburn Park was scheduled to receive a total of 174 Stirlings to relieve pressure at the parent MU at Brize Norton. Scrapping of these machines occupied much of 1946, the Park not being completely clear of the RAF until as late as May 1947. Incidentally, Woburn, along with Lennoxlove and Leanach in Scotland, is one of the few SLGs known to have been used by aircraft before the war, the Duchess of Bedford's Moth and other types operating from the Park on a regular basis. Brayton in Cumberland was cleared gradually of over 100 Wellingtons and closed in December 1945, whilst in South Wales, St Brides was de-requisitioned at the end of July 1945, except for a small strip of land on which a few Henleys and 18 Beaufighters were being broken up.

During the brief lives of these little airfields some large and sophisticated aircraft had flown in and out. Early in 1942 many of the SLGs were tested to establish their suitability for four-engined types. Most were found acceptable, if somewhat marginal, and it is a tribute to the skill of the MU test pilots and the ferry pilots of ATA that the movements of such types as the Halifax, Stirling and Fortress became routine. The operation of aircraft with the newfangled tricycle undercarriages on grass strips

was treated with misgivings at first, but this too became an everyday occurrence. Brayton's first such aircraft was a Mitchell in June 1943 and a few months later Bostons and Albemarles were to be seen at Chepstow. Fighter aircraft used the SLGs too, including Mustangs at Hornby Hall, Hellcats at Hoar Cross and Spitfires at a number of places. Oddest of all was perhaps the Westland Welkin, a handful of which ended their days at Lennoxlove at the hands of 18 MU.

Despite the cramped dimensions, there were few serious accidents, most being caused by RAF pilots unaccustomed to the short runways. In fact after several Hurricanes were damaged at Bodorgan by squadron pilots on collection duties, 48 MU decided that its own pilots would position the fighters to Hawarden when required! Some minor damage was also caused by natural hazards, sometimes of an unusual nature. At Lennoxlove several Wellingtons were damaged at various times when sheltering beech trees were blown down in gales, whilst misjudgements resulted in a number of bent wingtips when large aircraft were being taxied in confined spaces. At Woburn an Anson even managed to collide with a deer and the animals were subsequently kept in a compound.

Apart from the sites previously mentioned in Northern Ireland which were developed as full airfields, several on the mainland were expanded as well but never aspired to concrete runways. Findo Gask in Perthshire was intended to be 25 SLG but was handed over to Flying Training Command before being taken into use. It was then employed as an RLG for Tiger Moths from Perth, then housed 309 Squadron for a while and finally served as the home of the Naval Flight of 9 (Pilot) Advanced Flying Unit at Errol.

Ollerton in Shropshire became RNAS Hinstock in 1942 when the Admiralty, which had a very urgent need for an instrument training airfield in a central position, requested joint use of one of the SLGs. After due consideration it was decided that this would be impracticable so Ollerton was transferred entirely to the FAA as HMS *Godwit*. Another SLG in the area, Weston Park, was used jointly as HMS *Godwit II* in a satellite role. Tatton Park in Cheshire was shared with 1 Parachute Training School at Ringway but finally given up to this organization in May 1943 when the pace of training increased sharply as preparations for the invasion moved into top gear.

Several sites have been quoted as SLGs but these, although serving a similar function, were in fact managed by aircraft manufacturers to disperse output away from the vulnerable factory area. Marwell Hall, where four Robin hangars can still be seen, was run by Cunliffe-Owen so that new and modified aircraft could be moved outside the heavily defended port of Southampton where the company was based amidst the balloon barrage.

Cowdray Park was a satellite of Lee-on-Solent and was sometimes referred to as a 'Naval SLG'. In Warwickshire, the pre-war private strip at Heronfield was often seen to be occupied by Spitfires believed to be an overspill from the Castle Bromwich plant, whilst Baginton sent new Whitleys to the Leamington aerodrome at Bishops Tachbrook. Plans to build a mile-long taxi-way from Baginton to a dispersal at Stoneleigh were vetoed by the local landed gentry in defiance of the Government's sweeping powers of requisition.

A third category, the Sub-Storage Site, also causes confusion because official documents often refer to them as SLGs. They were in fact surplus airfields taken over by the MUs for storage and scrapping after their wartime occupants had disbanded or moved elsewhere. They were numbered from 100, this being the designation of Hooton Park in Cheshire. Other examples were 101 SSS at Maghabery, 102 SSS at Brackla, 103 SSS at West Freugh and 105 SSS at Castle Kennedy.

Evidence of almost all the SLGs can still be found if one knows just what to look for. The bungalow guardroom/watch offices, with a little modification, made excellent dwellings and many are still occupied, including those at Brinklow and Weston Park. They conform to a style of architecture common on the Scottish Borders but look slightly out of place in the English Midlands! The tractor which was so essential for moving aircraft on the ground was always kept in a small shed of standard pattern to facilitate maintenance and ease of starting, and these buildings are another frequent survivor. Barrack huts, mess rooms, armouries (the latter recognizable by their barred windows) and gun testing butts are good clues to the exact location of a particular site.

The best landmark, however, is the Robin hangar. Many of these, especially where the landing ground was centred on a farm, were left *in situ*, perhaps as part of a deal for compensation after de-requisitioning, and they make excellent grain stores or shelters for agricultural equipment. The fences should not

Robin hangar disguised as a gamekeeper's cottage at one of 9 MU Cosford's SLGs, probably Weston Park (PRO).

be ignored either, for they are often made from square mesh track runways which were torn up after the war and used to replace the original hedgerows. Wide fenced gaps in the latter sometimes mark the spots where aircraft were towed across roads. This was necessary because the storage area was often discreetly separated from the landing strip, good examples being viewable today at Barton Abbey and Hodnet.

Satellite Landing Grounds

No	Name	OS map ref	County	Remarks and representative aircraft types known to have been stored there
1	Slade Farm	164/509220	Oxon	In use from 1 December 1940 to at least December 1945. Nos 8, 15 and 39 MUs. Also by Hotspur gliders from the units at Kidlington for landing practice. Wellington.
2	Starveall Farm	164/412192	Oxon	In use from 14 June 1941 to 29 September 1945 by 39 MU. Hurricane.
3	Middle Farm	164/685171	Mixbury, Oxon	In use from 25 February 1941 to 31 December 1945 by 8 MU, also by Hotspurs from Kidlington for landing practice. Wellington.
4	Rudbaxton	158/960215	Pembs	In use from April 1941 to 25 September 1942 by 38 MU. De-requisitioned 1 July 1943. Spitfire.
5	Berrow	150/805340	Worcs	Also called Pendock Moor. Used by 5, 20 and 38 MUs from January 1942 (or earlier) until 31 May 1945. Also by Hotspurs from 5 GTS, Shobdon for landing practice in 1942 and liaison aircraft from TRE at Defford. Spitfire.
6	St Brides	154/900735	Glamorgan	Used by 19 MU from approx April 1941 until 26 September 1945. Spitfire, Beaufighter.
7	Chepstow	162/525955	Monmouth	Used by 19 and 38 MUs from 13 May 1941 to 31 May 1945. Spitfire, Albemarle, Boston.
8	Hutton-in-the-Forest	90/470350	Cumb	Used by 22 MU. First test landing 1 June 1941 by Anson. Closed August 1945. Blenheim, Botha, Mustang, Ventura.
9	Hornby Hall	91/575295	Cumb	Used by 12 and 22 MUs (briefly by 18 MU) from 17 March 1941 to 2 July 1945 then became POW Camp. Botha, Wellington, Hurricane, Anson.
10	Wath Head	85/297480	Cumb	Used by 18 MU. First test landing 23 March 1941, closed September 1945. Botha, Halifax, Wellington.

No	Name	OS map ref	County	Remarks and representative aircraft types known to have been stored there
11	Low Eldrig	82/112427	Wigtownshire	Used by 18 MU. First test landing 3 June 1941 by Dominie. Believed not used after 1942. Battle, Blenheim.
12	Beechwood Park	166/046145	Beds	Used by 5 and 15 MUs from at least May 1942 and still in use 16 October 1945. Hurricane, Seamew. Number allocated originally to Calmsden.
13	Tatton Park	109/756827	Ches	Used by 48 MU from 11 August 1941 until May 1943 when handed over to Airborne Forces (previously a joint-user) as a satellite and DZ for the PTS at Ringway. Wellington, Halifax, Lysander. Previous use as an ELG. Number allocated originally to Macaroni Down.
14	Overley	163/965045	Glos	Used by 10 and 20 MUs from 21 April 1941 to at least April 1944. Also used during 1942 as an RLG by 3 EFTS. Spitfire.
15	Bodorgan	114/400715	Anglesey	Originally known as Aberffraw. Used by 48 MU from 31 March 1941 until 30 December 1945. Also used for flying other than as an SLG. Botha, Wellington.
16	Ballywalter	15/J630675	Co Down	Used by 23 MU from 1 June 1941 to 14 March 1945. First test landing 25 April 1941 by Anson. Wellington.
17	Maydown	7/C485210	Co Londonderry	First test landing by an Anson on 10 April 1941. Used by 23 MU. Handed over to Air Ministry late 1941 for development as a satellite of Eglinton. Later became an RNAS. Wellington.
18	St Angelo	17/H230500	Co Fermanagh	Opened in April 1941 for 23 MU but actual use doubtful as it was soon developed as a full airfield.
19	Murlough	15/J405350	Nr Newcastle Co Down	Also known as Dundrum. Used by 23 MU from 15 March 1941 to 14 February 1945. Also used by 'A' Flight 88 Sqn with Battles 26 May to 23 June 1941 and 652 AOP Sqn in 1942. Wellington.
20	Langford Lodge	14/J100760	Co Antrim	Used by 23 MU from 9 May 1941 but closed 15 May 1942. Concrete runways had been laid because of wet ground so the site was developed as an airfield in its own right. Wellington.

No	Name	OS map ref	County	Remarks and representative aircraft types known to have been stored there
21	Ollerton	126/660267	Salop	Used by 27 and 37 MUs from at least 17 October 1941 but given up in August 1942 and developed as RNAS Hinstock. Master.
22	Barnsley Park	173/082062	Glos	Used by 5 and 6 MUs. Closed September 1945. Spitfire.
23	Down Farm	173/853908	Glos	Also known as Westonbirt. Used by 10 MU from 15 May 1941 until January 1946. Also used as an RLG by 15 (P) AFU, Babdown Farm. On 2 August 1945 there were 246 aircraft stored there.
24	Methven	58/050253	Perthshire	Used by 44 MU from June 1941 to at least April 1944. Also by Army Co-operation Squadrons such as 652 Sqn and naval communications aircraft. Wellington.
25	Findo Gask	58/010215	Perthshire	Built in 1941 for 44 MU but not used. Handed over to Flying Training Command.
26	Stravithie	59/537124	Fife	Used by 44 MU from 9 May 1941, closure date unknown. Defiant, Wellington.
27	Lennoxlove	66/523717	East Lothian	Also called Haddington. Used by 18 MU, first test landing 24 April 1941 by Battle L5797, closed September 1945. Hurricane, Wellington, Blenheim.
28	Barton Abbey	164/463248	Oxon	Also known as Lower Heyford and Hopcroft's Halt. Used by 8 and 39 MUs from 30 September 1941. Closure date unknown. Wellington, Spitfire.
29	Hodnet	127/615270	Salop	Used by 24, 27, 37 and 51 MUs from 12 June 1941 to February 1945. Master.
30	Brockton	127/791048	Salop	Used by 9 MU from 30 June 1941, closure date unknown. Spitfire, Beaufighter, Wildcat.
31	Everleigh	184/202532	Wilts	Used by 15 and 33 MUs from about November 1941 to at least December 1944. Hurricane. Previous use as an ELG.
32	Hoar Cross	128/128224	Nr Yoxall, Staffs	Used by 51 MU from 27 July 1941 until June 1945. Whitley, Hellcat, Boston.

No	Name	OS map ref	County	Remarks and representative aircraft types known to have been stored there
33	Weston Park	127/805104	Staffs	Used by 9 MU from at least June 1941. Later a satellite to RNAS Hinstock as HMS *Godwit II*. Spitfire.
34	Woburn Park	165/970340	Beds	Used by 6 and 8 MUs. Opening and closing dates unknown but breaking up of stored Stirlings went on until May 1947.
35	Blidworth	112/590540	Notts	Used by 51 MU in 1942 at least. Wellington. Previous use as an ELG.
36	Winterseugh	85/165706	Dumfries	Used by 18 MU, first test landing 30 April 1941. De-requisitioned 20 April 1944 since it was too small for aircraft types then in use. Battle, Wellington.
37	Hardwick Park	112/465635	Derbys	Used by 27 and 51 MUs. Opened May 1941, transferred to School of Airborne Forces 14 September 1943. Defiant.
38	Grove Park	174/412910	Notts	Used by 27 and 51 MUs from at least August 1942. De-requisitioned 29 April 1944 as too small for aircraft then in use. Hurricane.
39	Brayton	85/172425	Cumb	'Hall' or 'Park' sometimes appended to name. Built 1941 but not opened until 29 May 1942. Used by 12 MU and closed in December 1945. Spitfires, Fortress, Mitchell, Halifax.
40	Dornoch	21/800885	Sutherland	Used by 45 and 46 MUs from at least August 1941 until 27 September 1945. Spitfire, Wellington.
41	Kirkton	21/803983	Sutherland	Also called Golspie. Used by 45 MU from at least August 1941. Still in use October 1944, closure date unknown. Spitfire, Whitley.
42	Black Isle	21/716604	Ross and Cromarty	At Blackstand Farm. Used by 46 MU from 22 August 1941 until October 1945. Beaufighter.
43	Leanach	27/757455	Moray	Also called Culloden Moor. Used by 46 MU. First test landing 10 May 1941, handed over to 19 (P)AFU, which had earlier been a joint user, on 11 October 1943. Beaufighter, Hurricane.

No	Name	OS map ref	County	Remarks and representative aircraft types known to have been stored there
44	Bush Barn	158/360960	Nr Pusey, Oxon	Used by 5 MU from 22 September 1941. Also by 3 EFTS as an RLG and from 1 August 1944 as a satellite of RNAS Worthy Down — possibly as HMS *Kestrel II*. Closure date unknown.
45	Townsend	157/070725	Wilts	Used by 10 and 33 MUs from at least September 1941, closure date unknown. Spitfire.
46	Brinklow	140/436783	Warks	Used by 29 MU from 16 October 1941. Also by training aircraft from Ansty and Church Lawford. Closure date unknown. Hampden.
47	Southgrove	174/235585	Wilts	Planned to open 30 August 1941 under 15 MU but never used.
48	Teddesley Park	127/955155	Nr Penkridge, Staffs	Used by 29 MU from July 1941 to December 1945. Hudson, Ventura, Hotspur.
49	Knowsley Park	108/460960	Nr Prescott, Lancs	Used by 37 and 48 MUs. First test landing 14 October 1941 but not opened until 15 May 1942. Closed November 1944. Wellington.
50	Name not traced			

Other SLG Sites

Calmsden, Glos	Not used
Kayshill, Ayr	Under construction in November 1941 but abandoned.
Macaroni Down, Glos	Completed but later de-requisitioned.
Picton, Pembs	Not used.

Each SLG was considered as a sub-unit of a particular Maintenance Unit so, although they were frequently transferred from one unit to another, they usually held only aircraft from one MU at any given time.

Chapter 18

Bombing and gunnery ranges in the Second World War

The numerous bombing and firing ranges which supported the wartime training of aircrews have long since faded into obscurity, but the dedicated aviation archaeologist can still find evidence of their existence. The Army and Navy had their ranges as well and often required aircraft to tow targets for the gunners. Regrettably, no official list of these facilities seems to have survived and it is only with difficulty that I have been able to trace the following outline.

Prior to the expansion period of the mid-to-late 'thirties, a total of 17 ranges of various types existed. Additional facilities were urgently needed and it was not always easy to find suitable sites. The requirements of a typical air gunnery school, for example, normally involved the acquisition of about 80 acres of land for ground ranges and the various buildings and controls. Added to this was the provision of a sea area about 10 miles long and five miles deep, including the rights to the foreshore, which could then be regulated through by-laws and Admiralty and Board of Trade Orders.

The accommodation was comparatively small, consisting usually of a range party living building, control tower, quadrant shelters and a number of types of target for the different ranges. Housing for the supporting marine craft party was also necessary and was often located at some distance where suitable moorings were available. The planning procedure in respect of each range was considerable, entailing extensive reconnaissance surveys to find sites and close liaison with the appropriate Commands before plans could be drawn up.

Objections poured in on grounds as diverse as the effects on swans at Abbotsbury in Dorset and the disturbance of the peace at Holy Island and other possible sites. In a celebrated court case, three Welsh intellectuals were jailed for a minor act of arson at Penrhos in

protest against the building of a bombing school and ranges. Some of the objections were heeded but the sites were merely kept in abeyance and developed when war came.

During 1935, coastal ranges were constructed at Skipsea, Languard and Theddlethorpe, the latter being an integral part of the Air Armament School at Manby. Target launches were in use at some of the ranges, including Luce Bay and Christchurch Bay which served RAF Calshot. They had a crew of three protected by an armoured cabin. Bombing targets consisted of a simple wooden framework mounted on piles driven 6 ft into the sand. Often they were found unequal to the combined force of gales and high tides, so a new type was devised to overcome this deficiency.

One of the first was erected at Luce Bay, serving 4 Armament Training Camp at West Freugh. It was made from steel plates bolted together, forming three towers upon which the superstructure was built on steel girders filled to a height of 17 ft with concrete. The whole affair was built on timber piles driven about 18 ft into the sand and rising 64 ft above it, high tide in the area being 30 ft.

One site at Orford Ness in Suffolk was not for practice but for proving trials with various weaponry. In 1935 a series of tests were carried out with 500 lb general purpose bombs to ascertain the blast and fragmentation effects on concrete walls and other structures. As a result, much valuable data was obtained for the design, thickness and construction of the walls of hangars and technical buildings.

In April 1937 further tests were undertaken on the blast-resisting qualities of different types of wall and window coverings, with special regard to their gas tightness after explosion. It was imperative that the trials proceed as quickly as possible so that the design and construction of the new Expansion stations should not be delayed. One major fact emerged — for an above ground structure no window or special window covering or shutter was reliable against blast effect. Windows, from a gas protection point of view, were useless, and this information was duly incorporated in the windowless design of operations and decontamination blocks.

The pre-war ranges usually had an adjoining landing ground with basic refuelling and rearming facilities, administered by the associated Armament Training Station, as at Hell's Mouth, coming under Penrhos; Tain, under Evanton, and Donna Nook, under North Coates Fitties, for example.

In 1937 airfield ranges were provided at Marham, Feltwell, Scampton, Honington, Mildenhall and Hemswell, and in the following year 17 more ranges on bomber aerodromes were added. They were obviously of limited use because of the proximity of buildings and the restrictions on other traffic when in use. It was really an extension of the long-established 'bombing circle' of white chalk in the centre of most RAF aerodromes in the 1920s and early 1930s. When bomber OTUs were formed in wartime, a number of proper ranges were established in isolated places well away from the parent airfield.

The pre-war ranges catered for little more than practice and live bombing, and air-to-air and air-to-ground firing, but the war brought with it a requirement for a variety of other activities. Amongst these were rocket firing, torpedo and depth charge dropping, moving target bombing, air-to-sea firing and turret ranges.

Certain of the larger ranges, particularly of the coastal type, entailed the construction of three or more bombing targets, six or more quadrant shelters, about 10 air-ground targets and two rocket projectile ranges. There were also marker shelters, dive screen shelters and signals. During the war period, approval was given and construction undertaken on new sites for 13 turret ranges, 103 coastal ranges and 108 inland ranges. All the inland sites were re-surveyed for enlargement in 1943 and considerable re-siting and alteration was necessary.

It was the practice for the Air Ministry to take full possession of the target area itself. Outside this, within a certain radius, the land was considered to be a danger area and was appropriated for use of the range under the sweeping powers of Defence Regulation 52. At the same time, a set of by-laws was published which prohibited entry to the land while bombing was in progress. Indication as to whether or not the range was active was given by the usual signal, a red flag. When the flag was flying the area was dangerous, when it was down it was safe. By these means the occupier of the land was able to gain full access and continue with cultivation when the range was not in use.

The open flat expanse of many of the ranges was considered to offer a potential landing ground for enemy troop-carrying aircraft and steps were accordingly taken to obstruct them. At Tain in May 1940, for example, coils of barbed wire were stretched along the ground, intermingled with old cars and tractors.

Bombing ranges had two or more quadrant towers of a standard pattern overlooking the target area. The occupants were equipped to take bearings through telescopes as each practice bomb burst and, when the position was fixed, the result was radioed to the aircraft. One of these towers still stands near Grandborough in Warwickshire and has evidence of a repaired hole in the concrete roof. I discovered that one of the range personnel lost an arm here when a bomb came through the roof, so it could obviously have been quite a dangerous occupation.

These inland ranges were often alarmingly close to habitation and many bombs went astray. In his book *A Thousand Shall Fall*, Murray Peden gives an amusing account of

Surviving quadrant tower at Grandborough, Warks.

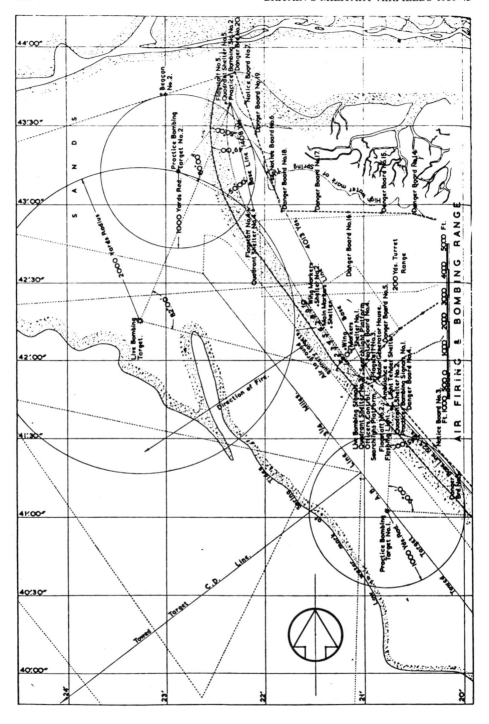

A typical coastal air firing and bombing range.

Concrete range direction arrow still to be seen at Drumburgh, Cumbria (G.J. Rothery).

how the villagers of Shotteswell near Banbury suffered more from the RAF than ever they did from the *Luftwaffe*. RAF stations were not immune either. A crew from 8 (O)AFU at Mona probably had a lot of explaining to do after they accidentally dropped a 10 lb flash bomb on Cark aerodrome when they were supposed to be aiming for the Warton Sands Range which lay about five miles to the south-east! Pinpoint accuracy was not popular either. When a crew from 81 OTU scored a direct hit at night on the Fenns Moss Range, they extinguished the target lamp to the annoyance of those on the ground who had to replace it!

The Wash was virtually ringed with ranges, as Eric Rhodes has described in his book *The Wash in Wartime — A Personal History*, published by Enthusiast Publications in 1981. The following are just a few extracts from the book relating to range activities.

'From a recorded interview with a retired fisherman in King's Lynn, it is known that he and his fellows had a sub-contract from a firm in Brightlingsea to carry out the placing and tying down of cork float targets at ranges from Holbeach and up the Lincolnshire coast as far as and including Donna Nook. The work was carried out for the Air Ministry using the fishing boat *Rachel*.

'Later, this work included the erection of steel portals with triangular super-structure and surmounting basket. In accordance with Ministry directives these baskets had to be produced by disabled people. I take it that these structures were in fact the markers to the various ranges. One was in evidence at Wolferton Marsh to the north-west of North Wooton. Presumably this work went on into the war when I believe it was taken over by service personnel. Painting of the various target markers was also carried out by civilian workers.

'The North Wootton range was established in the early 1940s and was administered by RAF Bircham Newton on behalf of Coastal Command. A "Ship" target was built from tubular scaffolding and painted canvas which looked quite effective even from fairly close range. It was placed on the "kink" in the outer bank but was falling into disrepair in 1942 and had been dismantled and cleared by 1944.

'Various targets were marked out from time to time on the mud flats and were bombed by various aircraft, including such types as Blenheims, Swordfish and Wellingtons. Later, a ship outline was made from oildrums on poles for attack by Beaufighters.

'There were air firing targets inside the outer bank to the north-west and an observation hut, with soil and grass protection on its concrete roof, was nearby. . . Observation huts were erected, one at each extremity of the outer bank. In these was a quadrant with a sighting telescope to make cross readings to check bomb hits. The telescopes were removed at the end of the war but I managed to rescue a quadrant and still have it . . . In 1944 a Cromwell tank arrived and was placed inside the bank, to the south-east of the old ship, for use as a target by RP equipped aircraft.'

Gilbert Rothery has discovered a little more about a range sited at Mawbray Bank, near Silloth in Cumbria. There were two arrows approximately 50 yd apart pointing in a direction of about 240°. The larger one (80 ft long) was painted white and signified 'smoke bombing', whereas the shorter (40 ft) arrow was coloured red and indicated live bombing practice. Canvas covers were fitted over associated concrete circles at the front and sides of the arrow not in use, to guide the aircraft crews, the targets being positioned out to sea.

A little to the north and on the shore were machine-gun targets in the form of red triangles suspended from small structures. In between all this on the edge of the sand dunes was an observation post which was inadver-

Seafire testing its guns at the stop butts at Culham in 1945 (FAA Museum).

tently 'shot up' by one of the trainee pilots during the early operation of the range. The base of this building can still be seen, as can the arrows.

The arrival of the 8th US Army Air Force in Britain brought a further requirement for bombing and air gunnery training to bring crews up to operational standard. The Air Ministry offered a number of ranges, but only Breast Sands in the south-east corner of The Wash was deemed acceptable for high altitude bombing practice. Others were suitable but necessitated long round trips from East Anglia.

As a result of further approaches, the Air Ministry offered Ot Moor in Oxfordshire, which became available in April 1943. Grassholm and Ynys Gwylanfach islets, off the coasts of Pembrokeshire and Caernarvonshire repectively, were allocated the previous month. Smaller ranges in East Anglia were earmarked for USAAF use, non-explosive M38 practice bombs being dropped here and at all other sites. They weighed 100 lb were sand-filled and contained a 3 lb charge of black powder for visual assessment of results.

Air-to-air gunnery training for the USAAF required a further allotment of ranges. The main one was Snettisham in Norfolk, but there were others in Cardigan Bay and the area of the Humber Estuary, serving the fighter training stations at Atcham and Goxhill, respectively. In Northern Ireland several locations on and around Lough Neagh catered for B-17 and B-24 gunners. For full details of the American use of ranges in the UK, the reader is recommended to consult Roger Freeman's *Mighty Eighth War Manual*.

The 3rd CCRC at Toome in Northern Ireland, which trained Marauder crews, made its own target on the tiny Skady Tower Island in Lough Neagh. Construction was the responsibility of the 1561st Ordnance Supply and Maintenance Company and, having been delayed by bad weather, this facility came into use early in 1944. Skady Tower was also used by FAA Seafires and other British aircraft for live dive-bombing practice.

Lough Neagh, the largest inland lake in Britain, was ideal for training and there were a variety of ranges on it. 1 Armament Practice Camp at Aldergrove controlled the activities which, apart from the bombing of fixed targets and air-to-air gunnery, included the low-level bombing of dummy periscopes towed by launches and Leigh Light exercises. The APCs, by the way, were lodged at various mainly coastal locations. They received squadrons on a rotational basis for attachments of about a week so that they could stay in practice with aerial gunnery, RP firing and other methods of weapon delivery.

Air-to-air gunnery, of course, required towed target sleeves and units such as fighter OTUs and Air Gunners' Schools had their own aircraft. Initially, these were Battles, Defiants, Henleys and Lysanders but most of these were replaced by the Martinet later in the war. The 8th Air Force was allotted some Lysanders and Masters by the RAF for its Gunnery and TT Flights but, by the spring of 1944, had standardized on the A-35 Vengeance plus a handful of P-47s and A-20s. It is an indication of the intensity of wartime training that 2 AGS at Dalcross expended over one million rounds of ammunition in May 1944 alone!

At certain ranges some of the bombing was live and this caused the loss of a Spitfire of the Fighter Leaders' School at Milfield, in a

Sea Hurricane V6556 of 759 Squadron at the butts at Yeovilton, 1942 (Via M.J. Burrow).

dive-bombing attack on 9 March 1944. During the build-up to D-Day, the FLS trained hundreds of pilots from both the RAF and USAAF in the techniques of close air support. The range at Goswick Sands in Northumberland featured six Churchill tanks for RP firing, a 10 ft square moving target, gun emplacements and 50 typical soft-skinned vehicles dispersed in convoy for strafing attacks with live ammunition. The site was near to Holy Island where the Air Ministry wished to place a range before the war but local objections forced them to look elsewhere.

Other special ranges included a disused railway tunnel at Maenclochog in south-west Wales, used for live attacks by Mosquitos, and a dummy factory on the moors above Stranraer. The latter was used by the Bombing Trials Unit at West Freugh and when I looked at the remains of the concrete edifice about 10 years ago, it was still surrounded by bomb craters. At Ashley Walk, east of Fordingbridge in Hampshire, *Tallboys* and other large bombs were tested. Presumably there is evidence of this even now, as the resulting craters were 80 ft deep!

With the carrier war moving to the Pacific in 1944, the FAA's Treligga Range in Cornwall was laid out to simulate a typical area of Japanese-held territory. It was modelled on the island of Tarawa and real dummy tanks, a bridge and a road convoy were provided near an airstrip. By December 1944 it was being used for the intensive training of squadron commanders and senior pilots of units destined to join the Pacific Fleet.

Various other places, not necessarily ranges, were used for special training, 617 Squadron

Lancasters making dummy attacks on dams in Derbyshire. At Loch Eriboll in the North of Scotland, 618 Squadron trained with *Highball* Mosquitos, dropping a smaller version of Barnes Wallis's bouncing bomb intended for use against shipping. Abandoned lead mine buildings near Hag Dyke in Yorkshire were used to simulate a hill target for an unspecified special operation.

Infra-red bombing was a procedure which eliminated the necessity of actually dropping anything and thus enabled 'attacks' to be made on real targets in urban areas or on pinpoints such as bridges. Little has been published concerning this simulated bombing, but it appears to have been pioneered by 16 OTU at Upper Heyford during April 1941.

It consisted of a device which projected an infra red beam upwards at the approximate angle and along the pre-determined line of the bombing run. In theory, if the bomb aimer was tracking correctly on his run and had the target centred in his sight, when he pressed the button and activated his camera, the invisible infra-red beam would leave a trace on the exposed film. Once the film was developed, the degree of accuracy or otherwise would be obvious.

The infra-red projectors were placed at a number of locations round the country, examples including Conway in North Wales, Aintree Racecourse, Liverpool and London's Green Park. They were often used in *Bullseye* exercises near the end of the night bomber OTU course, before crews were sent on *Nickels* — leaflet dropping raids to towns in Occupied France.

Bullseyes were introduced in August 1942 and were simulated operations covering about 800 miles on round-Britain routes. Sector Operations, the Royal Observer Corps, search-

lights and night fighters all co-operated in making the exercises as realistic as possible and gained useful experience themselves. Although the defences were imaginary, the dangers from bad weather, high ground and technical malfunctions were real enough, resulting in the deaths of many OTU crews in accidents.

That, then, is a summary of the use of ranges, indispensable to the effectiveness of the RAF's fighters and bombers. So far, I have not been able to trace a master list or map showing all the wartime ranges in the UK. The standard 'half-million' scale charts of the time show only airfields and one wonders how pilots were supposed to avoid flying through dangerous areas if they wandered off their briefed routes. The charts featured a warning on the top right-hand corner: 'areas dangerous to flying are not indicated on this sheet'.

In the event of infringement, black smoke shells were supposed to be fired to warn the intruder to leave the area as fast as possible. The indications were sometimes more positive, as the crew of Wellington LP927 of 81 OTU discovered on 28 February 1945. Straying into the Prohibited Area at Orford Ness, they were hit by AA fire but managed to return to base at Tilstock.

Today, a few of the wartime ranges remain

Top *Hudson starboard wing section close to old bombing target in Solway Firth* (John Huggon).

Above *Liberator VI of 311 Squadron at Tain, Highland, in 1945. The airfield is now derelict but on the edge of a very active bombing range* (Via Zdenek Hurt).

in use, including Pembrey, Aberporth, Holbeach, Wainfleet, Luce Bay, Jurby, Drurridge Bay, Tain and Manorbier, the latter occupied by the Army. The abandoned sites are worth investigation as there is often evidence of their former use. Quadrant towers are common while at some giant concrete arrows and other symbols conspicious to aircraft remain in place as described above. Beware, however, of explosive devices lying around. The ranges were cleared after the war, of course, but not always exhaustively. The wreckage of Hudson AM771 of 1 OTU, Silloth, can be seen where it force-landed on a sandbank in the Solway on 31 August 1942, right next to the bombing tower, which itself still stands.

I am told that seabirds drop shellfish on the concrete at the former Tentsmuir Range in order to break the shells. It is certainly the last bombing activity to be recorded here!

Known ranges 1939-45

Use shown where known plus representative units. Counties are as at the time.

Aberayron, Cardigan	13th Light AA Practice Camp
Aberporth, Cardigan	1st Heavy AA Practice Camp
Ainsdale, Lancashire	HMS *Queen Charlotte* RN AA Gunnery School. 776 Sqn
Amble, Northumberland	Air-to-Air firing, 4 AGS
Ashley Walk, Hampshire	Bombing. A and AEE Boscombe Down
Balcary Point, Kirkcudbright	Bombing. 10 B and GS
Ballaghennie, Isle of Man	Bombing
Ballaugh, Isle of Man	Bombing
Bearshanks Wood, Northants	Bombing by OTUs
Beversbrook, Wiltshire	Bombing 9 FTS
Braid Fell (Stranraer)	Bombing. Bombing Trials Unit, West Freugh
Breast Sands, The Wash	High level bombing. 8th Air Force. 1st Air Division
Burgh By Sands, Cumberland	Firing. 9 OTU
Burrow Head, Wigtownshire	6th Heavy AA Practice Camp. 290 Sqn
Caerlaverock, Dumfriesshire	Firing. 9 OTU
Cannock Chase, Staffordshire	Bombing. 30 OTU
Cherington Moor, Salop	Bombing. 83 OTU
Chesil Beach, Dorset	Bombing and firing. 6 ATS
Chisildon, Wiltshire	Bombing and firing
Cleave, Somerset	AA Practice Camp. 1 AACU
Criccieth, Caerns	Air-to-Air firing. USAAF
Crichel Down, Dorset	Bombing. A and AEE
Cushendall, Co. Antrim	Air-to-air firing. USAAF
Dee Marshes, Cheshire/Flints	Firing. 60 OTU
Dengie Flats, Essex	Bombing and firing
Derryogue, Co. Down	Ground-to-air firing. B-17 and B-24 gunners
Dirleton, East Lothian	Air-to-ground firing. 132 OTU
Dornoch, Sutherland	Air-to-air firing
Drurridge Bay, Northumberland	Bombing and gunnery. 7 ATS
Ducks Hall, Suffolk	Low-level bombing. USAAF B-26s
East Hartley, Cambridgeshire	Low-level bombing. USAAF B-26s
Eastney, Hampshire	Royal Navy AA. 1622 Flight
Fenns Moss, Salop	Bombing. 11 SFTS, 58 OTU
Goswick Sands, Northumberland	Bombing and firing. FLS, Milfield
Grandborough, Warwickshire	Bombing
Gransha Point, Co. Down	Bombing. FAA etc.
Grassholm, Pembrokeshire	Bombing, USAAF
Grendon, Bucks	Bombing. 13 OTU
Grimsthorpe, Lincolnshire	Bombing. 14 OTU
Hell's Mouth, Caernarvonshire	Bombing/firing. 5 ATC/9 B and GS

Hillmartin, Wiltshire	Air-to-ground firing
Holbeach, Lincolnshire	Bombing
Holmpton, Lincolnshire	Air-to-air firing. 496th Fighter Training Group
Imber, Wiltshire	Army ranges with occasional RAF involvement
Jurby, Isle of Man	Bombing. RAF Bomber Command, USAAF
Kessingland, Suffolk	Air-to-air firing. B-24 gunners
Kilkeel, County Down	USAAF Ground Gunnery School. 290 Sqn
Kinder Scout, Derbyshire	Air-to-air firing. 42 OTU
Lakenheath, Suffolk	Bombing
Lambourn Downs, Berkshire	Air-to-ground firing
Lavendon, Bucks	Bombing. 401st BG
Leysdown, Kent	Bombing and firing. 18 APC. 264 Sqn
Links of Innes, Morayshire	Bombing. 14 FTS
Llanbedr, Merioneth	Gunnery, bombs and rockets
Longdon, Worcestershire	Bombing. 23 OTU
Luce Bay, Kirkudbright	Bombing. 4 ATC
Lyme Bay, Dorset	Bombing. A and AEE, Boscombe Down
Manorbier, Pembrokeshire	School of Heavy AA, 1 AACU
Margam, Glamorgan	Air-to-air firing. 7AAGS
Millom, Cumb	Bombing and firing. 2 B and GS
Misson, Yorkshire	Bombing. 25 OTU
Montrose, Angus	Bombing/firing. 8 FTS
Mousehole, Cornwall	Ground-to-air firing. 8th AF Gunnery School
Mowsley, Rutland	Bombing. 85 OTU
North Channel (between N Ireland and Scotland)	Air-to-air firing. USAAF
North Wootton, Norfolk	Bombing. 17 OTU
Odstone, Berkshire	Bombing. 15 OTU
Oldbury Sands, Bristol Channel	Bombing
Ot Moor, Oxfordshire	Bombing. 16 OTU. 8th Air Force
Peel, Isle of Man	Bombing
Pembrey, Carmarthen	Bombing and firing. 1 AGS
Penhale, Cornwall	AA practice. 1 AACU
Pepperbox Hill, Wiltshire	Air-to-ground firing. 1 FTS, USAAF
Pilling Sands, Lincolnshire	Bombing and firing. FAA
Pilton, Northants	Bombing by OTUs
Poole Bay, Dorset	Air-to-air firing.
Prestatyn, Flintshire	Air-to-ground firing. 61 OTU
Preston Capes, Northants	Bombing. 16 OTU
Priors Hardwick, Warwickshire	Bombing. 22 OTU
Racks Moss, Dumfriesshire	Bombing. 10 (0) AFU
Ragdale, Leicestershire	Bombing. 28 OTU
Rams Island, Lough Neagh	Bombing and firing. 1 APC

Ramsey, Isle of Man	Bombing
Reculver, Kent	Bombing (including 'bouncing bomb' tests)
Redgrave Fen, Suffolk	Low level bombing. USAAF B-26s
Rose Valley, Morayshire	Bombing. 19 OTU
St Agnes, Cornwall	AA practice. 1 AACU
St John's Point, Co Down	AA practice. 290 Sqn
Sand Bay, Somerset	Gunnery
Scilly Isles	Firing. 286 Sqn
Seal Sands, Co Durham	Bombing and firing. 6 OTU
Shotteswell, Warwickshire	Bombing. 12 OTU
Shutlanger, Northants	Bombing. 17 OTU
Silloth, Cumberland	Bombing. 1 OTU
Sinclairs Bay, Caithness	Torpedo dropping. Wick units
Skady Tower Island, Lough Neagh	Bombing. CCRC, Toome. FAA Squadrons
Skipsea, Yorkshire	Bombing and firing
Snettisham, Norfolk	Ground-to-air firing, USAAF Gunnery School
Stiffkey, Norfolk	AA practice
Stockyard Green, Suffolk	Bombing. 8th Air Force 2nd Air Division
Stokes Bay, Hampshire	Air Torpedo Development Unit, Gosport
Strangford Lough, Co. Down	Air-to-air firing. 5 OTU, fighter sqns
Strensall, Yorkshire	Bombing
Steart Flat, Somerset	Air-to-ground firing
Sutton Walks, Suffolk	Bombing. 8th Air Force 2nd Air Division
Tain, Ross	Bombing and firing. 8 ATC. 8 B and GS. 8 AGS
Theddlethorpe, Lincolnshire	Bombing and gunnery
Tentsmuir, Fife	Bombing and firing. Leuchars units
Tollesbury, Essex	Bombing. 8th Air Force. 3rd Air Division
Tonfanau, Merioneth	Royal Artillery AA School
Trawsfynydd, Merioneth	Army (artillery). 41 OTU
Treligga, Cornwall	HMS *Vulture II*. Firing. St Merryn units
Ty Croes, Anglesey	No 4 Royal Artillery Practice Camp. 285 Sqn
Upnor, Kent	
Wainfleet Sands, Lincolnshire	Bombing
Wardley, Leicestershire	Bombing. 29 OTU
Warton Sands, Lancashire	Pathfinder Force range
Watchet, Somerset	Royal Artillery AA Practice Camp. 1 AACU
Wellsworthy, Devon	
Weybourne, Norfolk	Army AA gun and rocket firing. 1 AACU
Wigtown Bay, Kirkcudbright	Bombing. BTU
Ynys-Gwylanfach, Caerns	Bombing. USAAF

Chapter 19

Shadow factories

The term 'shadow factories' has always had slightly sinister overtones but they were, in fact, very ordinary manufacturing plants specifically intended to supplement the output of aircraft from existing facilities. Their distinction lay in the way they utilized the expertise of the motor industry in mass production and tapped unlikely sources of labour to do it. In the first years of the Second World War they made a great contribution to the build-up of the RAF.

RAF Expansion began in 1934 but, up to the end of the following year, the aircraft industry was left to meet increasing demand from its own factory capacity. The first re-equipment scheme of 2,400 aircraft in two years was well within the scope of the existing accommodation. The second programme, in May 1935, which required an output of at least 2,000 aircraft per year, led several firms to make some extensions to their factories, but there was no suggestion that the industry would not be able to meet the target. By February 1936, however, when a third and larger programme was announced, requiring 8,000 aircraft by 1939, it was beginning to seem unlikely that the industry could meet the second one, let alone this new figure.

It was at this stage that the formation of a shadow industry for aircraft production was announced in the Statement Relating to Defence in 1936. The term 'shadow factory' was probably first used in 1934 in the Weir memorandum on rearmament expansion, but it was then applied to proposed plans for the development of capacity for munitions production. It was not until 1936, when the new aircraft programme was discussed, that the term was applied specifically to the expansion of aircraft manufacturing capacity.

Although not described as such, a shadow industry had been planned for aircraft construction as early as 1929 and these plans were adopted in revised form in 1936. It was to consist of factories managed by firms from outside the aircraft industry and, initially, the title shadow factory was applied only to those plants planned as part of the shadow industry. However, from 1938, when it was decided to provide new factories at Government expense to be managed by aircraft firms for an agency fee, the term was extended to include these as well. By the end of 1939, there were at least as many shadow factories being run by the aircraft industry as by outside companies.

From the first hypothetical planning for aircraft expansion, the motor vehicle industry had been selected as most suitable for running the new factories. Direct commercial links were in fact few and related mainly to engine production, but the technological and engineering similarities provided obvious advantages. In addition, the motor industry, unlike its aircraft counterpart, was expanding rapidly and several firms were undoubted leaders in large scale production. Giving them some experience of the specialized work in aircraft production would provide a huge residue of productive power in the event of a national emergency.

Moreover, the motor car industry had by 1935 completed the conversion to metal fabricated bodies and structures. Thus the seven firms — Daimler, Humber, Standard, Rover, Bristol, Austin and Rootes — which entered the shadow industry in 1936 were all car manufacturers. They shared in the formation of the aero-engine section of the industry but at first only two, Austin and Rootes, entered the aircraft section.

Briefly, the Shadow Scheme meant that the parent aircraft manufacturer would concentrate on the development and bringing into production of any new type. The contractors would then take over and complete production with the parent supplying tooling, jigs and plenty of advice, including in some cases a pattern

RP590, the last Wellington to be delivered from a shadow factory flies over the Squires Gate plant on 25 October 1945 (Charles E. Brown).

aircraft which would be dismantled to study precisely how it was put together.

The Shadow Scheme inevitably created much debate and controversy, mainly about where the new factories were to be located. Up to 1938, with the solitary exception of the Bristol engine factory (which in the event, was one of the *Luftwaffe*'s earliest targets), all the engine shadow factories were concentrated in the West Midlands and so too were Austin at Longbridge and Nuffield at Castle Bromwich. Their positions had been determined by industrial factors, primarily management and the availability of skilled labour. Because of these requirements, the disadvantages of adding to the concentration of potential targets was accepted.

Another consideration, still apposite today, was to provide employment in depressed areas. This had the advantage of dispersing some of the factories to less vulnerable districts but, weighed against this, was the scarcity of skilled labour. The conflict of circumstances and policy is well shown in the controversy which developed over the location of the Rootes airframe shadow factory for Blenheim production.

On 21 January 1937, the Secretary of State for Air announced in the House of Commons that it had been definitely decided to erect an aircraft factory at White Waltham near Maidenhead. The House was not slow to express surprise at this apparent violation of the ground rules of location — vulnerability to air attack and the claims of the special areas for employment opportunities. Rootes declared that production could begin there more quickly than anywhere else, as local labour could be found without building new houses and also that the site was 'behind the defences of London'.

There was an outcry that local amenities would be ruined and rich farmland destroyed, *The Times* carrying columns of letters on the subject. However, the claims of the depressed areas had more influence on the opinion of the country and Parliament than the increasingly hypothetical problems of vulnerability in the face of modern long-range bombers.

In deference, Rootes turned to Lancashire, a site being found at Speke, on the edge of Liverpool's airport. The same year, two other shadow factories were chosen in the county, although the factories of the parent firms were in London and Wolverhampton respectively. These were the propeller shadow factory at Lostock, managed by de Havilland, and the carburettor factory at Woodstock Mill, Oldham, run by H.M. Hobson. At Lostock, the staff were trained to act as a nucleus of a much larger concern if emergency expansion became necessary.

Further dispersal and the search for new sources of labour resulted in a courageous move by Rolls-Royce. After an attempt to find labour and sub-contracting capacity near their

Above The Rootes shadow factory at Speke, Liverpool after the war. Located bottom right, traces of camouflage are still visible.

Above right The final Halifax to be produced by Rootes at Speke.

Right Halifax L9526 sent to Rootes, Speke, as a pattern aircraft in September 1941 seen with MAP Humbers. Note camouflage paint on the apron (Via P. Summerton).

factories at Crewe and Derby, the firm decided to venture into Scotland and open a plant at Hillington on the outskirts of Glasgow. Only a small fraction of the skilled labour was available and extensive training schemes had to be organized. Rolls-Royce had some qualms, groundless as it turned out, that a name that was synonymous with luxury might arouse the antagonism of the Clydeside workers but the factory eventually delivered over 50,000 Merlins.

Almost equally distant from the head-quarters of the management was the Vickers works at Chester. Throughout 1939 the greater use of the north-west continued. In September 1939 a site at Accrington was adopted for an engine shadow factory to be managed by the Bristol Aeroplane Co. The problems of administration at a distance were now having to give way to those of finding a large enough pool of local labour.

Thus, the approval of a second set of aero-engine factories adjacent to the first group in Coventry and Birmingham was contrary to all rules of vulnerability. However, this was un-avoidable as it was intended to draw the management and work force required for war expansion from the motor car works of the parent firms.

By the end of 1939 the choice of Lancashire for airframe construction had been extended to engine production. Bristol at Accrington has already been mentioned, but Ford was now to set up a Merlin factory at Trafford Park, Man-chester, far from their head office at Dagen-ham which was too exposed a location to risk on this vital work. It was soon proved that these new plants, far removed from their management, could function efficiently.

From the summer of 1938 much more atten-tion was given to the expansion of the factory capacity of the existing aircraft industry and no other shadow firms were introduced before the outbreak of war. During 1939-40 several smaller firms entered war production but mostly for rather circumstantial reasons. Stan-dard Motors at Coventry was adopted for Oxford manufacture in the first month of the war, because although the company was entirely committed to the Air Ministry it was not yet fully employed. At the same time Morris Motors undertook extensive sub-contract work on the Tiger Moth for de Havil-land at Cowley. During 1940 they graduated to final assembly and delivery of complete air-craft and thus became a fully-fledged shadow firm.

The only other major shadow capacity was

the London Aircraft Production Group. Early in 1940 it was proposed to recruit a large group of sub-contractors which would use several London Passenger Transport Board depots, buildings eminently suitable for the assembly of heavy bombers. At an early stage it was decided to form this into a shadow group with direct contracts for aircraft construction. An output of 32 Halifaxes per month was envisaged, assembled from components to be manufactured by members of the group.

These new factories obviously needed airfields for flight testing and delivery. Up to 1934 aircraft firms were located on their own airfield or near a municipal or service site which they could use. Since after 1936 it was usually necessary to site the factories in engineering centres which were often some distance from

the nearest aerodrome, this was not always a practical arrangement.

The most frequent solution of the problem was to choose a site adjacent to an existing airfield which could, if necessary, be extended to cater for the testing of larger types of aircraft. The other answer adopted more and more after 1938 was to separate the factory from the airfield and to erect flight and final assembly sheds at the latter. This was done with English Electric at Preston and Samlesbury respectively.

A combined site was unusual; for example Vickers at Chester (Hawarden) was eventually shared with the RAF. The work of some factories increased beyond the capacity of specially-constructed airfields. One example was the small landing ground at Longbridge,

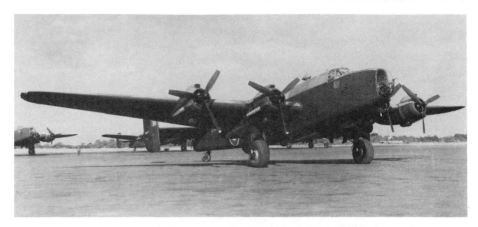

Top *Halifax NR134 just off the production line at Samlesbury, Lancashire, in August 1944* (British Aerospace).

Above *Flight shed at Hawarden, Clwyd, with Vickers-built Lancaster and Wellington XIV* (Vickers-Armstrong).

Left *Rudimentary pill-box at Hawarden for defence of shadow factory.*

originally laid out by First World War German PoWs, which was barely adequate for the Battle even when short asphalt strips were built. When Austin switched to building Stirlings, it was totally useless, and distant Elmdon became the place for final assembly, test and delivery.

In the Manchester area, separation of factory and airfield was practised from the start, Manchester's airport at Ringway playing host to up to three firms simultaneously, namely Metrovick, Fairey and Avro. It was therefore essential to carry out the final assembly of the airframe at the airfield, and large flight sheds had to be built there.

The construction of new factories took time and it was not until well into 1938 that the first aircraft built by the shadow industry took to the air. Probably the first was an Austin-built Battle which Squadron Leader T.H. England flew before the Secretary of State for Air on 22 July 1938. It was noted at the time that this was the first aircraft to be built in Birmingham since the First World War.

The first of the Rootes Blenheims flew from Speke in October 1938, which was quite an achievement since the enormous factory had been a 'green field site' only 20 months before. Well before the work was finished, Vickers at Chester assembled Wellington L7770 from parts supplied by Weybridge. A Bellman hangar was used, but flooding of the new aerodrome was so bad that the aircraft had to be flown to Weybridge on 2 August 1939 for further testing.

Certain of the shadow factories actually exceeded the output of the parent firm. Bristol began production of the Blenheim in March 1937 and A.V. Roe in September 1938, but the combined production of these two companies eventually made up only about half of the shadow output. By 1942 Rootes's production of the Blenheim had been transferred to the shadow factory at Blythe Bridge just across the road from Stoke (Meir) Airport and to a dispersal factory near Speke. This left the original plant free for Halifaxes, but by then the peak Blenheim figures during just one month in 1941 had reached 148 from Speke.

Similarly, the highest monthly delivery of 90 Beaufighters came from the shadow factory at Weston-super-Mare which had been built in 1940 solely for this purpose. The wooden Mosquito was eminently suitable for firms previously engaged in building trainers and Standard Motors switched from Oxford production, as did Airspeed and Percival. However, the numbers of Mosquitos built lagged far behind those of de Havilland itself.

Such was Bomber Command's demand for Lancasters in 1943 that parts of the Castle Bromwich Spitfire and Chester Wellington factories were set aside for their production. The final scheme came in May 1943 when it was decided to change the Austin plant at Longbridge from Stirlings to Lancasters. These three factories supplied a total of 900 aircraft in 1944-45 but they came too late to alter the main balance of output at the peak of war production.

Until it began to build Mosquitos, Standard Motors was one of only three shadow firms turning out trainers, the others being Morris Motors and Brush Coachworks at Loughborough. Since predominently wood and fabric aircraft made a much smaller demand on productive resources than operational aircraft, high outputs were achieved, Morris reaching a maximum of over 100 Tiger Moths a month at Cowley.

An indication of the level of efficiency at the factories is provided by the figures achieved by Vickers at Chester and Blackpool. These were Government-owned agency factories, rather than true shadow factories, but, as I explained above, by 1939 the latter term embraced the agency plants as well. The Chester works was in production in January 1940 and within little more than six months output exceeded that of Vickers at Weybridge.

Ground defence of the factories was the responsibility of the Army and the Home Guard. Many pillboxes were constructed, including a strange little concrete device which would have been proof against little more than small arms fire. Two of them survive at British Aerospace, Hawarden, once the Vickers Chester plant, but now producing BAe 125s and Airbus wings.

The first Air Ministry shadow factories were planned with a lavishness which contrasts with the austerity which was to be the rule later on. The architecture of the office blocks and ancilliary buildings is quite distinctive, being typically 'thirties in concept. Similar styles can be seen in many parts of London and the West Midlands, where factories for the motor and other industries were built at that time.

To disperse capacity and thus reduce the vulnerability of a shadow factory, there were often several separate plants in the same district. Rootes at Speke, for instance, had a No 2 Factory about half a mile away, Nos 4 and 5 Factories slightly further on and No 3 at Lister Drive, about four miles away in Liverpool city.

A further shadow activity is described fully in Aldon Ferguson's excellent history of RAF Burtonwood. This was the Burtonwood Repair Depot Ltd for the servicing and other technical support of US aircraft operated by the British. It was formed under Fairey and Bristol

Typical 'thirties shadow factory architecture at Speke. Both have since been demolished.

management and comprised four subsidiary companies, namely Rover, Rollason Aircraft Co, Sunbeam Talbot and BOAC. It was eventually taken over entirely by the USAAF.

After the war, the shadow industry ran down slowly to keep the work force occupied for as long as possible, even if it meant assembling aircraft from the stockpile of parts and flying them straight to an MU for scrapping. Some of them switched to making prefabricated aluminium houses, an ingenious interim measure to alleviate the post-war housing shortage.

Within a few years, only a handful were still producing aircraft. Others were in the hands of firms like GEC and Dunlop and one was even manufacturing wallpaper! The Vickers works at Chester was acquired by de Havilland, which became Hawker-Siddeley and is now part of British Aerospace. English Electric stayed in the aviation business, but the rest of the shadow firms reverted to their original place in the motor industry, all the stronger for having inherited vast new factories.

Chapter 20

The post-war years: development or dereliction?

The end of the war in Europe was followed almost immediately by mass closure of those RAF training stations which were now surplus to requirements. The departure of the bulk of the USAAF and VJ-Day gave further impetus to this trend but, for the moment, many airfields were retained on a care and maintenance basis pending a decision on their future. Their ultimate fate was subject to various conflicting interests, chiefly the farmers who wanted the return of their land, the RAF which required a strategic reserve of airfields, and local councils seeking future civil airports. For obvious reasons the grass RLGs and SLGs and the airfields in the more remote parts of Britain were the first to be relinquished.

Group Captain Leonard Cheshire VC, DSO, DFC estimated that in March 1946 there were currently 680 surplus aerodromes in the UK and that no one, not even the Government, knew what was going to happen to them. He devised a Utopian scheme to turn them into workshops and homes for demobilized ex-servicemen and their families. As Andrew Boyle observes in his biography of Cheshire, *No Passing Glory,*

> 'The decaying aerodromes of Britain were for Cheshire a striking symbol of the nation's imperceptible decline from its wartime greatness . . . There had once been laughter as well as tragedy in these ghostly surroundings and life had been simple; in four years the sense of purpose sustaining aircrews, groundcrews and a whole people behind them had withered. He saw the aerodromes as a mark of the futile emptiness of life without a common cause; a symbol of mute reproach like the untended grave of a lover.'

Cheshire's dream remained unrealized, although many of the domestic sites on abandoned airfields were occupied either by displaced persons from Europe or Britons escaping from the post-war housing shortage. The onset of the Cold War was reflected in a marked slowing-up in the rate of closure. Between 1950 and 1955 only 60 were closed, leaving 210 in operation. In the same period a number of airfields which had been retained under care and maintenance were refurbished for training and other purposes. They included Long Marston in Gloucestershire and Halfpenny Green and Lichfield in Staffordshire.

A considerable number of airfields were earmarked for the USAF, many of them on a reserve basis. They included some unlikely sites, for example Winfield in Berwickshire, East Fortune near Edinburgh and the grass-surfaced Chipping Norton in Oxfordshire, all of which would have required large scale reconstruction. Desborough in Northamptonshire was listed in October 1952 as a possible B-47 base, as were Gransden Lodge and Podington in the same general area. Work was carried out at quite a few sites, but most were never occupied by the USAF and eventually reverted to Air Ministry control.

The bases which *were* taken over by the Americans included Lakenheath, Woodbridge, Bentwaters and Shepherds Grove, all of them for fighters. The bombers were stationed to their rear in the south-west Midlands, at Fairford, Brize Norton, Greenham Common and Upper Heyford, all four being provided with the 9 to 10,000 ft runways essential for B-47 operations. Several reserve airfields including Chelveston and Bruntingthorpe in the Midlands, both rebuilt wartime sites, were made available for USAF units expelled from France in 1959.

The reappraisal of defence requirements in the Government's 1957 White Paper led to the redundancy of a large number of service airfields. Closures for the first time began to

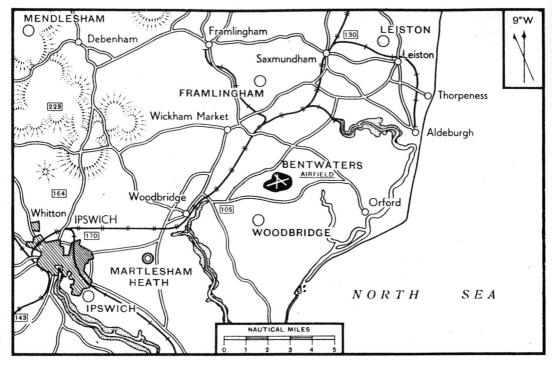

ALL HEIGHTS IN FEET ABOVE MEAN SEA LEVEL

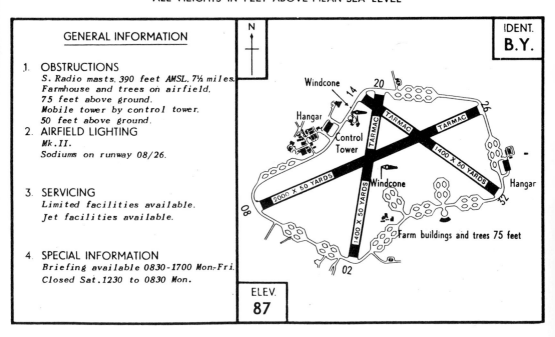

GENERAL INFORMATION

1. OBSTRUCTIONS
   S. Radio masts, 390 feet AMSL, 7½ miles.
   Farmhouse and trees on airfield,
   75 feet above ground.
   Mobile tower by control tower,
   50 feet above ground.

2. AIRFIELD LIGHTING
   Mk.II.
   Sodiums on runway 08/26.

3. SERVICING
   Limited facilities available.
   Jet facilities available.

4. SPECIAL INFORMATION
   Briefing available 0830-1700 Mon-Fri.
   Closed Sat.1230 to 0830 Mon.

IDENT.
B.Y.

ELEV.
87

Bentwaters, Suffolk, a very late Second World War site which was developed for the USAF and is still in use today.

Above *The 'J' and 'T2' hangars are still in good condition, but the tower is a house and the airfield is under the plough once more. Honeybourne, Worcs, once a night bomber OTU* (Tony Hooper).

Right *518/40 Type tower at Hawarden, Clwyd, modernized with visual control room on roof. Compare with the photograph on page 101.*

affect many of the smaller stations originating before 1935, for example Biggin Hill, Hendon, Digby and Gosport, and the last surviving flying boat bases at Calshot, Felixstowe, Pembroke Dock and Mount Batten. In the five years after 1960, about 30 more were closed, including other early stations such as Martlesham Heath, Duxford and Abbotsinch. Not surprisingly the airfields of the Expansion Period with their fine buildings and facilities were those retained longest by the RAF, but by the early 'seventies many were de-activated. Among them, Horsham St Faith and Middleton St George became Norwich and Tees-side Airports, respectively; Stradishall was turned into a prison and Bassingbourn was handed over to the Army.

The policy of 'scattering' the bomber force

in time of war was not new and it became policy in the 'fifties to equip many service airfields with so-called medium bomber dispersals situated close to the main runway. Intended for use by Canberras and the V-force, adjacent buildings for crews and supporting equipment enabled them to operate independently of the station. Air defence bases were provided with Operational Readiness Platforms (ORPs) at each end of the longest runway so that fighters could be scrambled with the minimum of taxiing. The ORPs were built on the same side of the runway to allow free passage on the opposite grass shoulder for emergency landings.

In the early 'sixties, the RAF divided its permanent airfields into six categories to indicate the role for which they were either designed or primarily intended.

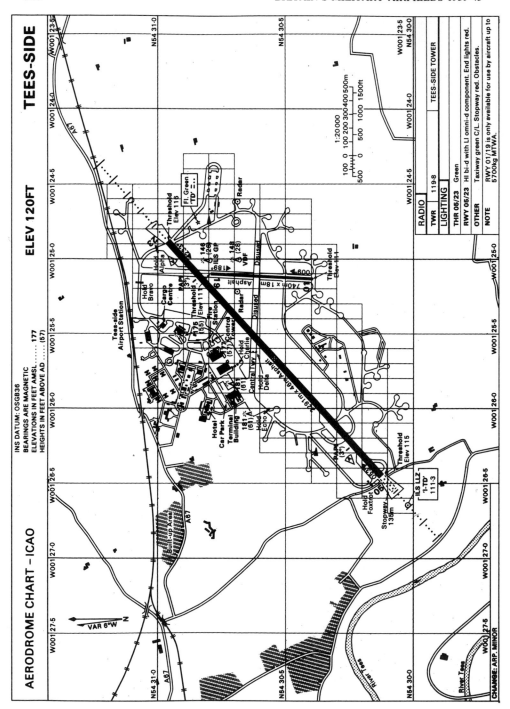

Teesside Airport, formerly RAF Middleton St George. The various stages of its development can be traced through the successive runway and taxiway extensions, the dispersals and the post-war ORP (CAA).

Above *The modern style of RAF tower seen here at Valley owes much to its wartime counterpart.*

Category	Role	Main runway	Subsidiary runway	Taxiway width
1	Medium bomber, Strategic Transport, Strategic Reconnaissance, Long Range Maritime Patrol (Jet), Tankers, Long Range Strike/Attack	3,000 x 67 yd	Not provided	20 yd
2	Light Bomber, Tactical Transport	2,000 x 50 yd	1,600 x 50 yd	17 yd
3	Fighter, Offensive Support, Tactical Reconnaissance	2,500 x 50 yd	Not provided	17 yd
4	Long Range Maritime Patrol (Piston)	2,500 x 50 yd	Not provided	20 yd
5	Advanced Flying Schools	2,000 x 50 yd	1,800 x 50 yd	17 yd
6	Basic Flying Schools	1,500 x 50 yd	1,300 x 50 yd	17 yd

From March 1981 the categories were simplified, now being based on runway length and width instead of role.

Category	Main runway length	Main runway width
1	9,000 ft and over	200 ft
2	7,500 ft to 9,000 ft	150 ft
3	6,000 ft to 7,500 ft	150 ft
4	4,500 ft to 6,000 ft	150 ft
5	Grass	

Above *Gaydon Hangar at Valley with cut-out in roof to allow large aircraft such as the Vulcan to enter.*

Left *Sea Vampire over Ford, Sussex, with its 'cross-bow' layout and extended runways for jet operations* (Roy Bonser Collection).

Below *Lightnings do not look out of place on an Expansion Station of the 'thirties. Leconfield, Yorks, in July 1963* (P.H.T. Green Collection).

Above *Wartime tower converted into a nightclub at Haverford-west, Dyfed.*

Right *Coningsby, Lincs* circa *1972 with Gaydon Hangars and apron. 'T2' hangars to right and frying pan hard-standings reveal its wartime ancestry* (P.H.T. Green Collection).

At the beginning of 1988 there were approximately 75 active military airfields in Britain, although this total includes RLGs like Mona and Elvington and gliding sites such as Sealand and Halton. In the meantime the de-requisitioned airfields have gradually been reclaimed for agriculture, but although their buildings could be adapted easily for farming purposes, the runways and taxi-ways were a major problem. It was generally uneconomical to pay for their removal but the boom in motorway construction from 1960 onwards brought with it a voracious appetite for hardcore. Many landowners were able to arrange for the paving to be removed *en masse* at no cost to themselves, leaving only narrow strips for field access.

Apart from farming, disused airfields have attracted a remarkable variety of other uses. Prior to disposal many were offered first to government departments, nuclear research being one of the most significant adaptations. Harwell and Aldermaston in the Oxford area are well-known but there is also Dounreay in the north of Scotland. Nuclear power stations have been built on several airfield sites, including Annan, Dumfriesshire and Bradwell in Essex. Other research establishments include the bridge design testing centre at Drem, East Lothian and the steerable radio aerial unit at Chilbolton, Hampshire. Prisons have been built on Ford, Sussex, Market Harborough, Leicestershire, and Long Kesh and Maghaberry in Northern Ireland.

Small depots at strategic points around the country are used for emergency bulk food storage, reserve fire fighting appliances and storage of EEC grain surpluses. The industrial applications of disused aerodromes are many, the larger operations utilizing hangars and runways for container and other storage, while the minor ones such as car repairers require perhaps merely a single hut. Practically every old aerodrome supports some light industry which maintains a precarious existence in the face of local planning regulations.

Some airfields have been engulfed by industrial or housing development. A few of them are Hooton Park, Cheshire (Vauxhall car factory), Usworth, Tyne and Wear (Nissan car factory), Grangemouth, Central (oil refinery), Gravesend, Thornaby, and Castle Bromwich (housing estates). Others have already become industrial estates and still more are being developed as such. Examples are Ayr, Stretton and Burtonwood, Cheshire, Donibristle, Fife and Evanton, Highland.

A number of airfields have been turned into motor racing circuits, notably Silverstone, Northants, Snetterton Heath, Norfolk, Thruxton, Hants, and Croft in North Yorkshire. Go-karting takes place at Crail and Tain in Scotland and Andreas on the Isle of Man, amongst others. Many aerodromes in coastal and scenic areas including Penrhos in North Wales, St Merryn in Cornwall and Carew Cheriton in Dyfed, now support caravan sites; others continue to serve a useful aeronautical function, that of a navigation aid, and in the vicinity of active airfields they are often utilized as reporting points for aircraft joining the circuit visually.

It remains to give credit to one of the unsung heroes of the Second World War; the private citizen who had his land and farm requisitioned, his house demolished and his fields covered with acres of concrete. He was given financial compensation but his lost heritage could never be satisfactorily replaced by the State, particularly if his family had farmed the land for generations and had their roots in the soil. To some in remote villages, the airfields brought benefits which otherwise would have been far off in the future, namely piped water, main sewerage, bus services and sometimes even electricity. Britain's greatest civil engineering project has left an imprint on the landscape which will be discernible for centuries.

Chapter 21

Airfield history research

Readers familiar with PSL's *Action Stations* series, to which I contributed Volumes three and seven, may assume that there is little left to say on the subject of airfield histories. However, myself and the other three authors are the first to admit that the series merely scratches the surface, presenting a brief outline of happenings at each location in an easily digested form. A book of *Action Stations* length could be written about virtually every airfield and in fact many have already been produced. This chapter is an attempt to summarize the sources of information available to a would-be historian and it is hoped that it will encourage some original research.

Interest in airfield histories is not a recent phenomenon, of course, the enthusiasts' organization *Air-Britain** having had an Airfield Historical Research Section for several decades. The curiosity about the subject was obvious from the number of readers' letters in the aviation press over the years, particularly in *Air Pictorial*'s 'Your Questions Answered' column. The early endeavours in producing specialized histories were poor as they were written without recourse to official records which were at that time generally unavailable.

Amongst the first really comprehensive volumes were Aldon P. Ferguson's histories of Sealand, Shawbury and Woodvale for the Merseyside Aviation Society. These were xeroxed but the latest standard for airfield histories is exemplified by the same author's *Burtonwood*, Malcolm Giddings's *Ashbourne* and B A Stait's *Rivenhall*. All are professionally printed, the first-named being a hard-back, and show just what can be done by an enthusiast concentrating on a single airfield, previously unresearched in any detail.

The basic sources of reference for an airfield history are the station and unit Form 540s, better known as Operations Record Books (ORBs), which are readily accessible at the Public Record Office at Kew in London's south-west suburbs. One must start with a skeleton list of squadrons and other units known to have been based at the object of one's studies, together with the relevant dates. This information is obtainable from books such as MacDonald's trilogy on RAF Bomber, Fighter and Support Squadrons, although the first two are out-of-print, or the *Air-Britain* publication by James J. Halley, *The Squadrons of the Royal Air Force*. The appropriate *Action Stations* volume will help too, particularly with training and support units, and Ray Sturtivant's occasional series in *Aviation News* on RAF training is indispensible, as is his book *The Squadrons of the Fleet Air Arm*.

At this point confusion may arise when various authoritative sources provide conflicting information, in particular the dates for unit moves. It may be thought that the ORB entry will be the final arbiter but these can be frustratingly vague. It should be remembered also that moving a large training school, for example, might take several days. Ground personnel would travel by train or road and as many as 150 aircraft would have to be ferried across the country by instructors and advanced pupils. A spell of bad weather could result in stragglers landing in all sorts of places, and inevitably there were unserviceable aircraft left behind with a small working party. Details of formation and disbandment of units can nor-

* Air Britain is the International Association of Aviation Historians. Membership is open to all persons with an interest in history, and details can be obtained from The Membership Secretary, Air-Britain, 19 The Pastures, Westwood, Bradford-on-Avon, Wiltshire BA15 2BH.

mally be found in the Form SD 155s which
are held by PRO under Class AIR 10. Not all
appear therein and it is necessary to search
forward to find possible amendments to earlier
promulgations. When in doubt it is better to
omit the day and substitute a less definite alternative such as 'the first week in August', rather
than perpetuate an error.

Going back to ORBs, major operational airfields had one compiled by Station Headquarters which supplemented and often
duplicated those kept by resident units. Training organizations like OTUs usually administered the station themselves and therefore only
one ORB would be maintained. Happenings
at satellite aerodromes would be recorded in
the main ORB, the location being carefully
identified in the left-hand margin. Unfortunately, it is usually difficult to find out much
about occurrences at Relief Landing Grounds
for Advanced Flying Units and Flying Training Schools, apart from accidents. Some

ORBs, however, summarize at the end of each
month the activities at satellites or RLGs, often
tabulated with headings like Night Flying, Flying Control, Maintenance, Medical etc.

Having perused the contents of all relevant
ORBs, it is time to look at the peripheral
sources. They include the appropriate Group
and Command ORBs and the bewildering
mass of files which can hold gems of information or may be totally uninteresting. A systematic search of the indices at PRO will reveal
what is likely to be of use but do not be put
off by misleading titles. A file on compensation paid to landowners for the requisitioning
of an Advanced Landing Ground in Hampshire
proved to contain a vast amount of detail on
ALGs in general. Each unit came under the
jurisdiction of a particular Group which in turn
served the appropriate Command and numerous references to airfields can be found in their
records.

Some locations were under the control of

Plan and aerial views of RNAS Inskip, Lancs, from a 1944 navigational publication (FAA
Museum).

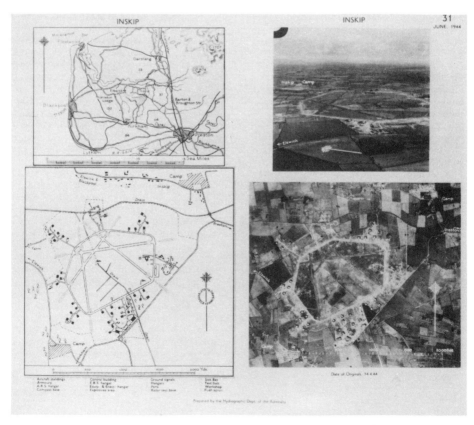

'Human interest' pictures are often valuable in airfield histories. Here a Firefly crewman at Burscough, Lancs, adopts a familiar fighter pilot's pose (V.M.G. Bennett).

the Ministry of Aircraft Production (MAP) whose records are in the AVIA section at PRO. Unfortunately, these are not always very helpful, so delving into events at a place like Helensburgh where the Marine Aircraft Experimental Establishment had its headquarters is particularly difficult. The Saunders-Roe facility at Beaumaris on Anglesey is another example.

Readers of airfield histories might be forgiven for thinking that the only events of any interest happened between 1939 and 1945. Certainly, the most momentous things occurred then, eclipsing anything before or since, but the availability of official information for these years is partly responsible. Prior to 1939, ORBs were not very detailed and the 30-Year Rule renders those of the late 1950s and 1960s unobtainable for the time being. Accredited authors, however, may be allowed access to them at Air Historical Branch with the condition that any resulting manuscript must first be vetted by AHB before publication. Another method is to convince the Commanding Officer of an RAF station that you can write a comprehensive history for him. His influence may then produce access to current material of an unclassified nature.

Contractor's airfields, such as Leavesden, Brooklands, Woodford and Samlesbury where there were no RAF lodger units, obviously kept no ORB or its equivalent. Records of visiting aircraft were maintained but it is unlikely that any of these have survived, apart from the ones for Woodford which were discovered by Harry Holmes. It may be possible to piece together some aircraft movements from pilots' log books, especially those of ferry pilots with the Air Transport Auxiliary,

but compiling detailed histories of this category of aerodrome will inevitably be difficult, if not impossible.

First World War aerodromes are another area of extreme difficulty. The PRO has some files and sketch plans of many sites can be found here, and a number of enthusiasts specialize in First World War aerodromes, and have made significant progress in tracking down these long-forgotten landing grounds whose exact location was previously unknown.

It is common knowledge that the majority of records for Fleet Air Arm units were destroyed after the war and this is reflected in the dearth of information on Royal Naval Air Stations, most histories being limited to a list of squadrons, types flown and dates. Flying logs and personal reminiscences are the only means of improving the material, Ray Sturtivant being the expert in this field. Some information on the origins of naval sites can be found in the ADM files at PRO and there are interesting comments such as: 'Abbotsinch — a grass airfield built on low land which frequently becomes unserviceable due to flooding. Bad weather in winter months. Some limited extension might be practicable. Convenient to Clyde; future use as a Repair Yard and Packing Unit probably practicable.' Whoever wrote this would be amazed to see Glasgow Airport today!

The MoD's Air Historical Branch has now passed most of its records of wartime aerodromes, including the ORBs, to the PRO. Amongst the material still held is a file of badges for defunct units and stations, few of which have ever been published. AHB also holds two separate collections of index cards, one containing the service histories of almost

Most ex-RAF personnel have photographs like this one but unfortunately they do not often show aircraft as well. Two pilots and the three WAAF groundcrew responsible for the 1665 HCU Fighter Affiliation Flight's Hurricane at Tilstock, Shropshire, in 1944 (R.R. Glass).

every RAF aircraft and the other the accidents which befell them. Many illuminating statements can be found about the aerodromes from which they flew and research is possible by prior arrangement.

Local records, usually held at County Record Offices, are a further useful source of information, but unfortunately they are not always very comprehensive and often consist merely of press cuttings of fairly recent vintage. Some of the CROs keep wartime police and Civil Defence records, many of them very detailed where aircraft accidents or air raid incidents are described. If these documents have not been transferred to the appropriate CRO, they are probably still in the hands of the regional police headquarters. The police are normally reluctant to allow access to them because of the crime records mixed in. However, if you can convince the Chief Constable of your *bona fides* he may grant permission to peruse them, the official attitude varying from one area to another.

Civil Defence, or Air Raid Precautions as it was more usually known, was a loosely-organized local function of the county councils. One of its more important duties was to anticipate air raids in response to telephoned code words from Fighter Command HQ at Stanmore in Middlesex. In Flintshire, now part of the county of Clwyd, the responsibility for receiving and acting upon these messages was vested in the police whose log sheets are now preserved in the CRO at Hawarden. The log contains precise times of all messages, including false alarms, and a summary of any subsequent enemy air activity.

A typical entry referring to a local aerodrome reads as follows:

'November 14 1940 — 2200 hours, 19 High Explosive and 300-350 Incendiary Bombs on Hawarden aerodrome and No 48 MU, RAF. 14 of the HE fell on the site seriously damaging two hangars and eight aircraft housed therein and slightly damaging other aircraft. Two aircraft on the ground seriously damaged. The other five HE fell in the fields of Well House Farm, two near the railway track. One horse and 14 cattle injured and one heifer killed.'

Of related interest are the National Fire Service, Home Guard and Royal Observer Corps records which sometimes give a lot of information about crashes, air raids and other incidents. Unfortunately not many of these seem to have survived, although I suspect that some of them are in private hands. I have seen, for example, a fire watcher's diary for Pilkington's Glassworks at St Helens in Lancashire which relates all the RAF and enemy air activity in the district during 1941. This sort of thing may not always be relevant to airfield histories but valuable 'background' may be picked up in this way.

A further repository of knowledge is *Hansard*, the verbatim record of day-to-day business in the House of Commons. It is published at regular intervals under the title *Parliamentary Debates* and reference libraries in the larger cities are likely to have them on their shelves. The airfield researcher will find background which is not necessarily hard fact but it can reveal something of the contemporary social impact of, say, RAF Expansion. The following extract, taken at random, is representative of many of the exchanges. It took place on 21 November 1929 when the Under-Secretary of State for Air was asked 'if his attention had been called to the protests against the establishment of a great aerodrome for military purposes in the immediate proximity of Oxford and, if so, whether His Majesty's Government propose to continue a project which will go far in destroying the amenities of the University and in increasing the danger to which it might be subjected in time of war?' The reply was:

'My Noble Friend is aware that objections have been raised and they very naturally received his most careful consideration. The site at Abingdon was, however, only decided upon after an exhaustive reconnaissance had failed to discover any feasible alternative in the vicinity, and the aerodrome now under construction is an essential part of the scheme for the air defence of this country. It is, in fact, more than five miles distant from the centre of the city of Oxford and arrangements will be made that transport proceeding from and to the aerodrome will normally avoid passing Oxford and thus adding to the traffic congestion. It is not admitted that the establishment of this aerodrome will have either of the results which the honourable and gallant Member fears, and indeed, to judge by their tenor, the representations which have been made are largely due to misinformation.'

Typical of the anodyne reply beloved of politicians, this one proved to be correct. Abingdon did *not* attract much in the way of fire and destruction to Oxford. However, I shall not repeat the name of the politician who claimed in 1937 that Coventry was not an especially vulnerable target! There are many other discussions of potential airfield sites, including Barningham Parva in Norfolk and Carlton Miniot in Yorkshire. In November 1935, according to *Hansard*, one was planned in Cannock Chase, Staffordshire, on the site of a First World War army camp, but did not progress beyond the discussion stages.

Casualties from flying accidents and enemy action are a valid part of any airfield history and it has become customary to tabulate in an appendix those buried in local churchyards and cemeteries. The Commonwealth War Graves Commission at Maidenhead produces registers of graves for each county in Great Britain and these can be purchased direct from the Commission. Large counties such as Lancashire may run to five volumes, but North Wales is covered in two and several counties in the more remote parts of Britain are combined into one book. Full name, rank and service number, place of origin and next of kin are listed, together with the date of death and sometimes the squadron number.

Cross-checking with ORBs should trace details of the accident but remember that RAF casualties later in the war were often interred in regional cemeteries rather than in plots in the district where they perished. Relatives, unless they lived overseas, were also given the choice of having their loved ones buried in their home area. The regional cemetery for RAF casualties in north Wales and north-west England was, for example, at Chester.

Civil Coroner's records in a Death Register also give war casualties but normally without any amplifying data on the circumstances. However, these may not be available to the general public and, if they are, a search fee may be levied. Some Coroner's Offices may let you look through the Registers unhindered; it all depends if the individual coroner sympathizes with your reasons.

British newspapers were not, as is generally believed, censored during the Second World War, editors merely being instructed not to publish anything which was likely to assist the enemy. In practice this probably worked better than official censorship as an editor, aware that there could be heavy penalties for any indiscretion, was doubly careful what he printed. Photographs were, however, subject to censorship. Anything which helped morale was fair game and extensive coverage can be found of *Luftwaffe* losses over Britain. Accidents to our own aircraft could not be mentioned unless they gave rise to public concern, such as when people on the ground were killed. Local newspapers are very informative on these matters but of course units and bases are not given.

During the First World War, newspaper censorship appears to have varied, accounts of aviation incidents on the Home Front being quite comprehensive in some cases. The upsurge of civil flying resulted in the publication of reams of information about the new airports springing up all over the country in the late 1920s and early 1930s. More can be traced in town council files, normally with the Engineers Department, if they have not been passed to a library or record office for safekeeping.

The problem with newspaper research is the sheer mass of data which must be combed for relevant items. Fortunately nowadays, most of it is on microfilm but many libraries still keep copies of local newspapers in bulk. Reading old papers is a fascinating pastime but one can soon become lost in the trivia of days gone by, one's original purpose long forgotten! The British Newspaper Library at Hendon may be worth a visit in the unlikely event of old newspaper files being unavailable in your home area.

The Times newspaper is commonly available at major reference libraries together with a series of index volumes covering three months at a time. (Six for the war years when paper shortages reduced the content). Simply look up the *Aeronautics* or, in later years, the *Aviation* section, and you will find brief details of the subject matter with date, page and column numbers. Local newspaper files rarely incorporate an index but some libraries are attempting to compile one as a long-term project. Libraries may have other aviation material so it is a good idea to explain your requirements.

For every Roger Freeman and Mike Bowyer who visited all the aerodromes within cycling range and kept meticulous logs, there must have been scores of other enthusiasts who noted down what they saw but have not yet shared these gems with the rest of us. I have traced a handful of these people and their revelations are sometimes astounding! An appeal in the newspaper is a good way of contacting those who kept records at the time.

This brings me to the subject of interviewing local residents on a random basis. Aircraft wreck investigators will be familiar with this method but it can also be rewarding if questions are asked about wartime activities at the local aerodrome. Although the stories may have to be taken with a pinch of salt, you can gain an insight into the flavour of life around a busy station but some of them may be unprintable!

The persons who can really help you are those who worked at or were attached to the airfield. One way to contact them is via the Royal Air Force Association's *Airmail* magazine. It is published quarterly and carries a *Help* column which is always full of appeals from researchers in many fields of aviation history. Looking through back issues, it is surprising how many diverse subjects have been investigated and how few have appeared subsequently in print. In my experience, replies to these appeals are few, the average being three or four, but just one of these may tell you all you want to know. Often, it is possible to insert a letter verbatim into your manuscript, there being no substitute for the memories of 'one who was there'.

For illustrating the work one always hopes that photographs will be forthcoming but they are generally rare. Apart from the fact that film was very difficult to obtain, photography was officially forbidden on and around aircraft and airfields. Luckily for historians there were many delinquents who ignored this regulation, especially on operational squadrons where discipline was more relaxed. Others acquired prints taken by the Station Photographic Section, but the problem is to find the material and copy it before it disappears for ever. Mortality, alas, thins the ranks of the veterans day by day and in 20 years or so only a handful will be left. Their memories will go with them and their relatives will probably destroy any photographs.

It is said that one's memories of earlier events are much easier to recall as one gets older and this certainly seems true of some people to whom I have spoken. They admit to being forgetful and vague about present day happenings but can recall names and places of nearly 50 years ago in vivid detail. Writing letters is always a chore but the casette tape provides a much better means of setting down reminiscences, giving far more scope for embellishment and the inevitable digressions as other incidents spring to mind.

Membership of the Airfield Research Group will put you in contact with several hundreds of enthusiasts with similar interests. The group was formed in 1978 by Roy Walters of Leicester with the support of David Benfield of Market Deeping, Lincolnshire, and produces a regular magazine full of information on histories, architecture, memorials and related subjects. Known as *Airfield Review*, it is edited jointly by Aldon P. Ferguson and Julian C. Temple, both being well-known in the aviation historical field. If you would like to find out more about the ARG, write to the secretary Rex Moore at 22 Rolleston Avenue, Petts Wood, Orpington, Kent BR5 1AH.

A lot of useful information can be culled from published sources; the wider your aviation reading the more you are likely to find. Amongst the hundreds of books of flying memoirs which have appeared since the war, there is a good chance that the focus of your research is mentioned at least once. It may perhaps be simply a paragraph containing an anecdote which you can incorporate, with acknowledgement of course, into your manuscript. Furthermore the author may be persuaded to elaborate on his reminiscences of a particular place. Any public library will have a good selection of such books which is beneficial because few of us can afford to buy more than a fraction of those in print.

The Inter-Library Lending Service will enable your local branch to find a copy of almost any book, even if it has been out of print for many years. Information required is the title,

Above *A bit of history in one photograph; Usworth, near Sunderland, is now obliterated by the Nissan factory.*

Right *Artwork and Czech graffiti on 312 Squadron's Magister at Penrhos, North Wales, in April 1941. Note local 'postmark'* (Via Zdenek Hurt).

author, publisher and date, although the last two are not essential. There is a small charge to cover the cost of a postcard to advise you when the book is ready for collection. This can take anything from a few weeks to several months and in the last resort the volume may come from the British Library's almost exhaustive archives.

Turning to American sources, the US National Archives in Washington DC apparently have much which would help British airfield historians, including aerial photographs, but finding out the exact nature of the material would necessitate a trip over there. More accessible are the holdings of the USAF's Albert F. Simpson Historical Research Center at Maxwell Air Force Base in Alabama. Unit histories can be purchased on microfilm and the records for each can be found, with some duplication, on separate reels for squadron, group and, sometimes, base. To take as an

example the 495th Fighter Training Group at Atcham in Shropshire, there is a reel for the Group and its HQ Squadron, one covering the constituent 551st and 552nd Squadrons and one for Station 342, the official code for the airfield.

British aviation photographic sources are numerous, one of the most useful being the RAF Museum which has negatives of a series of aerial views of aerodromes taken in 1942. Since these were designed to show the effectiveness or otherwise of the camouflage of these sites, many are not very clear but some are remarkable, with aircraft and buildings showing up well. They were usually taken obliquely from about 2,000 ft, the aircraft being an Anson or Tiger Moth as parts of these types intrude into some of the photographs.

Views of aircraft on the ground at particular airfields are held by the Museum and copies of these and the aerodrome shots can be ordered. Since the collection is so large, a personal visit by prior arrangement is necessary to establish what is likely to be of interest. The Museum also has files of press releases for RAF stations, and an arrangement with Military Aircraft Photographs of Lossiemouth, Scotland allows a selection of Museum prints to be offered in the monthly catalogue issued by this firm.

The Department of the Environment has negatives covering vertical views of virtually the whole of the British Isles. The first series of these was taken between 1945 and 1947 by Spitfires and Mosquitoes of the RAF's photo-reconnaissance squadrons and some of the prints show hundreds of surplus aircraft awaiting the axe at Maintenance Units. Further coverage was undertaken in the 1960s and 1970s, the whole process being an on-going operation which is now generally done by civil companies under contract to the Ordnance Survey. Prints are easily obtainable, the only snag being the cost; around £10 each at the time of writing. The DOE's address is Air Photographic Unit, Prince Consort House, Albert Embankment, London SE1 7TF.

The Fleet Air Arm Museum at Yeovilton is able to supply copies from its extensive collection of aircraft and airfield photos. There are some very good aerial views but there are also reproductions from wartime air information publications in the form of a rudimentary site plan and miniscule oblique and vertical

photographs. For some of the more obscure Royal Naval Air Stations the latter will be all that has survived!

The Imperial War Museum's photographic files are well-known but many are poorly captioned with no hint of where or when. Some, however, can be identified with a little deduction and local knowledge. There is, for example, a small series on the Blackburn Botha with no amplifying details. Comparison with the backgrounds as they are today confirms that the aircraft were from 1 OTU at Silloth. Again, a pre-arranged visit will be useful but remember that IWM has tens of thousands of aeronautical negatives! The IWM's only airfield photographs are of Greencastle, Hardwick, Husbands Bosworth, Shipdham, Snetterton Heath, Woodbridge, Marham, Prestwick and Benson, most being verticals. Related subjects include a sequence showing airfield construction but with no clue as to where.

ORBs occasionally contain photographs but most of them are of limited interest, service funerals being a popular subject! The PRO has several albums of vertical airfield views but they vary in clarity. Some are excellent, a selection having been published in Air-Britain's *Militaria* publication, but the majority are fuzzy and not really worth the large fee asked for copying.

You can of course take your own aerial photos from a light aircraft but it is difficult

The Banff Strike Wing taxiing out to the runway in the snow of January 1945. A fine photograph from the Strike Wing's album held at the Public Record Office.

A particularly good airfield shot taken by Tony Hooper, Chief Flying Instructor at the South Warwickshire Flying School, Wellesbourne Mountford. This is Moreton-in-Marsh, once a Wellington OTU but now the Home Office Fire Brigades School.

to obtain really good results with the average 35 mm camera. High-winged aircraft make the best camera ships, especially the Cessna 150 with its side windows opening upwards so that you can eliminate reflections. A certain amount of luck as well as technical knowledge seems to be necessary because of the vagaries of lighting and angle.

Having completed your opus, how do you go about getting it published? There are a number of ways of doing this, the cheapest being to type it yourself and have it duplicated. The result is inevitably amateurish, although the use of an electric typewriter will improve it, and reproduction of photographs will be poor. However, you stand a good chance of at least breaking even on the modest outlay. True enthusiasts, it is often said, want good, original 'gen' no matter how it is presented! Setting a price is another problem. Since most publications are sold through the trade, this will have to allow for the 30 per cent or more expected as a discount.

There is little point in approaching a commercial publisher, since individual airfield histories are too specialized for them. Bear in mind that PSL's *Action Stations* series began as something of an experiment and the company is delighted with its success. However, it is believed that this is only because of each volume's coverage of a wide geographical area.

Midland Counties Publications, the well-known aviation book specialists, have been producing their own books for a number of years and have now reached a standard equal to that of the bigger publishing houses. Their definitive volume *The Airfields of Lincolnshire* shows what can be achieved, as does their well-illustrated softback *Aviation in Birmingham*. They still have grave misgivings about the commercial viability of histories on less than a county basis. Having said that, MCP are always willing to read and comment on a manuscript.

A further suggested method is to approach a major library in your area and ask for sponsorship. There is usually a small budget set aside for local history projects but you will have some difficulty in convincing them that aviation is a valid subject. Michael Gibson managed to do this, however, the result being his magnificent *Aviation in Northamptonshire* published by the Northamptonshire Libraries.

Even if you never publish your history you may, like a number of people have done already, lodge the manuscript and background notes with local archives. They will become valuable information for future aviation researchers and you will have the satisfaction of recording a facet of local history generally ignored in favour of much earlier events. Because many of their runways and taxi-tracks have become roads and farm tracks, derelict airfields are permanently imprinted on the landscape. One wonders what future generations will make of them when they are as far in the past as the English Civil War is to us today!

Chapter 22

Airfield investigation

Interest in old wartime airfields has never been greater than it is today and this chapter is intended to suggest possible lines of investigation and exploration when engaged in fieldwork on the sites. There is much still to be seen, even after decades of dereliction, but the uninitiated eye will probably fail to realize the significance of what it sees or worse, miss it completely. An essential document with which to equip oneself before walking the ground is a site plan. These are obtainable for most abandoned aerodromes, and for quite a number of those in current use, from the RAF Museum.

Since the average airfield and its dispersed sites had anything up to 600 separate buildings, a master plan to a large scale was obvi-

ously essential. It marked also the runway safeguarded areas which were to be kept clear of obstacles. Towards the end of the war the Air Ministry Directorate General of Works produced from the original drawings a series of Record Site Plans to a scale of 1:2500, which is approximately 6 in to the mile. They show all the surface features including buildings, roads, runways, taxiways and the boundaries of Air Ministry property.

Within the last 12 years the RAF Museum Department of Records has acquired the site plans and has made copies available to the general public at reasonable prices. At first these were very large and unwieldy, being up to 4 ft square, but smaller sizes were offered later, along with 45 mm microfilm cards. The

The site plan for Pembroke Dock does not identify this hangar type. It appears to be a hybrid, having the features of both the 'A' and 'C' Types.

microfilms can be examined on a special viewer and are easy to store, but of course are useless for fieldwork.

Legibility is often a problem but this was overcome when *After The Battle* magazine began to reproduce many of the plans with the co-operation of Hendon. Each moderately-priced plan is produced to a common size of 16½ by 23½ in and, for ease of handling in the field in all weathers, comes folded in a plastic wallet punched ready for filing in a binder. At the time of writing, a total of 150 plans has been published covering the entire country and including both the obscure and the famous. *After the Battle* is to be congratulated on this venture bearing in mind the dubious commercial viability of such plans as Dallachy's dispersed sites in 1944! Some are from pre-war originals and show the early layouts of such stations as Leuchars, Biggin Hill, Cardington and Upper Heyford.

Unfortunately, plans no longer exist for some sites and for security reasons those for certain airfields still in use have not been declassified. I have been unable to trace those for Wrexham and Connel near Oban and there are no doubt others which are missing. Some, however, go under alternative names and it is wise to check this in the Museum's master list before assuming that they are no longer available.

Many of the plans contrive to fit the airfield and its dispersed sites on the same sheet, while others cover as many as three. There are also some oddities, such as the site of the infra-red projector at Malpas in Cornwall used for bombing practice. There is at least one Royal Naval Air Station, namely Twatt in Orkney, drawn by the Civil Engineer-in-Chief's Department Admiralty. 'Seaplane Base Plans' are also on file for such locations as Pembroke Dock and Felixstowe.

All the buildings on the plans are numbered and the key divides them up by site. The sites themselves are sometimes merely identified by number but more often by their function, for example, Instructional Site, Bomb Store Site, Communal Site and Sleeping Site. Defence structures are not always individually identified but marked BS (blast shelter), GP (gun post) and ARS (air raid shelter). A particularly useful feature is the indication of the type of construction of each building, eg PB (permanent brick), N (Nissen), L (Laing), S (Seco), R (Romney) and so on. There is even the occasional APC (aircraft packing case construction) where office accommodation had to be improvized when materials were scarce!

The Directorate of Works drawing numbers for many of the building types are given but comparison between plans reveals many

Entrance to the old station cinema at Hawarden, Clwyd.

differences although the buildings are outwardly identical. A typical drawing number is 8254/40 for the T2 hangar, the 40 indicating the year 1940. Often serving to confuse rather than inform, the numbers nevertheless are useful in comparing structures at different airfields. Where buildings were of a local design, they were given an appropriate code, an example being the Instrument Repair Shop at RAF Penrhos, PEN/124 on the plan.

It must be emphasized that even though the plans follow the same format, there are subtle differences in detail and each must be studied minutely to gain the maximum value, preferably *before* taking it out on a windy airfield. Apart from the example above, plans for Fleet Air Arm airfields are not generally available but rudimentary drawings of each are held by the PRO and the FAA Museum at Yeovilton. Extracted from a wartime air navigation publication, they show the runways, taxiways, dispersals and also the hangars and other important technical buildings. Unfortunately, the types of buildings are not identified, although there is an indication of their basic function.

Having arrived at the aerodrome, do ensure that you obtain permission from the landowner before entering. In my experience farmers are generally amenable provided you shut gates and observe other rules of the Country Code. Many disused airfields are now adapted for

Top *Watch office of local design at Carew Cheriton, Dyfed, with the remains of the stone and earth wall protection.*

Above *Another 'one-off' — the watch office at Hinton-in-the-Hedges, Northants, alas recently demolished.*

industrial rather than agricultural purposes, container depots being an example. In such instances it may not be possible to gain access on a casual basis but a formal letter to the manager will usually be effective.

By far the most rewarding method of investigating a site is on foot, with a bicycle a close second. Cars are useless unless one's time is limited because one is usually watching for obstructions and potholes and it is easy to miss some interesting relic, especially if it is overgrown. So leave your vehicle and walk round the perimeter track, wandering at will to check

any structures. If they have been demolished, the site plan will show where they once stood and often there will be tangible evidence of their presence, even if it is only a pile of rubble.

Assuming they have been left undisturbed, the dominant buildings on an old airfield will obviously be the hangars. Where they have been dismantled the concrete floors are normally left, complete with grooves for the sliding door runners. Many have been re-erected on farms in the locality so keep your eyes open for them. Blister hangars are the favourite as

Above *Most of the internal door inscriptions are still legible at Twinwood Farm, Bedfordshire. This is the control room.*

Right *A fine inscription survives in the tower at Babdown Farm, Glos.*

they make ideal barns. There were a number of different types of hangar and many are identified in Chapter 7.

Control towers, or more accurately, watch offices, are the other prominent buildings, standing out as they generally do on the aerodrome close to the runways. Again, there are different designs, identifiable only by the Air Ministry Works drawing number, and the type provided at a particular airfield will give a good clue as to the original use for which it was planned. Some aerodromes have, for no clear reason, one-off designs of tower which fall into no particular category, Hinton-in-the-Hedges in Northamptonshire and Kirkbride in Cumbria being two of them. Naval stations had a unique three-storey design unless they were inherited from the RAF, whereupon the original ancestry will be obvious. The former RNAS Stretton in Cheshire, for example, still has the RAF tower which betrays that the airfield was built for the night-fighter defence of the North-West before events rendered it surplus to requirements.

Watch for original inscriptions on the walls and any remaining doors. 'Visiting Pilots Report Here' is a common survivor but one can often find 'Flying Control' and an arrow pointing up the stairs where one enters the main door at the rear. A faded 'Chief Instructor' notice can still be seen on an internal tower door at Babdown Farm in Gloucestershire, once a busy Oxford Advanced Flying Unit. The backless iron cabinet which is often to be

seen in the control room on the first floor puzzles many people but it was merely a store for Very cartridges, the window or asbestos panel behind being designed to blow out safely into the open air if the contents were inadvertently ignited.

Whilst at the tower, check for any remains of the ground signal square in front of it. Most have long since disappeared but there are a few exceptions. The square was also the usual position for a mortar which could fire a large pyrotechnic vertically above the aerodrome in

Above *No more equipment will ever be issued from the parachute store at Long Newnton, Wiltshire. Surviving board seen in 1983.*

Left *Wartime inscription on the corner of Hangar No 1 at Liverpool Airport. I must have passed it scores of times before noticing it!*

Below *Notice inside a building at Twinwood Farm, Bedfordshire.*

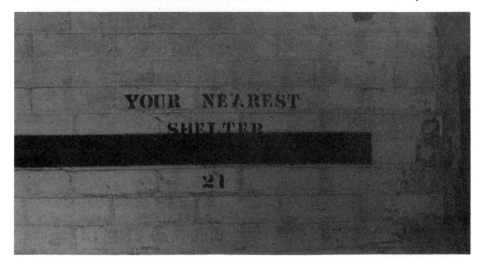

bad weather. It was something of a last ditch emergency method to find the airfield but was undoubtedly very effective. The only one I have seen is at Halfpenny Green in the West Midlands.

A word of warning at this point; these tumbledown buildings can be highly dangerous, so do not venture on to balconies or up iron ladders to the roof unless you are absolutely certain that they will bear your weight. Similar caution applies to defence structures which may be water-filled. Since disused airfields are a haven for wild-life, do not be too surprised if an owl or other roosting predator hurtles past your nose when you wander into a ruined hut. Beware also of farm animals which are often kept in old buildings. Most are docile but pigs with young are potentially lethal. I once came face-to-snout with one at Greencastle in Ulster and had to beat a very undignified and hasty retreat. Pigs are said to be more voracious than goats and will eat anything, even aviation historians!

Alongside the perimeter track at certain aerodromes you may find dispersal pens, or revetments as the Americans called them. Wartime airfields were supplied with liberal quantities of air raid shelters mainly of the Stanton type in pre-cast concrete. Blast shelters are another common sight, normally in the technical area so that taking cover could be deferred until the last moment, thus avoiding time wasted in the shelters. Overground sleeping shelters were built at some fighter stations to protect pilots at readiness.

PSP and other types of temporary metal tracking were often used to form extra parking areas and, at some places, for runway extensions and access taxi-ways. Sections can be found on many old airfields, either lying about or serving as fencing. A late-war design known as Channel Grid was somewhat uneconomical in material and was never produced in any quantity. However, pieces can be seen at Penkridge in Staffordshire, once a Tiger Moth RLG and an unlikely candidate for metal surfacing, as well as Gaydon in Warwickshire, a Wellington OTU satellite. Strangely enough, some Square Mesh Track 'fencing' still exists near the railway station at Rugby.

In the most remote part of the aerodrome the gun test butts will be found, the site plan usually annotating them as the machine-gun or cannon harmonization range. They consisted of a stout buttressed brick and concrete wall with sand piled against it. Most of this has been removed by now, but where it remains digs have produced bullets and cannon shell fragments. However, the possibility of turning up an unexploded shell makes this a dangerous pastime. A red flag was flown from the butts when firing was in progress and the original mast is often still in place. Sometimes a grooved block remains, with a pulley wheel to enable a fighter to be pulled up by its tailwheel so that its guns could be aligned. Separate small arms ranges were also built at many aerodromes.

Similarly tucked away as far as possible from the hangars and living sites was the bomb

A building of more than average interest: the tower at Twinwood Farm, Bedfordshire. Glenn Miller was last seen alive here on 15 December 1944 immediately before his mysterious disappearance over the Channel.

Battle HQ close to the tower at the old night fighter field at Charmy Down on the hills above Bath.

dump. These were built at many airfields which, as things turned out, were never used by bombers at all. On new stations constructed within the first two years of the war, facilities for bomb storage were of substantially simpler and more economical design than the pre-war ones. As the bombing offensive intensified, new methods of housing and handling had to be devised. Open bomb dumps, each of 200 tons capacity, were made up of four 50 ton bays separated by grass covered blast walls.

This made it easier to manhandle all except the largest bomb from incoming lorries to the dumps and from the dumps to the bombing-up trolleys. Efficient movement of vehicles was ensured by circulating roads from bomb storage, component stores, pyrotechnic store-houses and other ancillary explosive buildings in hutted construction, through the fusing sheds and thence to the aircraft dispersals. Today the bomb dumps are not very interesting, most, if not all, of the buildings having been demolished leaving only the blast walls.

Defensive works were often elaborate and by the very nature of their construction tend to have survived better than lesser structures. The hexagonal pill-box is the most common but there were also mushroom-shaped ones which were built at many of the bomber airfields laid out in 1942. Some types of defensive position appear to have been of local design, several former stations in Northern Ireland having a complicated concrete trench and blockhouse type which can be seen nowhere else in Britain. The oddly named 'Seagull Trench' saw widespread use, however, its flattened 'W' planform when viewed from above explaining its title. Many still have machine-gun mountings in place and at one location I found an old ammunition box.

Defence structures are not always marked on site plans as they were not finalized in the planning stage but sited at a later date on the advice of the local Army commander. It is therefore worth looking out for them, hidden as they often are in hedgerows and on the fringes of woodland. Even more difficult to find are the Pickett-Hamilton retractable forts which were installed at many airfields before they were deemed to be of only limited value. These devices are now widely known since several have been discovered and removed for preservation. Their entrances resemble a drainage manhole and they are normally emplaced out on the airfield. Equally obscure are the smoke generators provided at some sites to indicate wind direction and, reputedly, to lay a smokescreen when necessary. They consisted of a slotted metal cover over a pit, the smoke being produced by vaporizing oil or paraffin over a hot surface.

Barbed wire fencing enclosed many airfields and rusty strands and sometimes quite large coils can be found. Other defensive remains are anti-aircraft positions, often with adjacent accommodation for the gun crews and ammunition stores. The defences were co-ordinated by a Battle Headquarters, an underground building with an observation cupola just above the surface, giving a 360° view through a horizontal slot. The favourite situation for these was on the highest point of the perimeter, preferably on a hillock and in a hedge line to render them as inconspicuous as possible.

While walking on an old airfield, keep a careful eye out for discarded aircraft parts, spent cartridge cases and the other small debris which tends to remain unnoticed for decades. Ploughing on former 8th Air Force bomber bases always unearths old .50 calibre shell cases. They were literally shovelled out of the aircraft in thousands after a mission, not a few being dropped in the grass, and one can speculate that a particular shell case may have been fired in anger in the skies over the Third Reich. Alongside the threshold of each runway there was usually a small hard-standing for the runway caravan, around which it is sometimes possible to pick up the remains of discarded Very cartridges.

Other common items are screw pickets used for tying down aircraft and similar steel pickets for staking out barbed wire. I once found a small bomb rack lying on a taxi-way at Kingston Bagpuize in Berkshire and was able to identify it as coming from a Hawker Hector by means of the part numbers stamped on it. People I know have found much more impressive relics, ranging from propellor blades to whole undercarriage units. Enormous numbers of surplus aircraft were scrapped at Maintenance Units in the late 1940s and many pieces found their way on to local farms and into cottage gardens, cockpit canopies making very useful cloches for vegetables!

Every aerodrome most probably had a dump where damaged or redundant equipment and even whole aircraft were deposited to await salvage and to act as a store of spare parts. Judging by some well-authenticated reports, many of the airframes were simply buried at the end of the war in a hurried tidying-up operation.

So far, no one has found anything substantial but I am convinced that some very interesting and otherwise extinct aircraft await discovery. There is supposed to be the hulk of a Fortress buried at Deenethorpe and at Penrhos in North Wales I am told that an aircraft was disposed of by bulldozing a hole into the hillside behind the hangars.

This brings me to the subject of the Instructional Sites which were provided at OTU and other airfields as described in Chapter 8. Some of them incorporated early forms of flight simulator for crew procedures training using cockpits and even entire fuselages from aircraft damaged beyond repair. This is how the Wartime Aircraft Recovery Group acquired a Hampden nose section from Peplow in Shropshire and there may be other survivors lurking unseen in huts somewhere. The Hawarden Trainer, for example, named after the OTU station where it was invented, centred around an actual Spitfire cockpit and there are photographs in the PRO to prove it.

Numerous specialized buildings were developed to meet the progress made in synthetic training but common to most stations were navigation and armament lecture rooms and Link Trainer buildings. As standard policy under the dispersal scheme, Instructional Sites

The famous B-17 mural, 'The Big Picture', on the wall of a building at Podington, Bedfordshire, seen about 20 years ago. Badly faded, it still looks down on a room full of sows and their piglets (P.S. Lamb).

Mustang 1 on wall of former 41 OTU Flight Office at Hawarden, Clwyd.

were located between the technical and domestic groups. Traces of their original purpose can be seen in many of the huts, clouds and blue sky painted on the walls being quite common!

Again, it is useful to make a careful study of doors and walls for any wartime inscriptions. These need not necessarily be official ones as an entire sub-branch of aviation archaeology has grown up devoted to vintage graffiti and murals. They range from the telephone numbers of Carlisle 'popsies' (all grandmothers by now, no doubt) pencilled on walls at Crosby-on-Eden, to some very skilful aircraft paintings at East Anglian bases. There are probably more waiting for rediscovery but examining every building is a time-consuming operation so many must have escaped detection so far.

Dispersed domestic sites tend to be overlooked by airfield explorers in favour of the more obvious attractions of the airfield itself, but they are worthy of more than a cursory glance as some may contain wall art. The buildings themselves were completely utilitarian in concept and construction, providing only the bare necessities for their purpose. Typical accomodation consisted of officers' and sergeants' messes and quarters, barrack huts and dining rooms for the airmen and various types of WAAF quarters. There were also NAAFIs, store and bath houses and latrines. The fittings are sometimes still *in situ* and a good collection of 1940s RAF porcelain could soon be built up if one so desired! The infamous pot-bellied stoves are almost extinct but the concrete plinths show where they once stood.

Each RAF station had its own sewage disposal site to a common pattern but few of us find this very interesting! Water supply was another mundane but essential service. The proliferation of new aerodromes and expansion of existing ones severely strained rural water supplies and it was often necessary for the Air Ministry to find new and independent sources, which were frequently converted to local civilian use after the war. The storage reservoirs and fixed booster installation which were normal equipment on permanent stations for fire-fighting purposes were considered impracticable for the dispersed layout of the war years. A modified form of fire protection was therefore employed which relied upon storage in the station high-level tank to feed fire hydrants on all the main sites, which then used mobile fire pumps. Static water tanks were located at strategic points to supplement the supply available from the distribution centre. These static tanks were convenient for dumping stolen bicycles, I am told, and a delve in the sludge might prove rewarding!

Placed well away from the airfield was the operations block. Many bases used for training were originally intended to house operational aircraft, hence these buildings can also be seen at a number of unlikely places. Since they are windowless, a good torch is essential to explore them, particularly as many have uncovered drainage channels and debris-strewn floors. In one design the main operations room resembles a small theatre with a raised dais for the controller and the remainder of the building is a maze of offices and storerooms.

Sometimes, the operations board for the local squadrons is still in place and at Banff in north-east Scotland the score of shipping successes credited to the Strike Wing is just decipherable. As most of these inscriptions are painted directly on to the walls, removal for preservation is regrettably not feasible but they can at least be recorded on film.

Somewhat similar to an operations block and often confused with it is the decontamination centre. These large buildings were a product of the gas warfare obsession of the 1930s, a fear which thankfully was never realized. In the event of a gas attack, ground personnel protected by respirators could wash off any skin contamination and change into the clean clothing stored in readiness. In common with ops blocks the centres had tall chimneys to extract air from above the gas layer and circulate it through extensive ducting. Site plans often show gas chambers which were used for anti-gas training and the testing of masks.

Finally, it might be assumed that delapidated or torn-up runways and taxi-ways are of no interest, but the cross-section of construction methods thus revealed ranges from mere hardcore with a top-dressing of tarmac to the concrete slabs of the standard bomber airfield. If you wish to save an armoured runway light fitting for posterity, be warned, they are plentiful but extremely heavy!

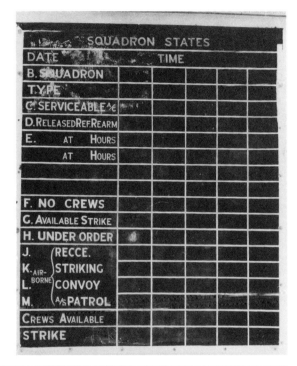

Board still to be seen inside the operations block at Limavady, Northern Ireland, once a Coastal Command station (E.A. Cromie).

Grangemouth, Scotland. Scottish Aviation Ltd relinquished this airfield at least 10 years ago but the company's emblem is still on one of the buildings (John Walker).

Chapter 23

Airfield memorials

During the past decade there has been a tremendous increase in the number of aerodromes whose history has been commemorated in some way. It may be a simple stone, a stained glass window in a village church, an aircraft propellor or an impressive structure like the breached dam in memory of 617 Squadron. The following list is not claimed to be exhaustive, research into aviation memorials often being difficult and heavily dependent upon local knowledge. For ease of reference, I have listed them under the airfield name even though the memorial may be in a nearby village bearing a different name.

Airfield	Remarks
Andrews Field, Essex	Amongst old people's bungalows in Great Saling a plaque detailing the building of the local aerodrome by US Army engineers.
Attlebridge, Norfolk	466th Bomb Group remembered on Weston Longville village sign.
Bardney, Lincs	In village, propellor memorial to 9 Sqn.
Barton, Greater Manchester	Road name Proctor Way commemorates local wartime production of the Percival Proctor.
Bassingbourn, Cambs	Propellor memorial to 91st Bomb Group and other USAAF units formerly based here. There is also a plaque to 91st Bomb Group on the fountain in nearby Royston.
Beaulieu, Hants	
Benson, Oxon	Plaque in memory of PR aircrew lost flying from here.
Biggin Hill, Kent	St. George's Chapel of Remembrance.
Binbrook, Lincs	Granite memorial to 460 Sqn (RAAF) and Roll of Honour at St Mary's Church. Stained glass window commemorates all Binbrook's Units.
Bodney, Norfolk	Memorial to 352nd Fighter Group.
Boreham, Essex	USAAF memorial pillar erected by Anglo-American Goodwill Association in 1948.
Bradwell Bay, Essex	Memorial to those lost flying from here.
Brockworth, Glos	Sayer Crescent is named after wartime Gloster test pilot, Gerry Sayer.

Above *819th Engineer Aviation Battalion memorial at Great Saling, Essex.*

Right *Propeller and marker commemorate USAAF units at Bassingbourn, Cambs.*

Brooklands, Surrey	Plaque commemorating its early racing and flying history.
Bungay, Suffolk	Plaque to 446th Bomb Group inside Community Centre (the former airmens' mess).
Bury St Edmunds, Suffolk	Memorial to 94th Bomb Group
Cardington, Beds	Ensign from R.101 hangs in church. The communal grave of the victims of the airship disaster is in the small cemetery across the road.
Castle Bromwich, West Midlands	Memorial to aerodrome and most of the roads and blocks of flats now on the site have names with aviation connotations.
Chalgrove, Oxon	Memorial to USAAF photo-recce units.
Cheddington, Bucks	Original runway light with dedication to 8th Air Force units stationed here.
Chelveston, Northants	Memorial tablet to 305th Bomb Group on wall of Chelveston church tower which the Group Memorial Association helped to restore.

Coningsby, Lincs	Chapel in village church in memory of 83 Sqn.
Christchurch, Dorset	Stars and stripes presented to Christchurch Abbey by 405th Fighter Group on their departure to France in July 1944. Some of the road names on the housing estate which covers part of the site reflect the earlier days, eg de Havilland Way and Ambassador Close.
Cottesmore, Leics	Plaque outside guardroom records USAAF Troop Carrier units which flew from here.
Croft, North Yorks	At nearby Dalton-on-Tees is a stone memorial to 431 and 434 Sqns, RCAF.
Dale, Dyfed	Roll of Honour for 300 (Polish) Sqn in Marloes Church.
Debden, Essex	USAAF memorial apse at Saffron Walden church.
Deenethorpe, Northants	In Weldon Church, stained glass window commemorating 401st Bomb Group.
Denham, Bucks	Memorial to glider pilot training here in the Second World War.
Down Ampney, Glos	Memorial window in church to Flight Lieutenant Lord VC DFC and a stone on the old airfield recalling its past.
Downham Market, Norfolk	Memorial at Bexwell Parish Church to aircrew lost flying from here.
Dunkeswell, Devon	Plaque in Dunkeswell Church listing US Navy men who died whilst flying from the base. Also a memorial organ given by US Navy personnel at Dunkeswell.
Dunsfold, Surrey	Stone in front of control tower commemorating the construction of the airfield by Canadian engineers.
Duxford, Cambs	78th Fighter Group memorial plaque beside old parade ground.
Eastchurch, Kent	In the village at the junction of the road leading to the camp and the A520, a large memorial to the first home of British aviation 1909.
East Fortune, Lothian	Memorial to R.34 which made the first double-crossing of the Atlantic by air.
East Wretham, Norfolk	Two memorials to 359th Fighter Group, one outside King's House, Thetford and the other in East Wretham Church. Plaque dedicated to 311 Squadron on wall of library, Thetford.
East Kirkby, Lincs	On the A155 east of the village a stone in memory of the dead of 57 and 603 Sqns.
Elgin, Grampian	20 OTU memorial incorporating the unit's badge.

An impressive 20 OTU badge close to the former Elgin satellite aerodrome, Grampian.

Elsham Wolds, Lincs	At Anglian Water Authority treatment works memorial garden to the former RAF station and its wartime units.
Elvington, Yorks	Memorial to French airmen killed on operations from here.
Farnborough, Hants	A replica of Cody's tree now replaces the original. At St Mark's Church some mementoes of Farnborough's early days can be seen.
Fiskerton, Lincs	Memorial plaque in village church to 49 and 576 Squadrons.
Ford, West Sussex	Airfield memorial garden.
Framlingham, Suffolk	Memorial to 390th Bomb Group
Glatton, Hunts	Conington churchyard. 457th Bomb Group memorial, stone head of an airman looking towards Glatton aerodrome.
Goxhill, Lincs	P-38 propellor memorial to USAAF personnel stationed here.
Grafton Underwood, Northants	384th Bomb Group memorial on the end of the old main runway.
Gravesend, Kent	Plaque at Thong Lane Sports Centre in memory of 14 pilots who died in the Battle of Britain whilst flying from Gravesend.
Great Ashfield, Suffolk	Memorial nave in village church to 385th Bomb Group. Also a Book of Remembrance to more than 400 airmen killed whilst flying from the base.
Great Dunmow, Essex	USAAF memorial erected by Anglo-American Goodwill Association in 1948.
Halesworth, Suffolk	Memorial to 489th Bomb Group.
Harrington, Northants	Memorial stone to 801st/492nd Bomb Group.
Harwell, Berks	Plaque commemorating departure from the former aerodrome of the first aircraft of 38 Group with airborne troops for the D-Day landings.

The 384th Bomb Group is remembered on this rock sited on what was once the threshold of the main runway at Grafton Underwood, Northants.

Hawkinge, Kent	Memorial stone which incorporates the original metal compass-swinging circle.
Headcorn, Kent	Plaque commemorating 403 and 421 Sqns, RCAF. Also three Canadian Maple trees.
Heathrow (London Airport)	In Central Area, statues of Alcock and Brown and a model of the Mustang in which Charles Blair pioneered the transpolar route.
Hemswell, Lincs	Memorial stone to those lost flying with 170 Sqn.
Hendon, Middlesex	Road names on former aerodrome site include some old RAF stations, for example Hemswell Drive, Dishforth Lane, Tangmere Way.
Heston, Middlesex	Road names Prestwick Close, Shannon Close etc commemorate local aviation connections.
Honington, Suffolk	12 Sqn sign at local public house.
Horham, Suffolk	Memorial to 95th Bomb Group near church. US Flag which once flew over 95th BG HQ can be seen at Stradbroke church.
Hornchurch, Essex	Memorial stone on site of former station HQ. Other memorials at public library and 'Good Intent' public house.
Horsham St Faith, Norfolk	Display about 458th Bomb Group in airport terminal.
Kelstern, Lincs	On western perimeter a memorial to 625 Sqn.
Kimbolton, Cambs	Memorial to 379th BG in Kimbolton church.

Kirkwall, Orkney

Plaque in airport terminal in memory of Captain E. E. Fresson who pioneered air services to Orkney and Shetland.

Kirmington, Lincs (Humberside Airport)

Parish Church, plaque to those lost flying with 166 Sqn. There is a similar memorial in the terminal building.

Kingscliffe, Northants

RAF/USAAF memorial on roadside adjacent to aerodrome.

Larkhill, Wilts

Concrete plinth at roadside records the site of the first British military aerodrome.

Lavenham, Suffolk

Plaque on wall in market place dedicated to those who lost their lives flying with the 487th Bomb Group.

Lee-on-Solent, Hants

Fleet Air Arm memorial at south-east corner of air station.

Leiston, Suffolk

357th Fighter Group memorial.

Leuchars, Fife

Memorial to Norwegian squadrons which flew from here with Coastal Command.

Lichfield, Staffs

Memorial seat in Cathedral to Australians who trained at 27 OTU

Lisset, Yorks

Memorial in village to 158 Sqn.

Little Rissington, Glos

Stained glass window commemorating all who flew from here.

Little Snoring, Norfolk

Memorial board in church showing enemy aircraft shot down and awards to RAF aircrew.

There are several RAF airfield memorials in this simple but effective style. This one is at Kelstern, Lincs.

Propeller memorial to 7th Photo Group which once flew from the nearby Mount Farm aerodrome.

Little Staughton, Cambs	In the village church, a tablet and Book of Remembrance dedicated to the Little Staughton Pathfinder squadrons.
Liverpool Airport, Merseyside	Plaque in terminal to 611 (West Lancs) Sqn.
Llandwrog, Gwynedd	Scots Guards airfield defence unit made a badge of sea-shells set in concrete which can still be seen.
Ludford Magna, Lincs	Memorial to 101 Sqn in centre of village. Also a Book of Remembrance in the church.
Marston Moor, Yorks	Memorial to wartime units.
Martlesham Heath, Suffolk	On old RAF parade ground in south-east corner of aerodrome, American memorial lists personnel lost flying with 356th Fighter Group.
Meir, Staffs	Roads on housing and industrial development reflect the site's original use as an aerodrome, eg Lysander Way, Mollison Road, Cobham Place.
Melbourne, Yorks	10 Sqn memorial.
Mendlesham, Suffolk	Beside the A140, an impressive memorial to the 34th Bomb Group.
Mepal, Cambs	Memorial to wartime units.
Methwold, Norfolk	Plaque to those who served here.
Middleton St George (now Tees-side Airport)	Memorial outside St George Hotel, formerly the Officers' Mess, honours 419, 420 and 428 RCAF Sqns.
Molesworth, Cambs	Plaque at Brington church recording the re-construction of the spire as a gift from American servicemen in memory of their fallen comrades.
Mona, Anglesey	Plaque in Shire Hall, Llangefni commemorates local First World War airship operations by RNAS.
Mount Farm, Oxon	On Berinsfield village green, a propellor memorial to the 7th Photo Recce Group. There is another 7th PRG memorial at the Abbey Church at nearby Dorchester.
Newmarket, Suffolk	Propellor memorial to 99 Sqn.
North Coates, Lincs	Roll of Honour in station church and stained glass window showing station badge.
Northolt, Middlesex	Beside North Circular Road, the Polish Memorial.
North Killingholme, Lincs	Stone in memory of 550 Sqn.
North Pickenham, Norfolk	Memorial to USAAF units based here. Road into industrial estate on former aerodrome is called Lancaster Approach.
North Weald, Essex	Stone monolith commemorates the Norwegians who served on the station. Village sign incorporates a Hurricane aircraft.

Nuthampstead, Herts	398th Bomb Group memorial
Odiham, Hants	Some mementoes of 4 Sqn are kept at Odiham Church.
Old Buckenham, Norfolk	Village hall extension with plaque to 453rd Bomb Group.
Pembroke Dock, Dyfed	Plaque in St John's Church commemorating local flying boat operations 1930-59.
Perton, Staffs	Memorial stone recalls site's previous use as an aerodrome.
Pocklington, Yorks	Memorial to 102 and 405 Sqns in front of Wolds Gliding Club HQ.
Polebrook, Northants	351st Bomb Group memorial on the old main runway.
Prestwick, Ayrshire	Plaque in terminal in memory of David F. McIntyre, AFC, founder of the airport.
Pulham, Norfolk	Village sign.
Rackheath, Norfolk	Village sign and seats commemorating 467th Bomb Group.
Rattlesden, Suffolk	Memorial to 447th Bomb Group near end of runway.
Renfrew, Strathclyde	Estate on former Glasgow Airport site has some appropriately named roads, eg Britannia Way, Viscount Way, Vanguard Way.
Ridgewell, Essex	381st Bomb Group memorial at old technical site entrance.
Ringway, Greater Manchester	Plaque in terminal commemorates Parachute Training School.
Saltby, Leics	Unidentified concrete badge here may have aviation connections.
Scampton, Lincs	Rose bed near guardroom commemorating Sergeant J. Hannah VC. Grave of Wing Commander Guy Gibson's dog Nigger outside 2 hangar.
Seething, Norfolk	Memorial stone on airfield and memorial in churchyard. Tower has been renovated and holds Honour Roll of the 448th Bomb Group.
Shawbury, Salop	Mosaic of 11 FTS badge based here 1938-42, outside Station HQ.
Shipdham, Norfolk	Memorial in Shipdham church-yard to dead of 8th Bomber Command.
Shoreham, Sussex	Plaque in terminal recording airport's longevity.
Silloth, Cumbria	Plaque in church incorporating badge of 22 MU.
Snaith, Yorks	Memorial to 51 Sqn.
Snetterton Heath, Norfolk	Quidenham church. Memorial chapel and stained glass window to 96th Bomb Group.
South Carlton, Lincs	Plaque in village church to those who died flying from the First World War aerodrome.

Spanhoe, Northants	Memorial obelisk to 315th Troop Carrier Group.
Stag Lane, Middlesex	Aeronautical road names on former site include Mollison Way and de Havilland Road.
Steeple Morden, Cambs	Large memorial with propellor to 355th Fighter Group.
Stonehenge, Wilts	Near site of First World War aerodrome is a stone marking the spot at which two airmen were killed in a crash in 1912.
Sudbury, Suffolk	Plaque in town hall presented by 486th Bomb Group personnel.
Sutton Bridge, Lincs	Memorial chapel and Roll of Honour in village church.
Swinderby, Lincs	In Norton Disney church a plaque to the Polish 300 and 301 Sqns.
Talbenny, Dyfed	Roll of Honour in Talbenny church to those lost flying from the Coastal Command Base.
Tangmere, West Sussex	Memorial stone on village green.
Tarrant Rushton, Dorset	Near old main gate a memorial to all who flew from here 1943-80.
Tatton Park, Cheshire	Plaque commemorates use as a DZ by Parachute Training School.
Tholthorpe, Yorks	Memorial on village green to RCAF personnel who served here.
Thornaby, Tees-side	Aerodrome is now Thornaby New Town but many streets and building names reflect its former role. For example, Bader Avenue, Halifax Road and Anson House.
Thorney Island, Hants	Plaque detailing how a Hawker Fury crash led to the discovery of the area's suitability for an aerodrome.
Thorpe Abbots, Norfolk	100th Bomb Group Memorial Museum in restored control tower.
Tuddenham, Suffolk	Memorial on village green.
Turnberry, Ayrshire	Obelisk listing 39 airmen who were killed whilst serving with the School of Aerial Gunnery and Fighting during 1917/18.
Upper Heyford, Oxon	Stone in village commemorating aircrew lost flying from the base.
Waddington, Lincs	Memorial clock to 463 and 467 Sqns, RAAF in village centre. Stone recalling 44 Sqn near station guardroom.
Waltham, Lincs	Memorial to 100 Sqn beside A16.
Watton, Norfolk	Memorial in Griston church to 3rd Strategic Air Depot.
Wendling, Norfolk	Beside minor road leading to Beeston off A47. Monument to 392nd Bomb Group and USAAF ground units at the base.
Westhampnett (Goodwood), Sussex	Stone in memory of 31st Fighter Group.

Above *One of the most elaborate of the numerous USAAF memorials; this is on the former fighter base at Steeple Morden, Cambs.*

SPANHOE AIRFIELD
1944 - 1945

THE SQUADRONS OF 315 TH TROOP CARRIER
GROUP U. S. ARMY AIR FORCES
FLEW FROM THIS SITE
ON AIRBORNE MISSIONS TO
NORMANDY, ARNHEM AND THE RHINE
FOR THE LIBERATION OF WESTERN EUROPE
AND THE DEFENSE OF FREEDOM
ERECTED BY THE W. W. II 315 TH
TROOP CARRIER ASSOCIATION
1983

Right *Plaque on an obelisk at Spanhoe, near Corby, commemorates the 315th Troop Carrier Group* (FlyPast).

Whitchurch, Avon	Some of the roads on the former Bristol Airport have an aeronautical theme, Dakota Drive being an example.
White Waltham, Berks	Air Transport Auxiliary flag in local church.
Wickenby, Lincs	Stone to dead of 12 and 626 Sqns.
Wing, Bucks	Spinney planted to commemorate local victory against proposal to site London's third airport here.
Woodhall Spa, Lincs	In Royal Square Gardens an impressive miniature dam commemorates 617 Sqn.

Bibliography

PSL Action Stations Series

1: *Military Airfields of East Anglia*, Michael J.F. Bowyer

2: *Military Airfields of Lincolnshire and the East Midlands*, Bruce Barrymore Halpenny

3: *Military Airfields of Wales and the North-west*, David J. Smith

4: *Military Airfields of Yorkshire*, Bruce Barrymore Halpenny

5: *Military Airfields of the South-west*, Chris Ashworth

6: *Military Airfields of the Cotswolds and the Central Midlands*, Michael J.F. Bowyer

7: *Military Airfields of Scotland, the North-east and Northern Ireland*, David J. Smith

8: *Military Airfields of Greater London*, Bruce Barrymore Halpenny

9: *Military Airfields of the Central South and South-east*, Chris Ashworth

10: *Supplement and index*, Bruce Quarrie

Action Stations: Cambridgeshire, Michael J.F. Bowyer

Action Stations, Oxfordshire, Michael J.F. Bowyer

Airfield History publications

This is a near-complete list of published airfield histories and closely related material. Some are now out of print but enquiries to the specialist aviation booksellers will probably establish availability.

Ferguson, J.D. *The Story of Aberdeen Airport 1934-1984* (Scottish Airports, 1984)

Pickavance, M.J. *Royal Air Force Abingdon, the First 50 Years* (RAF Abingdon, 1982)

Neanor, A. *Acton Aerodrome* (London Borough of Ealing Library Service, 1978)

Ramsey, W.G. Ed *Airfields of the Eighth Then & Now* (Battle of Britain Prints International, 1980)

Chiltern Aviation Group, *Airship to Concorde (Aviation in West London)*

Giddings, Malcolm L. *Royal Air Force Ashbourne* (Colerne Debden Publishing, 1984)

Coles, R. *History of Beaulieu Airfield* (R. Coles, 1981)

Wallace, G. *RAF Biggin Hill* (Reprinted 1979)

Kent Aviation Historical Research Society, *The Bump — A History of RAF Biggin Hill 1916-1980* (RAF Biggin Hill, 1980)

Negus, G. & Staddon, T. *Aviation in Birmingham* (Midland Counties Publications, 1984)

Ramsey, W.G. Ed *The Battle of Britain Then & Now* (Battle of Britain Prints International Ltd, 1980)

British Isles Airfield Guide (Merseyside Aviation Society, 10th Edition 1985)

Willis, S. & Hollis, B. *Military Airfields in the British Isles 1939-1945* (3 vols, subsequently combined in one volume) (Willis & Hollis, 1987)

Bond, S.J. *A History of Royal Air Force Brize Norton* (RAF Brize Norton, 1980)

Jackson, H. *Wings over Brooklands*

Ferguson, A.P. *Burtonwood — 8th Air Force Base Air Depot* (Airfield Publications, 1986)

Newell, M.D. *Castle Bromwich — Its Airfield & Aircraft Factory* (Enthusiasts Publications, 1982)

Hamlin, J.F. *Royal Air Force in Cambridgeshire Part 2* (J.F. Hamlin, 1987)

White, A. *Christchurch Airfield* (A. White, 1987)

Cownie, F/Lt A.G.H. *History of Royal Air Force Church Fenton 1937-1987* (RAF Church Fenton, 1987)

Haslam, G/C E.B. *History of RAF Cranwell* (HMSO, 1982)

Learmonth, B., Nash, J., & Cluett, D. *Croydon Airport 1928-1939* (Sutton Libraries and Arts Services, 1980)

Learmonth, B., Nash, J., & Cluett, D. *The First Croydon Airport 1915-1928* (Sutton Libraries and Arts Services, 1977)

Cluett, D., Bogle, J., Learmonth, B. *Croydon Airport and the Battle of Britain* (Sutton Libraries and Arts Services, 1985)

Connon, P. *An Aeronautical History of the Cumbria, Dumfries & Galloway Region Parts 1 & 2* (St Patrick's Press, 1982 and 1984)

Braybrooks, K. *Wingspan — A History of RAF Debden* (RAF Debden, 1956)

Montgomery, F/L B.G. and Longhurst, F/L E. *Royal Air Force Digby — A Short History* (RAF Digby, 1973)

Bowyer, Michael J.F. *Duxford, its First Year of War* (East Anglian Aviation Society, 1974)

Armstrong, R. *Wings Over Eastbourne* (Sound Forum, 1979)

Kinsey, G. *Seaplanes Felixstowe* (Dalton, 1978)

Anon. *A History of RAF Finningley 1936-1969* (RAF Finningley, 1969)

King, J. & Tait, G. *Golden Gatwick* (BAA, 1980)

King, J. *Gatwick — The Evolution of an Airport* (Gatwick Airport Ltd and Sussex Industrial Archaeology Society, 1987)

Bagley, J.A. *A Gazetteer of Hampshire Aerodromes* (Hampshire Field Club Archaelogical Society, 1972)

Smith, D.J. *Hawarden, a Welsh Airfield 1939-1979* (D.J. Smith, 1979)

Humphreys, R.S. *Hawkinge 1912-1961*

Anon. *The History of RAF Henlow* (Radio Engineering Unit, RAF Henlow, 1975)

Sutton, Sqdn Ldr H.T. *Raiders Approach* (Gale & Polden Ltd, 1956)

Lake, C. *Jersey Airport: The First 50 Years 1937-1987* (Michael Stephen, 1987)

Layzell, A. *Announcing the Arrival — Jersey Airport 1937-1987* (Channel TV, 1987)

Flint, P. *RAF Kenley*

Kent Airfields in the Battle of Britain (Kent Aviation Historical Research Society)

Brookes, R.S. *Aviation in Kent*

Collyer, D.G. *Flying — The First World War in Kent* (North Kent Book, 1982)

Flight in Kent (Kent Aviation Historical Research Society, 1985)

Wings Over Kent (Kent Aviation Historical Research Society, 1982)

Giddings, M.L. *Bomber Base: A History of RAF Lichfield & Church Broughton* (Colerne Debden Publishing, 1986)

Blake, R., Hodgson, M. & Taylor, W. *The Airfields of Lincolnshire since 1912* (Midland Counties Publications, 1984)

Hancock, T.N. *Bomber County, a History of the RAF in Lincolnshire* (Lincolnshire County Council, 1978)

Finn, S. *Lincolnshire Air War 1939-1945* (Aero Litho Co (Lincoln) Ltd, 1973) (Book 2 published in 1983)

Butler, P.H. *An Illustrated History of Liverpool Airport* (Merseyside Aviation Society, 1983)

Annand, RAF (Retd) Wg Cdr A.D. *RAF Llanbedr 1941-1945* (A.D. Annand, 1983)

Robinson, B.R. *Aviation in Manchester* (RAeS Manchester Branch, 1977)

Scholefield, R.A. and McDonald, S.D. *First and Foremost* (Manchester International Airport Authority, 1978)

Fraser, F/L W. *The Story of RAF Manston* (RAF Manston, 1969)

Stockman, R. *The History of RAF Manston* (RAF Manston, 1986)

Kniveton, G.N. *Manx Aviation in Peace & War* (The Manx Experience, 1986)

Kinsey, G. *Martlesham Heath* (Dalton, 1975)

Dring, C.M. *A History of RAF Mildenhall* (Mildenhall Museum Publications, 1980)

Teague, D. *Mountbatten Flying Boat Base, Plymouth* (West Way Publications, 1986)

Hamlin, J.F. *The Royal Air Force at Newmarket 1939-1947* (J.F. Hamlin, 1985)

Fairhead, H. & Tuffen, R. *Airfields of Norfolk & Suffolk (4 parts)* (Norfolk and Suffolk Aviation Museum, 1983)

Gibson, M.L. *Aviation in Northamptonshire* (Northamptonshire Libraries, 1982)

Hayward, K. & Norris, P. *A Short History of RAF Northolt* (Chiltern Aviation Society, 1980)

Hamlin, J.F. *The Royal Air Force in Cambridgeshire Part 1 Oakington & Bourn* (J.F. Hamlin, 1986)

Kinsey, G. *Orfordness* (Terence Dalton, 1981)

Crouther Gordon DFC, Dr T. *Early Flying in Orkney — Seaplanes in WWI* (BBC Radio Orkney, 1986)

Wright, P. *The Royal Flying Corps in Oxfordshire* (P. Wright, 1985)

Evans, J. *Flying Boat Haven* (Pembroke Dock) (Aviation and Maritime Research, 1985)

Tipton DFC, Wg Cdr J.E. *South Western Approaches. Air Operations from Pembrokeshire in The World Wars* (Tenby Museum, 1986)

Annand, RAF (Retd) Wg Cdr A.D. *RAF Penrhos 1937-45 and RAF Llandwrog 1940-45* (A.D. Annand, 1986)

Warren, G. *RAF Pershore, a History* (Enthusiast Publications, 1982)

Perth Aerodrome, Scone, Scotland (Compiled and published by Air Service Training, 1986)

Ewart, J. *Prestwick Airport — Golden Jubilee 1935-1985*

Tait, G. & Smith, P. *Redhill at War: The Lighter Side* (G. Tait and Associates Ltd, 1983)

Webb, R.J. *Early Ringway* (Webstar Graphics, 1978)

Stait, B.A. *Rivenhall: The History of an Essex Airfield* (Alan Sutton Publishing Ltd, 1984)

R Ae S Medway Branch *A Brief History of Rochester Airport* (RAeS Medway Branch)

Rennison, J.P. *Wings over Rutland* (Spiegl Press, 1980)

Jefford, F/L C.G. *A History of RAF Scampton* (RAF Scampton, 1968)

Baldwin, J. *40 Years of RAF Sculthorpe 1943-1983* (Jim Baldwin Publishing, 1986)

Ferguson, A.P. *A History of Royal Air Force Sealand* (Merseyside Aviation Society, 1978)

Ferguson, A.P. *A History of RAF Shawbury* (Merseyside Aviation Society, 1977)

Teague, D.C. & White, P.R. *A Guide to the Airfields of South Western England* (Baron Jay Ltd, 1982)

Paul, C. *Sywell — The Story of an English Aerodrome* (Sywell Aerodrome Ltd, 1978)

Wartime Tatton (Compiled and published by the Countryside and Recreation Division of Cheshire County Council, 1987)

Annand, RAF (Retd) Wg Cdr A.D. *RAF Towyn 1940-1945* (A.D. Annand, 1983)

Corlett, J. *Aviation in Ulster* (Blackstaff Press Ltd, 1981)

Williams, G. *Wings Over Westgate* (G. Williams, 1986)

Hall, P. *By Day & By Night — The Men & Machines of West Malling Airfield*

Rapier, B.J. *White Rose Base* (Aero Litho Co (Lincoln) Ltd, 1972)

Taylor, Bill *Royal Air Force Winthorpe* (Control Column, 1984)

Ferguson, A.P. *A History of Royal Air Force Woodvale* (Merseyside Aviation Society, 1980)

Peach, Flt Lt S. *The Pathfinder Station — A History of Wyton Airfield* (S. Peach, 1983)

Other publications of interest

Balfour, Lord *Wings over Westminster*

Boyle, Andrew *No Passing Glory* (Collins, 1955)

Calmel, Jean *Night Pilot* (William Kimber, 1955)

Charlewood, Don *No Moon Tonight* (Angus & Robertson, 1956)

Clarke, Arthur C. *Glide Path* (Sidgwick & Jackson, 1969)

Closterman, Pierre *The Big Show* (Chatto & Windus, 1951)

Dirst, C.S. *Meteorology of Airfields* (HMSO, 1949)

Freeman, Roger *Mighty Eighth War Manual* (Jane's, 1984)

Halley, James J. *The Squadrons of the Royal Air Force* (Air-Britain (Historians) Ltd, 1980)

Hough, Richard *One Boy's War*

Johnson, Robert *Thunderbolt*

Peden, Murray *A Thousand Shall Fall* (Canada's Wings, 1979)

Pooley, R. *UK & Ireland Air Touring Flight Guide* (Airtour International — updated annually)

Rhodes, Eric *The Wash in Wartime — A Personal History* (Enthusiasts Publication, 1981)

Settle, Mary Lee *All The Brave Promises*

Shute, Neville *Pastoral* (Heinemann, 1944)

Sturtivant, Ray *The Squadrons of the Fleet Air Arm* (Air-Britain (Historians) Ltd, 1984)

Wills, Henry *Pillboxes* (Leo Cooper, 1985)

Index